To Audie
  Who knows that this
book took nearly as long
to produce as it took to
produce the Polaris. Thank
you for the help

                Harry

The Polaris System Development

Bureaucratic and Programmatic Success in Government

The Polaris System Development
Bureaucratic and Programmatic Success in Government

Harvey M. Sapolsky

Harvard University Press
Cambridge, Massachusetts
1972

To my uncle,
Philip Selig

Preface

In May 1967 I was invited by the Special Projects Office (now the Strategic Systems Project Office) of the Department of the Navy to prepare a report on the history of the Fleet Ballistic Missile Program. This program, which involved the development, procurement, and deployment of the Polaris missile and a force of forty-one nuclear-powered missile submarines, was managed by the Special Projects Office. Currently, it includes the development of a successor missile, the Poseidon, the conversion of a number of the submarines to the new missile capability, and the initial research on an advanced weapon known as the Trident.

The Fleet Ballistic Missile Program, and particularly its Polaris component, is generally considered to be one of the nation's most successful weapon development projects. Certainly, it is the largest and one of the most important weapon projects ever undertaken by the Department of the Navy. Given my strong interest in organizational analysis and science and government relations, I found the invitation to be a rare opportunity to examine a large-scale technological development of the type which has come to dominate public administration since the Second World War.

Having read extensively in the captured literature on the history of business firms where errors of leadership are never mentioned and having glanced at a few of the available but easily avoidable books on similar government projects, I was reluctant to have the organization I was to study sponsor my research and determine the desirability of publication. I asked that some other organization or individual in the Navy act as sponsor. The Assistant Secretary of the Navy (Research and

Development) agreed then to extend the invitation for a study of the Fleet Ballistic Missile Program and the Special Projects Office. I also asked and was granted permission to publish the report without review other than for security purposes.

No specific task assignment was provided in the invitation. I was simply asked to examine the history of the program and discuss any lessons this history might hold for the development of future naval weapons and government policy in general. I was to be given access to all program records and permission to interview any civil servant or naval officer connected with the program. The identification of what records or persons were relevant to the study was to be my own.

The absence of official direction did not mean the inquiry was without guidance. Many people who work in the fields of national security, science and public policy, and organizational analysis kindly consented to assist me in identifying important aspects of the program for study. Carl Kaysen of the Institute for Advanced Studies, James Q. Wilson of Harvard University, and Ithiel de Sola Pool, Eugene Skolnikoff, Jack Ruina, and Jerome Wiesner of the Massachusetts Institute of Technology were among them. I also consulted with personnel at the Special Projects Office to discover what work had previously been done on the history of the program, whereby I met Wyndham Myles who was the official Special Projects Office historian in 1960–61. Dr. Myles kindly made available to me the drafts of an uncompleted history of the program and provided clues to the location of useful source materials. Also helpful in the initial stages of the study were a political analysis of the program prepared as a senior thesis at Wesleyan University by Robert Hunter, once a summer intern in the Special Projects Office, and the writings of Robert Perry and others at the RAND Corporation on the development of ballistic and cruise missiles in the Air Force.

The constraining influences on the direction of the study, however, had to be my own interests and training. I could envision several volumes being written on the development of the submarine-launched ballistic missile, only one of which I could write. For example, there could have been a volume analyzing the strategic consequences of the introduction of submarine-launched ballistic missiles and their possession by two or more nations. There also could have been a volume examining the contributions of research in various lines of technology to the overall achievement of the weapon system. Being neither a defense strategist nor a historian of technology, I could benefit from, but not produce, such works. Any study I prepared would necessarily focus on issues of government ororganization and research policy: In what way does the organization of the military affect the generation of weapon proposals? How do weapon proposals gain approval? What factors influence the development of approved projects? What type of government-contractor relations are most effective in large-scale technological projects? What is the role of science advisors in the formation of government policy? How can large-scale projects be controlled? What organizational structures and management policies facilitate the development of technology? Given the reputation the Polaris development has had within and outside of government, however, one basic question emerged: Why was the Polaris development successful?

In conducting the research for the study, I tried to take full advantage of the invitation to examine all program records and to meet with all persons who had some connection with the development effort. Over four hundred interviews were conducted ranging in length from a minimum of one hour to repeat sessions that total over forty hours with one individual. Among those interviewed were persons in other naval organizations, contractor organizations, the Army, the Air Force, the Department of Defense, the Atomic Energy Commission, the Congress, the General Accounting Office, the National Aeronautics and Space Administration, the Ceneral Intelligence Agency, and the British Admiralty. In order to ensure cooperation and openness, all interviewees were told that they would not be quoted in any report or book I would prepare, and their confidence has been respected. It is for this reason that I have in both the report and the book cited coded interview documents as references rather than identifying by name and title the individuals who provided the information. In the book the interview documents are footnoted so that the reader will be aware at all times of the type of sources that I am using. Only three persons refused my request for an interview.

No request for a program document was refused, but there were instances in which historical records had been destroyed in routine file purges.

The report was submitted to the Navy in October 1969. At that time I began revision for publication by soliciting comments on the report from interested scholars. Particularly helpful at this stage of my work were the suggestions of Eugene Skolnikoff and James Q. Wilson, mentioned earlier, and of Harvey Brooks, Max Hall, and Anthony Oettinger of Harvard University; Hayward Alker, Donald Marquis, and Stephen Weinberg of the Massachusetts Institute of Technology; and Frederick Scherer and Raymond Tanter of the University of Michigan. Neither they nor the Navy, which assisted by releasing certain documents for publication and correcting factual errors in the report, bear any responsibility for the structure of this book, its findings, or its conclusions.

The revisions centered on following through on certain arguments raised in the report and integrating a long historical appendix with the text. Nothing of importance which appeared in the report is missing in this volume, however. Once having committed myself to paper, I find it extraordinarily difficult to disown any wisdom conveyed. Although some additional research was conducted after October 1969, I cannot claim that all recent changes in defense procurement policies or the Fleet Ballistic Missile Program have been fully considered. This book, like the report, is essentially a historical case study; as such, it suffers from all the methodological limitations of historical case studies. I hope soon to prepare a more general work on the public management of technology which will compare the experiences of a number of major technological programs.

The entire effort has been an education for me, and I hope it has been of value to the Navy. Having personally enjoyed the research so much, I must thank those who helped make it possible. First among them must be my four able and dedicated research assistants: Mrs. Barbara F. Resnek, who worked with me through the entire study, and Mrs. Ardith Betts, Mrs. Maureen Aspin, and Mr. Sanford Weiner, who participated in important aspects of the study. Miss Eve Steinberg, Mrs. Jo Alice Kubarych, Miss Marcessia Gelowtski, and Miss Ellen Radtke provided cheer and secretarial assistance. Administrative facilities for the report were made available by the Instrumentation Laboratory at the Massachusetts Institute of Technology (now the Charles Stark Draper Laboratory). Among those at the laboratory who were particularly helpful were Sam Forter, whose knowledge of Polaris development is large and whose patience with slow writers is even larger, Mrs. Barbara Greene, whose ability to read scribblings and convert them into legible typing will be legendary, and Jean-Jacques Rivard, whose drawing and charting skills account for the report's and this volume's illustrations.

Dr. Robert Frosch, Assistant Secretary of the Navy (Research and Development) and Rear Admiral Levering Smith, Director of the Special Projects Office, are to be thanked both for extending the invitation to do the study and for being most generous with their time. Everyone in the Special Projects Office was most cooperative, but among them all I benefited most from the encouragement and aid of Dr. John Craven, Chief Scientist until 1969, and Thomas Aiken, who as Deputy Director of the Programs and Plans Division was the Special Projects Office contact for the study.

Finally, I must thank my wife who, for long months, then years, showed only the most moderate and understandable hostility to my other life. It was useful to know that I would always be welcomed back.

Harvey M. Sapolsky

Cambridge, Massachusetts
November 1971

Contents

Tables

Figures

Abbreviations

ABM	Antiballistic missile
CPM	Critical Path Method
DDR&E	Office of Director of Defense Research and Engineering, Department of Defense
DOD	Department of Defense
DSSP	Deep Submergence Systems Project, Department of the Navy
FBM	Fleet Ballistic Missile
ICBM	Intercontinental Ballistic Missile
IL	Instrumentation Laboratory of the Massachusetts Institute of Technology
IRBM	Intermediate Range Ballistic Missile
LOB	Line of Balance
MIRV	Multiple Independently Targeted Reentry Vehicles
n.m.	nautical miles
NMF	Navy Management Fund
NOBSKA	A study of antisubmarine warfare techniques conducted in the summer of 1956
NOTS	Naval Ordnance Test Station
OSD	Office of the Secretary of Defense
OSDBMC	Office of the Secretary of Defense Ballistic Missile Committee
PERT	Program Evaluation and Review Technique
PERT/COST	The extension of the Program Evaluation and Review Technique to consider dollar allocations
PMP	Program Management Plans
R&D	Research and Development
RMI	Reliability Management Index
SCN	Shipbuilding and Conversion, Navy
SPAN	System for Projection and Analysis
SRD	Secret, Restricted Data
STG	Steering Task Group

STL	Space Technology Laboratory, Inc.
U	Unclassified title
ULMS	Undersea Long-Range Missile System (Trident)
USA	United States Army
USAF	United States Air Force
USN	United States Navy
WDD	Western Development Division of the Air Research and Development Command

The Polaris System Development
Bureaucratic and Programmatic Success in Government

1 | Introduction

Government continually fails us. Laws which are passed with great expectation often cause larger problems than they were intended to solve. Programs which are announced with great ceremony and apparent commitment often are not implemented. Public agencies which are established to provide innovative and efficient approaches to major policy issues often act with an all too familiar rigidity and ineptitude.

At the local level we find schools which do not teach, police forces which are in league with organized crime, and public services which serve no one well. At the federal level we note that the State Department is unable to produce an effective foreign policy, the Post Office has trouble delivering the mail, and the Office of Economic Opportunity alienates both the rich and the poor. Turning to the defense agencies, we learn that the Air Force's C-5A transport development is likely to exceed its cost estimate by two or more billion dollars, that the Army's Cheyenne helicopter program, after an expenditure of several hundred million dollars, is unable to meet its performance specifications, and that the Navy's entire shipbuilding program is beset with cost overruns, performance flaws, and schedule slippages.

In this book, I am going to describe a government program which worked, a public bureaucracy which was successful. In doing so I will attempt to show what we can reasonably expect from government. The program is the Fleet Ballistic Missile (FBM) Program, which involved the development, procurement, and deployment of the Polaris missile, attendant subsystems, and a force of forty-one nuclear-powered submarines.

1

The successful bureaucracy is the Special Projects Office of the Department of the Navy, which managed the program.

The Polaris is a solid-fueled, intermediate range ballistic missile that is armed with a nuclear warhead and fired from a submerged submarine. It is, along with the Air Force's land-based Minuteman and Titan missiles and B-52 bombers, a major component of the strategic force of the United States, the force designed to strike at the heart of an enemy's social, industrial, and military structure.

There are two types of strategic missiles. One, the ballistic missile, expends essentially all of its energy in the early or boost phase of its flight and coasts the rest of the way to the target, as does a cannon shell. The other, the cruise missile, flies parallel to the earth's surface and uses energy all the way to the target, as does an airplane. Ballistic missiles require guidance only during the boost phase, whereas cruise missiles require guidance all along the flight path. Because ballistic missiles leave the earth's atmosphere during the boost phase of their flight, they are uniformly powered by rocket motors containing their own oxygen supply. Most cruise missiles, in contrast, are powered by air breathing jet-type engines. Ballistic missiles are capable of speeds exceeding 15,000 miles per hour; cruise missiles fly at the speed of a fast airplane, between 500 and 2,000 miles per hour.

Ballistic missiles are further classified by their range and rocket fuel. Missiles with a range of over 5,000 miles are known as Intercontinental Ballistic Missiles (ICBM); those with a shorter range are known as Intermediate Range Ballistic Missiles (IRBM). Ballistic missiles may use either solid or liquid fuel. Solid fuel is generally safer and easier to handle, but it has a lesser thrust and thus lesser lift capacity per pound than liquid fuel.

Nuclear-armed and quick to target, strategic missiles are obviously formidable weapons. The temptation to use them is deterred by the knowledge that the effectiveness of a counter-system capable of inflicting unacceptable damage cannot be significantly diminished in a surprise attack. Since land-based missile systems are deployed at fixed sites and since these sites now can be precisely located through satellite observation, most, if not all, of them could conceivably be destroyed in a coordinated attack by an enemy using powerful and accurate missiles. However, the nuclear-powered submarines that serve as Polaris launch platforms cannot as yet be detected and destroyed simultaneously in decisive numbers. Because the surviving Polaris missiles would be capable of delivering a certain and devastating retaliatory blow, the FBM system is considered to be the invulnerable deterrent.

The Polaris program has its origins in the technological advances of the Second World War and the uneasy peace that has marked postwar years.[1] During the war scientists ad engineers on both sides worked to improve old weapons and design new ones. In the United States the most notable achievements of scientists and engineers were in the development of the atomic bomb and in the advancement of aerial warfare; in Germany the most significant progress was made in missilery and in submarine warfare.

The Germans, appropriately, first thought of combining a missile and a submarine. In the summer of 1942, technicians from the German Army Weapons Department experiment station at Peenemündee fitted a U-boat with short-range bombardment rockets and launched several salvos from depths of

1. There are several historical accounts of the origins and management of the Polaris program. James Baar and William Howard, *POLARIS!* (New York: Harcourt, Brace and World, 1960) is a popular history of the development effort prepared at the height of the program. J. J. DiCerto, *Missile Base beneath the Sea: The Story of Polaris* (New York: St. Martin's Press, 1967) is a layman's explanation of the Polaris technologies and their development. *Adventure in Partnership: The Polaris Story* (Danbury, Conn.: Danbury Printing, n.d.) is an illustrated commemorative volume. Ed Rees, *The Seas and the Subs* (New York: Duell, Sloan & Pierce, 1961) is a popular discussion of the nuclear submarine and related programs including the Polaris. The most professional and accurate work is that of Vincent Davis, *The Politics of Innovation: Patterns in Navy Cases*, the Social Science Foundation and Graduate School of International Studies Monograph Series in World Affairs, IV, 3 (Denver, Colo.: University of Denver Press, 1967) and Wyndham D. Miles, "The Polaris," in Eugene M. Emme, editor, *The History of Rocket Technology: Essays on Research, Development, and Utility* (Detroit, Mich.: Wayne State University Press, 1964), pp. 162–175. Note also Dominic A. Paolucci, "The Development of Navy Strategic Offensive and Defensive Systems," *United States Naval Institute Proceedings*, 96 (May 1970), pp. 204–223. For an econometric analysis of the program, see Robert E. Kuenne, *The Polaris Missile Strike* (Columbus: Ohio State University Press, 1966).

thirty to fifty feet.[2] Refinements on the concept continued until several schemes for a submerged launching of the longer-range and heavier V-2 missile had been prepared.[3] Jurisdictional disputes that arose between the German Army Weapons Department and the German Navy Weapons Department prevented the concept from receiving serious attention, and no operational equipment was prepared.[4]

Later, in the United States, studies to assess the lessons of the waning war were independently initiated by each branch of the military and by the organization that directed the war research program. Although there were important differences in their conclusions, each of the studies interpreted the war as demonstrating the need for continuous vigilance, both militarily and technologically, if peace were to be maintained.[5] The unified opinion of the nation's military and leaders of its scientific community was that the United States should "never again be caught unprepared to meet an aggressor."[6] And for at least some of those involved in the assessments, recent actions of the Soviet Union suggested that there might soon be another aggressor.[7]

Impressed with technology's contribution to warfare, the armed services sought to continue on a permanent basis most research and development activities that had been established on an emergency basis during the war. German weapon research ideas and even German scientists and engineers were absorbed into the American defense effort. Within months of

2. Walter Dornberger, V-2, translated by James Cleugh and Geoffrey Halliday (New York: Ballantine Books, 1954), pp. 214–215; Baar and Howard, POLARIS!, pp. 4–5.

3. Interview Document [hereafter cited as Int] I-1. See also Ernst Klee and Otto Merk, The Birth of a Missile: The Secrets of Peenemünde, translated by T. Schoeters (New York: E. P. Dutton, 1962), pp. 106–107.

4. Dornberger, V-2, p. 215.

5. See Vincent Davis, Postwar Defense Policy and the U.S. Navy 1943–46 (Chapel Hill: University of North Carolina Press, 1962), Perry McCoy Smith, The Air Force Plans for Peace 1943–1946 (Baltimore, Md.: Johns Hopkins University Press, 1970), and Vannevar Bush, Science: The Endless Frontier (Washington: Government Printing Office, 1945, 1960).

6. Thomas A. Sturm, The USAF Scientific Advisory Board: Its First Twenty Years 1944–1964 (Washington: USAF Historical Division Liaison Office, 1967), chap. 2; Theodore Von Karman, The Wind and Beyond (Boston: Little, Brown, 1967), chaps. 33, 36, 37.

7. Smith, Air Force Plans.

the end of the war, parallel long-range missile projects, some based on V-2 technology, were established in the Navy and the other services.[8] Soon included was a project to develop a cruise missile capable of being launched from a submarine.[9]

The atomic bomb and air power, however, came to dominate military planning in the United States. Limited postwar defense budgets compelled the armed services and the newly established Department of Defense to choose among alternative weapon and manpower programs. Since nuclear weapons and the proven means of delivering them were then universally viewed as the essence of military strength, missile projects were allowed to languish while the armed services competed for access to nuclear technology and control over the strategic bombardment mission.[10]

In the late 1940's this competition culminated in controversy between the Air Force and the Navy over the B-36 versus the Super Carrier. The dispute involved national defense strategies as well as budget allocations for particular types of weapon systems. In urging the procurement of the new long-range B-36 bomber, which would necessarily have limited bombing accuracy, the Air Force was advocating a policy of using nuclear weapons against large urban areas in time of war. The Navy challenged both the effectiveness and the morality of this strategy and offered as an alternative increased reliance on carrier-based aircraft to pinpoint and de-

8. U.S. Congress, House, Committee on Science and Astronautics, *A Chronology of Missile and Astronautic Events*, 87th Cong., 1st Sess., 1961, House Report 67 (Washington: Government Printing Office, 1961), pp. 8–9.

9. Initial tests were conducted with the Loon missile. The program eventually led to the design of the nuclear-armed Regulus missile which was deployed in the mid-1950s on five submarines (Int 1-2). Paolucci, "The Development of Navy Strategic Offensive and Defensive Systems," pp. 210–213. Early research in naval missiles is discussed in Lee M. Pearson, "Naval Administration of Guided Missile Research and Development during World War II" (unpub. paper prepared for the Seminar on Science and Public Policy, Graduate School of Public Administration, Harvard University, May 1963).

10. For a description of the Navy's early interest in nuclear weapon and nuclear propulsion technologies, see Davis, "The Politics of Innovation" and Carl O. Holmquist and Russell S. Greenbaum, "The Development of Nuclear Propulsion in the Navy," *United States Naval Institute Proceedings*, 96 (September 1960), pp. 65–71. The state of missile programs in this period is discussed in Emme, editor, *The History of Rocket Technology*.

liver nuclear and conventional weapons to military targets. Though the Navy was not excluded from having a role in strategic warfare, the Air Force won the dispute and was given appropriations for the procurement of the new bomber.[11]

The attack against South Korea by North Korea in 1950 seemed to confirm the frequently stated warnings of the military and others that international Communism was dangerously aggressive. Defense appropriations quickly soared, not only to support United States and United Nations forces aiding the South Koreans, but also to expand generally the military capabilities of the United States. To discourage potential attacks by the Soviet Union, troop strength in Europe was increased, an aircraft defense network was constructed across northern Canada and the United States, and a worldwide system of bomber bases and support facilities was established for the Air Force's Strategic Air Command.

The national security situation, however, did not stabilize. Intelligence reports in the early and mid-1950's indicated that the Soviet Union was conducting tests of an ICBM. With ICBMs the Soviet Union would acquire the ability to bypass forward defenses and attack directly both the United States mainland and the Strategic Air Command bomber bases. This shift in weapon delivery technology from aircraft to missiles seemed to reduce the probability that the United States would respond to aggression against its allies since American cities and the strategic bomber force would be vulnerable to nuclear destruction.

The answer to this danger, it seemed obvious to many national leaders at the time, was for the United States to acquire its own strategic missiles. Threatened with the same or even greater potential nuclear destruction, the Soviet Union would be less likely to risk either an attack against the United States or a further probing expansion of Communism. Thus, the dormant ballistic missile programs were revived and placed on accelerated development schedules. In order to assure the early deployment of a ballistic missile, IRBM as well as ICBM

11. Paul Y. Hammond, "Super Carriers and B-36 Bombers: Appropriations, Strategy and Politics," in Harold Stein, editor, *American Civil-Military Decisions* (Birmingham: University of Alabama Press, 1961), pp. 299–300.

projects were given increased support. For interim protection, expansion of the bomber force continued.

In the mid-1950's the prospect that missile units might soon account for the largest share of the Unitied States strategic force stimulated renewed interservice rivalry. The Air Force had responsibility for long-range bombing, but the allocation of responsibility for strategic missiles was still uncertain. Each of the services sought to establish a claim for this responsibility through the control of one or more of the programs to develop a ballistic missile.

Rising defense expenditures, in part the result of accelerated and competing missile programs, became an even heavier burden on the conscience of the Eisenhower administration. It had taken office promising fiscal restraint and yet, largely because of increased defense costs, the federal budget had continued to grow. Initially, the administration's budget strategy was to limit expenditures for conventional military forces, particularly ground combat troops and their support, placing emphasis instead on the development and deployment of nuclear arms.[12] Later, the President and his advisors began to seek ways to hold down expenditures for even these activities.

The Navy was the last of the three services to propose a ballistic missile program and the first to feel the effect of the new budget policies. Jurisdictional disputes, conflicting technical advice, and lingering concerns about the use of weapons of mass destruction had delayed the formulation of a united position within the Navy on the establishment of a ballistic missile program. When the proposal for a naval missile was presented to defense officials in the early fall of 1955, the President had already approved four ballistic missile programs and was not willing to consider a fifth. The Navy was told that to gain a role in strategic missiles it would have to join either the Air Force or the Army in one of the development projects previously approved. With some reluctance arrangements were

12. Samuel Huntington, *The Common Defense: Strategic Programs in National Politics* (New York: Columbia University Press, 1961), pp. 88–106. Glenn H. Snyder, "The New Look of 1953," in P. Y. Hammond *et al.*, *Strategy, Politics, and Defense Budgets* (New York: Columbia University Press, 1962), pp. 436–524, and Malcolm W. Hoag, "What New Look in Defense?" *World Politics*, 22 (October 1969), pp. 1–3.

made with the Army to modify a liquid-fueled Jupiter missile for use aboard ships or submarines. Initial plans called for testing the missile in 1958, deployment aboard a Mariner-type freighter in 1960, test launching from a submarine in 1963, and deployment of a missile carrying submarine in 1965. In November 1955 the Secretary of the Navy established the Special Projects Office to manage the Navy's portion of the Joint Army-Navy Jupiter Program.[13]

The joint venture survived only a year. The most effective deployment of a strategic missile at sea is aboard a submarine since submarines are much more difficult to detect and destroy than surface ships. The Navy preferred the handling of safer solid-fueled rockets to liquid-fueled rockets in the confined spaces of a submarine, so it immediately initiated studies of a solid-fueled version of a Jupiter and an entirely new solid-fueled missile. On the basis of these studies, the Navy argued that the development of a new solid-fueled missile would be less costly and would produce a more effective weapon than any possible modification of the Jupiter, and the scientific community and the Department of Defense soon endorsed these conclusions. By December 1956 the Navy had been given permission to terminate the joint venture with the Army and the authority to begin an independent missile program, the Polaris.[14]

Defense policies, certainly at the center of national politics since the end of the Second World War, took on new political importance with the launching of the first space satellites by the Soviet Union in the fall of 1957. Though the American satellite program had a relatively low priority and was managed independently of the missile programs, its ostensible failures in the face of the obvious successes of the Soviet Sputniks were generally taken throughout the world as an indication that the United States lagged in missile technology.[15] Many

13. Secretary of the Navy Secret Memorandum to the Chief of the Bureau of Ordnance, Ser:0031P51, 17 November 1955, subj: Fleet Ballistic Missile (IRBM) Weapons System.

14. Secretary of Defense Secret Memorandum for the Secretary of the Navy, Ser: 121056 30041, 8 December 1956.

15. Constance M. Green and Milton Lomask, *Vanguard: A History* (Washington: National Aeronautics and Space Administration, 1970), discuss the problems of the United States satellite program. The Navy was its unfortunate manager. For an analysis of the reactions to the Sputniks and other Soviet achievements, see John N. Logsdon, *The Decision to Go to the Moon* (Cambridge, Mass.: M.I.T. Press, 1970).

political leaders felt that the President's fiscal conservatism had dangerously weakened the national defense, and they began at once to exert pressure to strengthen the military position of the United States through increased spending for weapons and space research.

The Navy's FBM Program benefited from these pressures. Twice in the late 1950's the Democratic-controlled Congress appropriated several hundred million dollars more for the construction of Polaris submarines than the President had requested. Arguing that the program was technologically unproven, the President initially impounded the extra funds. In both cases, however, the money was soon released to accelerate the program.[16]

The first test firing of a Polaris from a submerged submarine occurred on July 20, 1960. By the end of that year two FBM submarines were on patrol and twelve more were in various stages of outfitting or construction. This rapid progress permitted the abandonment of plans for the use of surface ships as missile platforms.

The existence of a "missile gap" was a central issue in the 1960 presidential election. The major candidates competed with one another in pledging to do more for defense and space. None was stronger in his statements than John Kennedy. Immediately upon taking office, President Kennedy redeemed some of the commitments he had made in the election campaign by ordering the construction of an additional five submarines. Soon he raised the total number to twenty-nine. During international confrontations such as the Berlin and Cuban crises the program was further accelerated. Eventually, forty-one FBM submarines, each carrying sixteen missiles, were authorized, constructed, and deployed; the last left on its maiden patrol in 1967.

The political significance of the FBM Program extended beyond the size of the fleet and its power for destruction. The

16. These incidents are recorded in "Democratic Sponsorship of the Polaris Program," Extension of the remarks of the Honorable John W. McCormack, *Congressional Record—House,* Vol. 106, Pt. 14 (September 1, 1960), pp. 19239–19240. Note also Robert E. Hunter, "Politics and Polaris: The Special Projects Office of the Navy as a Political Phenomenon" (unpub. Senior Honors Thesis, Wesleyan University, June 1962) and R. J. Kurth, "The Politics of Technological Innovation in the United States Navy" (unpub. diss., Harvard University, 1970).

submarines were named after famous American heroes and incumbent Presidents insisted on selecting those to be so honored. President Eisenhower, controlling the smallest list, found room for Theodore Roosevelt, Patrick Henry, Robert E. Lee, and Abraham Lincoln, as well as George Washington, but not for Andrew Jackson or Woodrow Wilson. These Democratic heroes and Sam Rayburn were included in the lists of Presidents Kennedy and Johnson, along with the heroes of the minorities: Tecumseh, Von Steuben, Casimir Pulaski, Kamehameha, George Washington Carver, and Mario G. Vallejo.

Three versions of the Polaris missile were produced. The Polaris A-1, with a range of 1,200 nautical miles (n.m.), was an interim weapon designed to meet accelerated deployment schedules. The originally programmed missile, with a range of 1,500 n.m., was designated the A-2 and was developed almost parallel with the A-1. Performance improvements discovered in the course of the A-1 and A-2 developments were incorporated into the more advanced Polaris A-3, which has a range of 2,500 n.m. Both the A-2 and A-3 are still in service.

Including the United States, four nations now possess ballistic missile submarines. The United Kingdom signed an agreement with the United States in 1963 for the purchase of Polaris A-3 missiles for a fleet of four British-built submarines. Independently, France began work on a fleet of five ballistic missile submarines similar in design to the Polaris submarines. The Soviet Union, which had previously constructed a number of short-range cruise and ballistic missile submarines, recently began to construct submarines similar in design to the Polaris boats. When completed, the new Soviet fleet is expected to equal or exceed in size that of the United States. Some of the new Soviet submarines have already taken patrol positions off the coast of the United States.

Although the deployment of Soviet ballistic missile submarines is necessarily disturbing to the operational commands in the Department of Defense, it is Soviet defensive measures against the United States strategic force that most directly affect the FBM Program. Fears in the early and mid-1960's that the Soviet Union would construct an antiballistic missile system around its cities and military bases led to the design of a new missile, the Poseidon. As each Poseidon is armed with a warhead that contains a dozen or so separately guided reentry vehicles (hydrogen bombs and their protective casings), it can easily saturate any possible missile defense. The missile was approved for development in 1965 and was first deployed in 1971. The Navy's plan is to convert thirty-one of the FBM submarines to carry Poseidon missiles. More recently, because of a concern that the Soviet Union might improve its antisubmarine warfare abilities to the point where the FBM fleet would be in jeopardy, design work has begun on an entirely new submarine-missile system, the Trident, which could replace the FBM in the 1980's.

The FBM program is awesome in terms of cost as well as purpose. To sustain the FBM fleet requires an extensive network of training, supply, and support facilities and the expenditure of over $600 million a year. The research, development, and investment cost of the Polaris portion of the program was about $10 billion. The Poseidon will cost at least $5 billion more. And although no official estimate exists for the Trident development, it is certain to be a multibillion-dollar project.

Because Vice Admiral Hyman G. Rickover is so well known as an innovator, he is often mistakenly identified in the press as the naval officer who directed the Polaris program. Admiral Rickover was responsible for the nuclear propulsion system used in FBM submarines, but he was not involved in the development of the missiles. The officer who held overall responsibility for the FBM Program from its inception through the development of the Polaris was Vice Admiral William F. Raborn. Two other admirals have served as the Director of the Special Projects Office. In 1962 Admiral Raborn was relieved by Admiral I. J. Galantin. In 1965 Rear Admiral Levering Smith, who for the previous nine years had been the Technical Director of the Special Projects Office, became the Director.

The Polaris program is considered an outstanding success. The missile was deployed several years ahead of the original FBM schedule. There has been no hint of a cost overrun. As frequent tests indicate, the missile works. The submarine building was completed rapidly. Not surprisingly, the Special Projects Office is widely regarded as one of the most effective agencies within government.

Figures 1 and 2 show the FBM submarine and missiles.

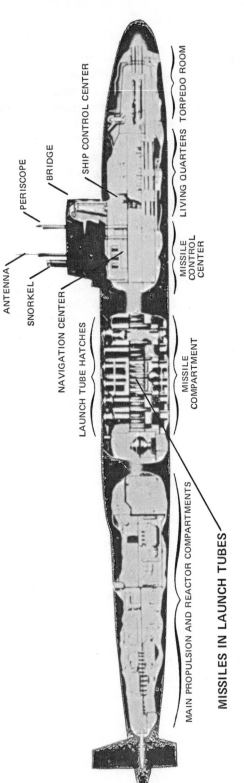

PERISCOPE

BRIDGE

SHIP CONTROL CENTER

ANTENNA

SNORKEL

NAVIGATION CENTER

LAUNCH TUBE HATCHES

TORPEDO ROOM

LIVING QUARTERS

MISSILE CONTROL CENTER

MISSILE COMPARTMENT

MAIN PROPULSION AND REACTOR COMPARTMENTS

MISSILES IN LAUNCH TUBES

Figure 1. A Polaris Fleet Ballistic Missile submarine

Figure 2. A comparison of the missiles of the Fleet Ballistic Missile Program

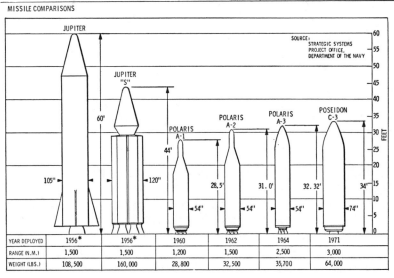

MISSILE COMPARISONS

	JUPITER	JUPITER "S"	POLARIS A-1	POLARIS A-2	POLARIS A-3	POSEIDON C-3
YEAR DEPLOYED	1956*	1956*	1960	1962	1964	1971
RANGE (N.M.)	1,500	1,500	1,200	1,500	2,500	3,000
WEIGHT (LBS.)	108,500	160,000	28,800	32,500	35,700	64,000

SOURCE:
STRATEGIC SYSTEMS
PROJECT OFFICE,
DEPARTMENT OF THE NAVY

2 | Promoting and Protecting the Program

A program's rank in official priorities is frequently used to explain its success or failure. Programs that rank high are said to be guaranteed the resources needed for their completion; those that rank low are guaranteed starvation. Once a program has been placed at the top of a priority list, many assume that its success is assured.

This explanation of success, however, neglects the question of feasibility. Some governmental ventures cannot be completed, regardless of the dollars committed to them, because the knowledge required for completion is unobtainable. Though we as a nation may be reluctant or unable to admit it, there are such things as impossible tasks.

More importantly, the explanation is inadequate because it begs the question of how a high priority status is obtained or maintained. The national agenda is crowded with programs competing for attention. Each agency and branch of government sets its own priorities by choosing from the available programs those that it is willing to support. A necessary condition for success, then, is the simultaneous agreement of the entire government, or at least its major components, on the high priority of a particular program. Apparently, this does not often happen.

Given the independence of governmental subunits, the process of achieving uniformity in priority rankings is necessarily political. Each agency and branch must be induced, cajoled, or persuaded to support a program not of its own invention. Since groups outside government influence the direction of public policy, their support must also be secured.

As a ballistic missile program proposed during the missile

scare of the mid-1950's, the FBM was obviously well situated to gain political support. Even before *Sputnik*, defense was the nation's number one priority and ballistic missiles headed the defense priority list. Each Soviet advance in missilery served both to reinforce the national consensus to build ballistic missiles and to demonstrate their feasibility.

Nevertheless, I will argue that the success of the FBM Program was dependent upon the great skill of its proponents in bureaucratic politics. Without their quick recognition of the political nature of decisions determining the procurement of weapons, I do not believe that sufficient resources could have been assembled to create the existing FBM fleet. Evidence to support this view exists in the early history of the FBM Program and in an analysis of the Special Projects Office's interactions with its environment.

TWO OBSTACLES TO A POLARIS

It may seem obvious, in retrospect, that the United States would choose to develop the Polaris missile. Given the theory of strategic deterrence that has guided national defense policy since the 1950's and given the technological constraints, the establishment of such a program appears to follow logically. The United States has sought both a certain and a secure deterrent. Ballistic missiles are a more certain deterrent than either cruise missiles or bombers because they are harder for an enemy to defend against. Submarine-launched missiles are more a secure deterrent than either land-based or other sea-based missiles because they are less vulnerable to destruction by a surprise attack, and, since solid-fueled missiles are less subject to dangerous accidents than liquid-fueled missiles, they are generally considered safer to handle aboard submarines. The solid-fueled Polaris, due to its smaller size and other characteristics, is a better missile to launch from a submarine than a solid-fueled Jupiter.

To initial proponents of the FBM system in the mid 1950's, however, it was not at all obvious that the United States would choose to develop the Polaris. There were two major obstacles to overcome: the Navy's indecisiveness about sponsoring a ballistic missile program and President Eisenhower's determination to limit the number of missile programs.

At least three organizations in the Navy sought jurisdiction over the development of long-range missiles, and each challenged the competence of the others to manage the task. The Naval Research Laboratory, a component unit of the Office of Naval Research, had been experimenting with high altitude rockets since the end of the Second World War. In 1949 and again in 1953, the laboratory had requested and had been refused appropriations to convert its test rockets into ballistic missiles.[1] The Bureau of Aeronautics had developed the Navy's first strategic missile, the Regulus I, a subsonic cruise missile fired from a surfaced submarine.[2] During the early 1950's, the bureau was working on a supersonic version of the Regulus and was considering both the development of more advanced cruise missiles and the design of a ballistic missile. The Bureau of Ordnance, long the rival of the Bureau of Aeronautics in the development of naval weapons, had been initially slow to assert itself in the area of strategic missiles. Prodded by the activities of others, however, the Bureau of Ordnance soon came forth with a proposal for the development of the faster Triton missile to replace the Regulus I and began also to explore designs for a ballistic missile.[3]

Throughout the Navy there was skepticism about the technical feasibility of basing ballistic missiles at sea. Ship navigation errors of ten miles or more were common then and yet the precise location of the launch point had to be known in order for a ballistic missile to be guided accurately to its target. More than one admiral wondered whether or not better navigation techniques could ever be perfected.[4] Though the safety advantages of solid propellants were acknowledged, there was great uncertainty about the chances of developing solid-fueled rockets with sufficient thrust to lift the weight of the existing missile warheads. On these and other technical problems, rival naval bureaus and laboratories provided contradictory advice.[5]

Related to the skepticism about technical feasibility was a

1. Vincent Davis, "The Politics of Innovation: Patterns in Navy Cases," The Social Science Foundation and Graduate School of International Studies Monograph Series in World Affairs, IV, 3 (Denver, Colo.: University of Denver, 1967), pp. 32–33.
2. The Regulus was first deployed in 1953.
3. Report of the Applied Physics Laboratory, Johns Hopkins University, on the Triton missile, June 1955.
4. Int I-63B.
5. Ints I-10A, 11, 12, 13.

concern over costs. Any serious effort to solve the technical problems of a sea-based ballistic missile was certain to be quite expensive. Since senior naval officers tended to believe that the Eisenhower administration was pursuing a policy of allocating fixed sums to the services, many of them were convinced that the costs of a ballistic missile would have to be absorbed in the Navy budget.[6] Some of these officers were responsible for programs that would likely be sacrificed, and they were not anxious to have the Navy propose the development of a ballistic missile.[7]

Other naval officers counseled against the endorsement of a ballistic missile program because they thought it was being promoted simply to compete with the Air Force for the strategic mission. Remembering the Navy's defeat in the controversy over the B-36 in 1949, they felt there was nothing to be gained by starting another interservice dispute. The Air Force would only win again. After all, there were other things to do militarily besides preparing for the war that seemed least likely to occur. Conventional warfare forces, for example, were being neglected, and the Navy could build its future by concentrating on these. Should a sea-based ballistic missile be needed, they preferred that its costs be charged against the Strategic Air Command appropriations.[8]

The 1949 dispute, besides making some naval officers timid in their dealings with the Air Force, imposed another major constraint on the Navy's promotion of a ballistic missile program. In the B-36 controversy, the Navy had argued that a national strategy centered upon the destruction of enemy cities and populations was both unwise and immoral. Now technological progress was threatening to reverse the services' positions in the target selection debate. Sea-based ballistic missiles, because of navigation problems, appeared certain to be inherently less accurate than comparable land-based missiles. The Navy would have to contradict its previous statements in order to promote a ballistic missile program.[9]

6. Int I-60.
7. Ints I-62A, B.
8. Charles J. V. Murphy, "U.S. Sea Power: 'The New Mix,'" 60 *Fortune* (August 1959), p. 187; also Int I-64.
9 Int I-65; Michael H. Armacost, *The Politics of Weapons Innovation: The Thor-Jupiter Controversy* (New York: Columbia University Press, 1969), p. 106; and Michael D. Intriligator, "The Debate Over Missile Strategy," *Orbis,* 11 (Winter 1968), pp. 1138–1139.

Finally, submariners were unenthusiastic about ballistic missiles. In their view, submarines were meant to sink ships with torpedoes, not to blast land targets with missiles; submarine warfare was a battle of wits against an opponent and not a demonstration of technological sophistication.[10]

Thus, when Commander Robert Freitag, Head of the Surface-Launch Missile Branch of the Bureau of Aeronautics, and Abraham Hyatt, Chief Scientist of the Bureau's Research Division, decided to seek the establishment of a ballistic missile program in the Navy in 1954, their prospects for achieving their goal were not good.[11] The document they needed to establish such a program was an "Operational Requirement" for a ballistic missile signed by the guided missile coordinator in the Office of the Chief of Naval Operations. Each previous request for such an Operational Requirement had been discouraged or denied.

Freitag and Hyatt began their quest by seeking support outside the Navy. In 1954 President Eisenhower had appointed a committee under the chairmanship of James R. Killian, Jr., of the Massachusetts Institute of Technology (officially, the Technological Capabilities Panel of the President's Science Advisory Committee) to conduct a secret assessment of potential developments in defense technology for the National Security Council. Through Captain Peter Aurand, the Navy's liaison representative, Freitag and Hyatt passed on to the committee's working panels their analysis of the strategic benefits offered by a sea-based ballistic missile. The Killian Committee strongly endorsed the priority development of both IRBMs and ICBMs in its report, which became widely available within the government in the early months of 1955. Included

10. Admiral Rickover has testified before the Senate Armed Services Committee that his early proposals for guided missile submarines were blocked by the submariners who let it be known that they would accept a cancellation of a new submarine rather than have it equipped with guided missiles. See U.S. Congress, Senate Preparedness Investigation Subcommittee of the Committee on Armed Services, *Hearings, Inquiry into Satellite and Missile Programs*, 86th Cong., 1st Sess., Pt. II, January 6, 1958, p. 1396, and John D. Morris, "Gavin Charges Pentagon with Barring Promotion; Rickover Scores Red Tape," *New York Times* (January 7, 1958), p. 1. He also has been quoted as telling the Chief of Naval Operations that submariners should not be allowed to direct the FBM Program as they lack sufficient imagination (Int I-59).

11. Davis, "The Politics of Innovation," p. 34; also Ints I-6, 7, 8, 9.

among the specific recommendations was a statement that a national requirement existed for a sea-based ballistic missile.[12]

Although the support of outside scientists did not produce the required endorsement of the program by the Chief of Naval Operations, it did help legitimize the concept of a sea-based ballistic missile within the Navy. Soon, Captain Alfred B. Metsger, the Chief of the Guided Missile Division in the Bureau of Aeronautics, and Rear Admiral James S. Russell, Chief of the Bureau of Aeronautics, joined Freitag and Hyatt in promoting the program.

Frustrated by the continued inaction of the naval planning staffs, Admiral Russell decided in early July 1955 to act on his own authority to establish a program. In a memorandum to the Chief of Naval Operations, he stated that, under authorization of the Operational Requirement for the Regulus missile, the Bureau of Aeronautics was proceeding (that is, not waiting for approval) with the development of a ballistic missile to be ready in five to seven years. The Chief of Naval Operations replied by directing the Bureau of Aeronautics to discontinue any efforts which would expand interest in the program. It was too late, however, for the bureau had already sent out letters to approximately twenty industrial firms and government laboratories inviting them to submit, by the fall of 1955, informal technical proposals for a liquid-fueled ballistic missile to be launched from a ship, preferably a submarine.[13]

The technical proposals received by the Bureau of Aeronautics were generally enthusiastic, though the magnitude and difficulty of the task were stressed. Organizations involved in competing ventures for the other services, such as cruise missiles or land-based ballistic missiles, not surprisingly thought that the Navy ballistic missile, or Fleet Ballistic Missile as it was coming to be known, would take a longer time to develop than Aeronautics had envisioned.[14] Other organizations, less busy with missile work but eager to become so, were willing to undertake the task within the minimum time period specified.[15]

12. Davis, "The Politics of Innovation," p. 34; also Int I-9.
13. Davis, "The Politics of Innovation," p. 37; also Ints I-15A, B.
14. For example, V-403 Navy Long Range Ballistic Missile Feasibility Summary (U) (Chance Vought Corp., 1955) (Secret), and Ballistic Missile Report (U) (Redstone Arsenal, 7 September 1955) (Secret).
15. A Preliminary Study, Fleet Ballistic Missile (U) (Lockheed Missile Systems Division LMSD-1399, 1 November 1955) (Secret).

Several mentioned the desirability of solid-fueled missiles in naval missions and noted the possibility of important advances in solid propellants within the coming year.

While these reports were being prepared, Admiral Russell and others in Aeronautics set out to gain support for the ballistic missile concept in the civilian Secretariat of the Navy. Using his prerogative as Chief of Bureau to bypass the Chief of Naval Operations, Admiral Russell approached James H. Smith, Jr., Assistant Secretary of the Navy for Air, and, through him, Charles Thomas, Secretary of the Navy, with the Bureau of Aeronautics' plan for an FBM capability. Although the backing the plan soon received from the civilian leadership of the Department of the Navy irritated several senior admirals, it prevented the abandonment of the FBM concept in its most vulnerable stage.[16]

The interests of other missile development groups in the Navy had begun by July and August of 1955 to undermine the efforts of the Bureau of Aeronautics to promote the FBM Program. The Bureau of Ordnance, for example, opposed the assignment of responsibility for the development of a ship-launched ballistic missile to Aeronautics, but did not itself immediately seek the task. Instead, it urged that the Navy both increase support for the Ordnance-directed program to perfect the use of solid propellants in large-scale rockets and accelerate the development of an Ordnance-designed cruise missile.[17] The Naval Research Laboratory, now seeking a role in developing earth satellites, would at inopportune moments point to the navigation and guidance difficulties that beset a sea-based ballistic missile.[18]

Knowledge of the divergent technical assessments within the Navy reached Reuben Robertson, Deputy Secretary of Defense, just as he was seeking ways to limit the cost of ballistic missile programs. Robertson was already disposed to ignore the Army's claim for a role in strategic missiles. Assuming that the Navy would not be able to reconcile its internal conflicts, he prepared a memorandum for the Secretary of Defense

16. Davis, "The Politics of Innovation," p. 38; also Int I-16.
17. Ints I-11, 12.
18. Int I-14.

recommending that the Air Force be given exclusive jurisdiction over the development of ballistic missiles.[19] Only the strong protests of the Navy Secretariat prevented the memorandum from being sent.[20]

The appointment of Admiral Arleigh Burke as Chief of Naval Operations in August 1955 marked the end to indecisiveness in the naval planning staffs. Admiral Burke was a veteran of the bureaucratic fights with the Air Force; he had been in charge of preparing part of the Navy's case in the B-36 controversy. Moreover, he was concerned about the Navy's past failure to seize technological opportunities. In the first week of his new assignment, Admiral Burke reviewed the problem and decided to support the FBM Program. Convening a series of meetings of naval officers responsible for development of missiles in early September, he formulated a consensus position: the Navy would seek both a ballistic missile capability and a continued cruise missile capability. Important questions of jurisdiction and budget allocations were put aside for the sake of unity.

The consensus was achieved too late for an independent Navy program, however. The President and Department of Defense officials had decided by early September not only to assign the highest priority to the ballistic missile programs, but also to limit their number to four. Already approved were three Air Force programs: the Atlas ICBM, the backup Titan ICBM, and the Thor land-based IRBM. Left for consideration as the fourth program were the Army's Jupiter and the Navy's FBM, both IRBMs. At the same time, the selection of a satellite launch vehicle for United States participation in the International Geophysical Year was to be made from candidates submitted by each of the services. In this competition, the Air Force and Army offered their ballistic missiles as satellite launchers whereas the Navy, using the Naval Research Laboratory as its representative, offered to build an entirely new launch vehicle, the Vanguard. Using the criterion of least direct interference with the military missile program, the Vanguard was chosen as the national entry in the unrecog-

19. Davis, "The Politics of Innovation," p. 38.
20. Int I-1S.

nized race to place a satellite in orbit.[21] Built around German rocket engineers, the Army's missile research group was judged to be more experienced in ballistic missiles than any of the Navy's remaining missile groups. As the President had decided to reserve the nation's best technical capabilities for the ballistic missile race, the Army was assigned responsibility for the backup IRBM, the fourth program.[22] There were to be only four ballistic missile programs. In order to have a role in strategic missiles, the Navy was going to have to find a partner among the other services.

The Navy first approached the Air Force for a seagoing version of the Thor and was turned down when the Air Force learned that the Navy would require major engineering changes for shipboard adoption of the missile.[23] The Navy's technical needs did not appeal very much to the Army, either, but the Army was in a more precarious position that the Air Force in their grasp on the strategic mission.[24] According to the Killian Committee, there was a national requirement for a Navy sponsored sea-based missile, but none for an Army-developed missile. The Army thought an arrangement with the Navy for a joint project to develop the sea-based missile might strengthen Army claims to the operational control of ballistic missiles. When the Navy promised to transfer funds to the Army which would more than compensate for the alterations in the Jupiter missile, a bargain was struck.[25] Though some naval officers remained skeptical about both the feasibility of a joint project and the use of the liquid-fueled Jupiter aboard ship,[26] the Navy Secretariat and Admiral Burke were convinced that a combined program with the Army was the only possible way to obtain approval for the development of an FBM. On November 8, 1955, the Secretary of Defense established ". . .

21. Kurt R. Stehling, *Project Vanguard* (Garden City, N.Y.: Doubleday & Co., Inc., 1961) and Constance M. Green and Milton Lomask, *Vanguard: A History* (Washington: National Aeronautics and Space Administration, 1970).

22. Armacost, *The Politics of Weapons Innovation*, p. 71.

23. Ints I-17, 18. See also Arleigh Burke, "Polaris," in *Adventure in Partnership: The Story of Polaris* (Danbury, Conn.: Danbury Printing, n.d.), pp. 8–11.

24. Armacost, *The Politics of Weapons Innovation*, p. 72.

25. Int I-18.

26. Admiral Sides personal letter to Admiral Galantin, January 31, 1964, SPO historical files.

a joint Army-Navy IRBM program (designated the IRBM #2 program) having the dual objective of achieving an early shipboard ballistic missile capability and providing an alternative to the Air Force IRBM program (designated the IRBM #1 program)."[27]

With unity having been maintained during the crucial external negotiations to establish the FBM Program, the Navy Secretariat and Admiral Burke could turn to questions of jurisdictions and budget allocations. A decision assigning responsibility for the FBM to either the Bureau of Aeronautics or the Bureau of Ordnance was certain to cause dissension since both had important supporters at the highest levels of the Navy. The solution was to assign the task to neither. A new organization, the Special Projects Office, was established to manage the program,[28] and Admiral Raborn, an aviator who had served in the Bureau of Ordnance, was selected as its first director. Budgetary pressures were alleviated by obtaining a commitment from the Office of the Secretary of Defense to support the FBM portion of the joint program outside the regular Navy allocations.[29]

The FBM fuel issue was also settled, but not in favor of liquid propulsion as many first thought. Most of the missile specialists recruited for the Special Projects Office had research background in solid-fueled rockets. Though they would work to adapt the liquid-fueled Jupiter for shipboard use, the Navy's goal was a solid-fueled FBM.[30]

The Navy was frank with the Army. At an early meeting of the joint project, senior naval officers informed their Army

27. Secretary of Defense Secret Memorandum for the Secretary of the Navy and the Secretary of the Army, Log. No. 55-2415, 8 November 1955, subj: Management of the IRBM #2 Development Program.

28. Secretary of the Navy Secret Memorandum to the Chief of the Bureau of Ordnance, Ser: 0031P51, 17 November 1955, subj: Fleet Ballistic Missile (IRBM) Weapon System (Secret). The jurisdictional issue is further considered in Chapter Three, below.

29. Secretary of the Navy Secret Memorandum, Ser: 0031P51, 17 November 1955, subj: Fleet Ballistic Missile (IRBM) Weapon System (SECRET), p. 1; also Int I-57B. Chapter Six, below, examines the problem of budget allocations in detail.

30. It should be noted that the problems of using liquid fuels in naval missiles were not insurmountable. The Soviet FBM fleet was for a long period built exclusively around liquid-fueled missiles. The development of storable liquid fuels now make liquid-fueled missiles as safe to handle as solid-fueled missiles.

counterparts that the Navy would switch to a solid-fueled missile as soon as advances in technology permitted. The Army was told that it would be invited to join the Navy in the development of such a missile when the opportunity arose, but, in any event, the Army should recognize that the Navy's interest in the Jupiter was only expedient.[31] Initially surprised by the Navy's position, the Army soon conceded the advantages of solid propellants for shipboard environments. Nevertheless, the Army could hardly have felt that the Jupiter program was threatened since, in their view, the likelihood of major short-run advances in solid propellant missiles was so slight as to make the Navy look naïve. Wernher von Braun, the famed German rocket engineer who worked for the Army on the Jupiter project, was quoted as saying that the farthest east the Navy could hope to reach with a solid-fueled missile fired from the Atlantic Coast of Europe would be the Simplon railway tunnel in Switzerland, a very improbable target for United States forces.[32]

Despite the revelations about the Navy's long-term intentions, cooperation at the working level between the Army Ballistic Missile Agency and the Navy Special Projects Office seems to have been excellent.[33] The Army, for example, considerably modified the dimensions of the Jupiter in an effort to accommodate the Navy, making the missile nearly ten feet shorter and ten inches larger in diameter than the original design. Moreover, some of the Army engineers were apparently so intrigued with the complexities of shipboard launch, fire control, and navigation that they spent considerable time seeking solutions to these problems. Only infrequently would their military superiors remind them that the Army's main objective was to build a land-based IRBM that would be ready sooner than the Air Force's Thor. The Special Projects Office, for its part, selected the Chrysler Corporation, the Army's production

31. Ints I-19, 20, 21A, B, C.
32. Int I-22.
33. Ints I-23, 24. Note also the testimony of Wernher von Braun, Director, Development Division, Army Ballistic Missile Agency on December 14, 1957, before the Preparedness Investigating Subcommittee of the Committee on Armed Services, U.S. Congress, Senate, *Hearings, Inquiry into Satellite and Missile Programs,* 85th Cong., 1st and 2nd Sess., Pt. I, 1958 (Washington: Government Printing Office, 1958), p. 614.

contractor for the Jupiter, as its weapon system contractor in order to facilitate interservice communication. On the request of the Special Projects Office, the Bureau of Ships drew up plans for the conversion of several Mariner-class cargo ships to Jupiter launch platforms and considered designs for the construction of submarines to carry the missile.[34]

The Navy did not wait long to begin its effort to obtain a solid-fueled missile, however. At the first meeting of the Office of the Secretary of Defense Ballistic Missile Committee (OSDBMC), the group charged with the coordination of all military missile projects,[35] Navy representatives requested approval for an accelerated research and development program to test the feasibility of solid-fueled ballistic missiles.[36] Though their request soon won the endorsement of the Secretary of Defense's Science Advisory Committee,[37] the OSDBMC sought to delay action on it.[38] First, the OSDBMC questioned the need for a priority program in solid-fueled ballistic missiles, given the Navy's continued development of the Regulus II and Triton cruise missiles.[39] When the Navy's representatives refused to withdraw their request, the OSDBMC then suggested that the Navy work with the Air Force in a combined program to explore the possibilities in solid-propellant technology.[40]

Since the two services had quite different views about the

34. Cmdr. H. A. Jackson, USN, and E. Ralph Lacey, "Milestone in the Development of the New Navy," *Bureau of Ships Journal*, 7 (September 1958), pp. 2ff.

35. Included on the committee were the Deputy Secretary of Defense, the Assistant Secretaries of Defense for Research and Development, Applications Engineering, Properties and Installation, the Comptroller, and a representative of the Bureau of the Budget. Secretary of Defense Secret Memorandum for all Assistant Secretaries of Defense, All Service Secretaries, Chairman, Joint Chiefs of Staff, Log. No. 55-2413, 8 November 1955, subj: Establishment of the OSD Ballistic Missiles Committee (OSDBMC).

36. Minutes of the OSDBMC, First Meeting, 9 December 1955, Log. No. 55-2703 (Secret).

37. Office of the Secretary of Defense Science Advisory Committee, *First Report on Ballistic Missiles to the Secretary of Defense*, 11 February 1956 (Secret), attached to the agenda of the Fourth Meeting of OSDBMC, 14 February 1956, Log. No. 56-403 (Secret).

38. Minutes of the OSDBMC, Fourth Meeting held 15 February 1956, 13 March 1956, Log. No. 56-648 (Secret).

39. Minutes of the OSDBMC, First Meeting.

40. Minutes of the OSDBMC, Second Meeting held 14 December 1955, 16 January 1956, Log. No. 56-92 (Secret), and Minutes of the OSDBMC Fourth Meeting.

opportunities in the field, a combined research program at this point in time was certain to stifle the Navy's ambitions. The Air Force was much less optimistic about the immediate prospects for overcoming the technoiogical problems afflicting the development of solid-fueled rockets and much more concerned that solid propellant efforts would interfere with existing ICBM and IRBM programs than was the Navy.[41] While the Air Force envisioned that a solid-fueled rocket as a possible follow-on to its first generation of ballistic missiles which were liquid-fueled, the Navy was seeking to initiate a fifth ballistic missile program, a program rejected by the Secretary of Defense only a few months earlier. Despite the Navy's pledges to use Jupiter components in any test rockets that would be designed, the OSDBMC recognized the Navy's real goal and sought to block its implementation.

Senior naval officers, however, had already decided to act on their own initiative to begin a new FBM Program. Without obtaining the approval of either the Department of Defense or the Navy Secretariat, in early January of 1956 they approached the Aerojet-General Corporation and the Lockheed Missile and Space Division for technical assistance in developing a solid-fueled ballistic missile.[42] These firms, with the collaboration of consultants and the Special Projects Office, quickly prepared a missile design, euphemistically called the Jupiter S, which provided sufficient thrust to carry a standard nuclear warhead by clustering six solid-fueled rockets in a first stage and using a single rocket in a second stage. The action of the uniformed Navy soon received the support of the Navy Secretariat and the "Six Plus One" design became the Navy's official interim FBM objective.[43]

By late February, the Air Force, despite frequently ex-

41. Among the then unsolved technical problems of solid-fueled ballistic missiles were unstable combustion of solid propellants, inability to insure termination of combustion at the precise velocity to be gained, thrust vector control of solid-fueled missiles, nozzle reliability, and the construction of large combustion chambers (Int I-25). See also Minutes of the OSDBMC, Fourth Meeting, and Ints I-26, 27, 28.

42. Int I-29. As there could be no guarantee that the firms would be paid, this was a risky undertaking for them. Both firms, however, were likely to be quite responsive to requests for assistance from the Navy. Aerojet had long ties to the Navy with one of its Presidents being a former Secretary. The Lockheed Missile and Space Division was a newly formed organization eager for the prospect of business.

43. Int I-30.

pressed "grave doubts that the Navy's program . . . [would] result in a tactically usable missile,"[44] was persuaded to state that the Navy's solid fuel research plans complimented rather than conflicted with its own. A memorandum of agreement on solid-fuel data exchanges between the services was soon signed. In March, the OSDBMC, somewhat outmaneuvered, approved the Navy's solid-fuel "backup program" for IRBM #2, but provided only $850,000 for system studies.[45]

Although still tied to the Army and Chrysler, the Navy had gained the opportunity to build a solid-fueled ballistic missile, if only as a successor to the Jupiter. The meager OSDBMC allocation was quickly supplemented by the reprogramming of Navy funds. Official relationships with Aerojet and Lockheed could now begin. Captain Levering Smith, a naval officer with long experience in missile research, was brought into the Special Projects Office to direct their efforts. The Navy now had to ask itself whether or not it was worthwhile to build the Jupiter S.

The Jupiter S was a monster. Designed around the same reentry body as the liquid-fueled Jupiter, it was, because of the limits of solid propellant technology, going to be a very large missile. It would stand 44 feet high, would be 120 inches in diameter, and would weigh 160,000 pounds. These working dimensions could hardly be expected to bring any relief to those concerned about the development of launch equipment for the missile. The best the submarine designer could prepare for the Jupiter S was a plan for an 8,500-ton boat carrying four missiles in an awkward housing attached to the sail.[46]

Most naval officers doubted the potential usefulness of the Jupiter S as a weapon. A favorite rhetorical question asked in the Special Projects Office during this period was, "What are you going to do with the submarine with the big holes?"[47]

44. Department of the Air Force Confidential Letter to the Assistant Secretary of Defense (R & D), 2 March 1956, subj: Large Solid Rocket Development for FBM (Confidential).

45. Secretary of the Navy Confidential Letter to the Chief of the Bureau of Ordnance, 13 April 1956, subj: Proposed Navy Solid Propellant Program (Confidential) and Minutes of the OSDBMC, Fifth Meeting, 20 March 1956, 22 March 1956, Log. No. 56-760 (Secret).

46. Transcript of an interview of Wyndham Miles with Captain Arentzen, USN (ret.), p. 9.

47. Int I-31.

Nevertheless, given the extreme difficulty involved in first initiating the FBM Program and then in introducing the Jupiter S into the FBM Program, there seemed nothing else to do but go ahead with Jupiter S and be prepared to proceed with a second-generation missile when the major limitations of the approved program were recognized in the Office of the Secretary of Defense.

The search for a potential successor to Jupiter S began with Captain Levering Smith's involvement in the FBM Program. He requested the Naval Ordnance Test Station at China Lake, California, to conduct a variety of system improvement studies. Initial results of this work indicated that no significant reduction in missile weight could be achieved without a critical examination of every missile component, including those that made up the reentry vehicle and the guidance package.[48] A study of component weight reductions pointed to the feasibility of a 30,000-pound missile having performance characteristics equal to the Jupiter S that could be developed on nearly the same schedule.[49] At the time, however, the probability of losing the entire program appeared greater than the probability of gaining approval for a new missile development that would strain the state-of-the-art in numerous fields. The Special Projects Office went on with the plans to test a liquid-fueled Jupiter on a surface ship in 1958 and to build the Jupiter S for a submarine to be deployed in 1965.[50]

It was fortuitous that, in the summer of 1956, the Navy sponsored a scientific study on antisubmarine warfare that changed the nature of the entire program. The study resulted from a request of the Chief of Naval Operations made in the fall of the previous year that the National Academy of Sciences' Committee on Undersea Warfare look into the "growing Russian submarine menace."[51] The committee decided to approach the problem through the now famous summer study method—a national gathering of scientists (and their families) at some attractive location to work intensively on an

48. Frank E. Bothwell, *The Origin of Atlantis* (U) (NOTS Doc. 12-208, 13 January 1958) (SRD), p. 2.

49. *Ibid.*, and D. H. Witcher, "Discussions of a Large Ballistic Missile Program" (U) (NOTS Tech Note 123-6, 13 April 1956) (SRD).

50. Int I-32.

51. Ints I-34, 35, 36.

important policy problem during the summer vacation.[52] Nobska Point at Woods Hole, Massachusetts, was chosen as the attractive location, and the study became known as Project NOBSKA.

The committee thought that, if scientists were to assist the Navy, the study would have to consider new technological and strategic uses of the ocean as well as the more traditional components of antisubmarine warfare which held the attention of most naval officers. Accordingly, the committee invited scientists knowledgeable in nuclear propulsion and weapons to participate in the study. Frank E. Bothwell, who was in charge of missile targeting and design work being done at the Naval Ordnance Test Station for the Special Projects Office, was among them. Through Bothwell the NOBSKA panel on the Strategic Uses of the Underseas learned of the possibility of a new lightweight missile. Calculating the drain on Soviet resources a countersystem would require, the panel concluded that a fleet of nuclear submarines armed with the new missile would be a much more effective strategic deterrent than the weapon system the Navy was committed to building.[53]

The Navy's ability to acquire such a fleet was, however, contingent upon progress in several technologies. Warhead technology seemed particularly crucial. Studies at the Naval Ordnance Test Station had indicated the incapacitating effects of damage resulting from fractional megaton weapon attacks on Soviet cities,[54] but military preferences remained fixed on larger weapons. Although the possibility of lightweight weapons of significant yield suitable for small missiles was being explored, warheads then in or on the way to the arsenal were too bulky for anything but a Jupiter-type missile.

The NOBSKA study soon altered dramatically the technological outlook for an FBM, not so much by its identification of potential breakthroughs in technology as by its recognition of the rapid obsolescence of past breakthroughs in technology. The first participant to focus NOBSKA's attention on the technological trend rather than the technological event was Dr. Edward Teller of the Lawrence Radiation Laboratory. He had

52. See J. R. Marvin and F. J. Weyl, "The Summer Study," *Naval Research Reviws,* 20 (August 1966), pp. 1–12.
53. Ints I-34, 35, 36.
54. Witcher, "Discussions of a Large Ballistic Missile Program," p. 2.

been asked to take part in a symposium on antisubmarine weapons, and, challenged by a naval officer for suggesting that powerful nuclear weapons be substituted for conventional torpedoes, Teller asserted that a significant yield weapon could be obtained to fit the size and weight constraints of torpedoes. To many present, this seemed a ridiculous statement since existing weapons of the same yield required a much larger housing.[55] Teller justified the statement by pointing to the trend in warhead technology which indicated major weight reductions in each generation of warheads. Although the weights required were not then available, they probably would be soon. Questioned after the symposium on the applicability of his statement to the Navy's ballistic missile program, Teller was quoted as asking in turn, "Why use a 1958 warhead in a 1965 weapon system?"[56]

The approved Navy program, as of the summer of 1956, did call for building a missile based on performance characteristics attainable in 1958, to be used with a submarine scheduled to be ready for service in 1965. There was a clear mismatch between the missile and the missile's major platform.[57] The panel on the Strategic Use of the Underseas, seeking to design a more reasonable FBM Program, prepared extrapolations of the major missile subsystem technologies. Taken separately, any improvement in any particular system component, including the warhead, would have little effect on overall weapon system performance; taken together, there was the promise of an extremely effective system by 1960–1961 and an even more effective one by 1963–1965. On the basis of these extrapolations, the panel recommended that the Navy build a solid-fueled ballistic missile whose basic features would be a weight of eight to fifteen tons, a range of from 1,000 to 1,500 miles, and a low-yield warhead.

The panel's recommendation was not greeted enthusiastically in all quarters. Some NOBSKA participants felt it unwise for the summer study to endorse the plan for the new missile and argued that it went beyond the bounds of the Navy's request.

55. Int I-37.
56. William F. Whitmore, "Military Operations Research—A Personal Retrospect," *Operations Research*, 9 (March–April 1961), p. 263; also Int I-38.
57. Int I-39.

Others questioned the supporting data, thereby forcing an independent recalculation that only confirmed their validity.[58] Violent objections to the panel's work were heard from the senior Navy representative in residence at NOBSKA, partly because he thought it might jeopardize an existing priority Navy program and partly because he thought his charge was to get scientists to find ways to kill submarines, not ways to promote them.[59] In the final study report, the recommendation appeared with little to distinguish it from numerous others dealing with torpedoes, sonars, communications, and the like. One year later it was clear that the NOBSKA study would be remembered for its missile recommendation and little else.[60]

The study was saved from obscurity because the Chief of Naval Operations and the Special Projects Office liked this particular recommendation. Between them, they had sufficient political and organizational resources to gain internal Navy acceptance for the new missile. Unlike other NOBSKA participants, the Strategic Use of the Underseas panel members did not have to choose between the dangers of fighting for their conclusions or the comforts of their regular careers. The Chief of Naval Operations was willing to risk the Navy's future to obtain a viable ballistic missile system. And top officials in the Special Projects Office were more than willing to abandon the burdens of Jupiter.

Through Bothwell and others, Captain Smith at the Special Projects Office kept informed of events at NOBSKA affecting the FBM. The summer study extrapolations were rechecked by Special Projects Office contractors, and more detailed justifications for switching to the new missile—named the Polaris— were prepared. Many naval officers were reluctant to push for the Polaris until the Atomic Energy Commission officially confirmed the informal warhead weight estimates of the Lawrence Radiation Laboratory. In the past the Atomic Energy Commission had gained the reputation of being more conservative (and less accurate) than its laboratories in estimating technological progress. Yet, without the promise of a significant

58. Int I-39.
59. Int I-40.
60. *Review of Project NOBSKA, Final Report*, August 5–9, 1957 (U) NRC:cuw: (Committee on Undersea Warfare, National Academy of Sciences, Washington, D.C., November 1, 1957) (SRD).

reduction in the yield/weight ratio, the military would not be sufficiently impressed with the advantages of the small ballistic missile. Surprisingly, the Commission backed Lawrence in this instance and wired Admiral Raborn the necessary confirmation in early September 1956.[61] The Polaris was to replace the unfinished Jupiter S.

The Army had known of the Navy's interest in a smaller, more advanced, solid-fueled missile, but it had considered the missile only as a possible follow-on to the modified joint program. When informed of the Navy's intention to terminate any Jupiter-type development, the Army's missile people were shocked. They had come to rely upon their tie to the Navy's official requirement for a sea-based IRBM to bolster their own claims for control over the development and deployment of a land-based IRBM.[62] To those who could recall Peenemünde, the U.S. Navy appeared to be acting now as much on the basis of service pride as the German Navy did when it refused the offer of a submarine-launched missile from the German Army.[63] As it had promised, the Navy offered the Army the opportunity to join in the development of the new missile, but the Army's organizational investment in the Jupiter was too large to permit its abandonment. The Army, arguing that the development of the Polaris would take ten years, maintained that national policy as expressed in the Killian Committee report required the immediate deployment of an IRBM.[64] The Army decided to continue alone in the competition with the Air Force for the right to provide the initial U.S. ballistic missile capability.

The Navy Secretariat provided vigorous support for the shift to Polaris. Garrison Norton, Assistant Secretary of the Navy

61. Ints I-41, 42.
62. See the testimony of Reuben B. Robertson, Deputy Secretary of Defense, before the U.S. Congress, House of Representatives, Subcommittee of the Committee on Appropriations, *Hearings, Department of Defense Appropriations for 1958*, 85th Cong., 1st Sess., Pt. II, p. 1375; Maj. Gen. John B. Medaris, USA (ret.), *Countdown for Decision* (New York: G. P. Putnam's Sons, 1964), p. 64; Armacost, *The Politics of Weapons Innovation*, p. 118.
63. Int I-43. To General Medaris, who headed the Army Ballistic Missile Agency, it seemed that the Navy was stabbing the Army in the back with its decision, also a German image. Note his *Countdown for Decision*.
64. Ints I-21B, I-44.

for Air, could, as a former civilian aide in the Air Force, re-member Air Force documents that showed the significant ad-vantages of a sea-based missile. Using his contacts in the Air Force and the Department of Defense, he worked full time during the summer and fall of 1956 on a realignment of the FBM Program.[65] Firmly convinced the project was feasible, Secretary Thomas and Under Secretary Gates added their en-dorsements to the Polaris proposal.[66] The Navy, once again preparing to present a case for its own missile development, was even more united than it had been a year earlier.

Persuading the Department of Defense to approve a new missile development in 1956 was no easier than it had been in 1955. The problems of weapon costs and organizational dupli-cation still concerned defense officials. This time, however, the Navy was more politically astute. First, it prepared a proposal that indicated a savings of one-third of the program's develop-ment cost (an estimated reduction of $500 million) if Polaris were substituted for the Jupiter S.[67] Second, it voted with the Air Force in the Joint Chiefs of Staff to assign land-based IRBM responsibility to the Air Force rather than the Army.[68] In late November 1956, Secretary of Defense Charles E. Wil-son issued a directive that gave the Air Force control over land-based missiles with a range of 200 or more miles.[69] By early December he had authorized the Navy to initiate the Polaris FBM development while terminating all collaborative efforts with the Army involving either the liquid or solid

65. Armacost, *The Politics of Weapons Innovation*, p. 108; also Int I-45.
66. Int I-46.
67. Admiral J. E. Clark Secret Memorandum to Chairman Standing Committee Appropriation Category SCN, OP515 c/nc, Ser: 00612P51, 15 November 1956. See also Jack Raymond, "Man of the Polaris," *New York Times Magazine* (February 19, 1961), p. 28, and James Baar and William Howard, *POLARIS!* (New York: Harcourt, Brace and World, 1960), p. 72.
68. Dr. T. C. Muse Secret Memorandum to Dr. C. C. Furnas, 19 November 1956, Log. No. 56-3127, subj: Twenty-Third Meeting Ballis-tic Missile Committee (Secret) and Armacost, *The Politics of Weapons Innovation*, p. 118.
69. "Memorandum for Members of Armed Forces Policy Council: Clarification of Roles and Missions to Improve the Effectiveness of the Operation of the Department of Defense," *New York Times* (November 27, 1956), p. 22. The Army would continue to develop the Jupiter, but it would not have any operational responsibility for IRBMs. See also Armacost, *The Politics of Weapons Innovation*, pp. 117–124.

versions of the Jupiter missile.[70] It had been a difficult struggle, but there was at last a Polaris Program.

THE MANY POTENTIAL OBSTACLES TO SUCCESS

The advantages of possessing the highest national priorities accrued initially to the overall ballistic missile program and not to any one of its component projects in particular.[71] The very existence of several similar projects made each the competitor of the other, and questions of comparative military utility were continually raised. Moreover, since the high cost of developing a ballistic missile was to be absorbed in the budget of the sponsoring organization, each of the services had reason to be hesitant in supporting a project, irrespective of the national need. In the mid-1950s nearly everyone said the nation had to build ballistic missiles, but relatively few said that, among the ballistic missiles built, there had to be an Atlas, a Jupiter, or a Polaris.

Despite the great concern over the Soviet effort in ballistic missiles, it was possible to be against the FBM. Potential opposition existed both within and outside the Navy. The program's progress—its ability to obtain the resources necessary to complete the Polaris development—depended upon how skillfully the program's proponents could neutralize the threatened opposition.

Some potential opposition to the Polaris can be attributed simply to the difficulty naval officers had in adjusting to change. As a major innovation in naval weapons, the FBM would be certain to alter career opportunities within the officer corps, favoring particular types of training over others. It is not surprising that naval officers tied to outmoded tech-

70. Secretary of Defense Secret Memorandum for the Secretary of the Navy, Ser: 121056 30041, 8 December 1956.

71. Actually, for six months after its establishment the Polaris program was not included in the list of the highest priority programs. Because the sea-based system was due to be operational at a date later than the land-based systems, defense officials had reserved the highest priority category exclusively for the Air Force projects. The Special Projects Office eventually won the highest rank for the Polaris by arguing that a lower-priority status would only further delay its deployment date (Int I-47). Minutes of the OSDBMC, Thirty-second Meeting, 16 April 1957, 15 May 1957, Log. No. 57-1550 (Secret).

nologies found it difficult to appreciate the benefits of an innovation which challenged their role in life.

Organizations as well as people seek stability. Traditions, the preservation of stable relationships, are important in the Navy; witness the retention of dress swords and Filipino mess boys. FBM submarines, if deployed, would challenge a sacred naval tradition—that of naval ships having but one commanding officer and crew. In order to increase the effectiveness of the FBM fleet, it was necessary to develop a two-crew concept for the submarines. The Blue and Gold concept, as it is known, calls for the relief of a commanding officer and crew on completion of a patrol by a second commanding officer and crew so that the submarine can resume its mission without the delay required to rest a single crew. Two crews instead of one are permanently assigned to the submarine. Though naval aircraft had always been exchanged among pilots and crews, naval vessels had not. Some senior officers, perhaps thinking that the break with tradition might arouse unacceptable expectations in an economy-minded administration, were prepared to oppose both the concept and the program that developed it.

Greater danger to the program grew directly from the conflict over budget allocations. The promised supplements to the Navy budget for the Polaris program were not made by the Department of Defense. As the program increased in size, favored Navy projects had to be canceled or postponed. First the Triton, then the Regulus II, and then the Seamaster (a $330-million jet-powered seaplane program) were sacrificed. The long-sought program to construct nuclear-powered attack submarines was further delayed so as not to interfere with the construction of the FBM submarines. The scope of the Polaris program was so enormous that only a few parts of the Navy were not in jeopardy. Even the Air Navy's position of dominance was challenged as the Polaris grew to a tenth of the Navy's budget.

Money was not the only resource whose reallocation could provoke opposition. The Chief of Naval Operations, because of the national urgency associated with the program, authorized Admiral Raborn to order into the Special Projects Office any naval officer he thought best able to assist him in the effort to develop the FBM.[72] In addition, the Civil Service Commission was persuaded to rate civilian positions in the Special Projects Office so high that the most able civil servants in the Navy could easily be attracted to the newly created organization.[73] Senior admirals for the first time saw themselves bypassed in personnel matters as their most valuable military and civilian assistants were removed from their commands and transferred to the Special Projects Office.[74] Programs hurt by reduced appropriations now lost the men most able to gain new support. Those officers left out of the FBM Program were being told that they as well as the programs they worked on were second-rate.

Perhaps the most dangerous internal threat to the program, however, came, ironically, from those who were apparently among its most vigorous supporters. Within the Navy there were many who sought to improve the program by suggesting technological and operational changes. In promoting their suggestions, these "friends" identified deficiencies or problems in the program and thus aided those who might have wanted to block the FBM development. Criticism did not have to be malicious to be damaging, as the following examples show.

The Naval Ordnance Test Station continued to explore independently advanced missile systems while contributing to the approved FBM program. The test station's reputation had been gained in the development of the Sidewinder, an extremely cheap and effective air-to-air missile, and its strategic missile work followed the pattern of emphasizing low cost and high performance. One proposal offered by the test station called for the placement of launchers for small missiles in the ballast tanks of fleet (diesel) submarines. This would, it was claimed, provide an immediate workable deterrent for 2 percent of the potential cost of the Polaris program.[75] Another proposal stated that the range of the Polaris missile could be dramatically improved without significant additional cost. Such an improvement would, it was argued, permit the FBM system to avoid a major threat to its invulnerability posed by

72. Int A-1.
73. Int A-2.
74. Int I-63A.
75. Ints I-66A, B.

a small number of Soviet antisubmarine warfare aircraft.[76]

The Applied Physics Laboratory at Johns Hopkins University, a Navy-affiliated facility, independently developed a satellite navigation system as the product of tracking the first Sputniks. With some refinement it seemed likely that the navigation satellite could achieve extremely accurate position fixes useful for launching missiles at sea. In promoting this costly innovation, the many weaknesses in the planned navigation aids for the FBM submarines necessarily had to be highlighted.[77]

Naval vessels had traditionally been designed and equipped for multipurpose activity. A submarine, for example, could be used for rescue missions and landing secret agents as well as sinking ships. Short of funds for ship construction, senior naval officers saw the possibility of gaining several submarines for the price of one in the FBM program by assigning several tasks besides strategic deterrence.[78] Diverting an FBM submarine from its patrol to perform, say, a search and rescue mission, however, could cause the submarine to reveal its position or move out of target range, thus eliminating its effectiveness as a strategic deterrent. Helping the Navy meet its pressing submarine needs would not help the program meet national strategic needs.

External threats to the Polaris, at least until the FBM fleet was deployed, can be described, without much distortion, as Air Force threats. From the mid-1950's to the mid-1960's, any argument against Polaris had to be almost automatically an argument in favor of another ballistic missile. Though some naval officers may not have wanted the Navy to build a ballistic missile system, another service would certainly have been given the assignment. The Air Force, despite its own internal doubts about ballistic missile projects,[79] directed the largest, and after 1956 the only, land-based ballistic missile programs. External opposition to the Polaris stemmed largely from, and would clearly benefit, the Air Force.

76. Bothwell, *The Origin of Atlantis; Atlantis: A Study of Range Improvement in the Polaris System* (U) (Weapons Planning Group, NOTS Report 1902, January 1958) (SRD).

77. Ints I-67A, D.

78. Ints I-67B, C.

79. Int I-68.

Before the end of 1956, the Air Force paid little attention to the efforts promoting an FBM system. Its main struggle for the strategic missile mission was with the Army, and in that phase of the dispute the Air Force needed at least Navy neutrality if not Navy support. Moreover, until then the Navy's own program, as had been noted, did not appear particularly realistic, and thus not particularly threatening, to the Air Force.

With the demise of the Army's role in long-range ballistic missiles, however, the Air Force and the Navy became direct competitors for national missile allocations. The revolution in defense management that marked the 1960's notwithstanding, the strategic missile programs have apparently long felt the pressure of comparative analysis or else their efforts to undermine each other would not have been as intense. The Department of Defense's use of systems analysis has reduced the level of competition by accepting the value of multiple methods of delivering warheads—the trinity of bombers, land-based missiles, and sea-based missiles—something that was not explicitly recognized in the late 1950's.

Constrained by its own internal studies which showed the strategic value of sea-based missile systems,[80] the Air Force began its attacks on the FBM Program by questioning the technical feasibility of the undertaking. Particularly vulnerable points in the Polaris development were solid rocket propulsion, navigation accuracy, and submerged communication, all of which tested the state-of-the-art. The Air Force continually reminded defense officials and Congressmen that Polaris was a very large technological gamble based on the uncertain extrapolations of engineering achievement. Similar to all other missile developments, the Polaris program suffered major setbacks: rocket fuel plants blew up, missiles burned on the pad or flew erratically, and some schedule milestones were missed. The first five Polaris test vehicles launched from Cape Kennedy were either complete failures or what is euphemistically referred to as partial successes. At each setback, the question was raised as to whether or not it was wise to continue to pour large amounts of scarce dollars into the program.

80. E. P. Oliver, "POLARIS Weapon System," (U) (RAND Report RM-2311, 28 October 1958) (SRD); also Int I-45.

The Air Force did, however, come to stress what it considered to be the one major strategic weakness in the planned FBM system. Because of the expected limitation in thrust of solid fuels, the Polaris was to carry a relatively low-yield warhead. Though the Navy's analytical studies had shown the cataclysmic effect of fractional megaton nuclear weapons on urban centers, a significant portion of the defense community still favored a "big bang" type of weapon.[81] In contrast, the Air Force systems existing or programmed at the time were all rated in the multimegaton range.

Information on the FBM system problems and limitations was available to the Air Force from a number of sources: internal Navy conflicts, traveling scientists, official Navy reports, dissident contractors, and trade publications. It also appears that the Navy inadvertently sold some of this data to its rival. In late 1957, the Air Force, stating that it might have a land-based requirement for the Polaris, requested the Navy to prepare a study of possible system characteristics with Air Force funds.[82] The Navy complied with the request and, in the process, turned over extensive information on the advantages and disadvantages of Polaris components and the overall system. The land-based application did not live much longer, but, since the Navy was already publicizing all of the advantages of the FBM, the Air Force thought it was necessary to reveal only the disadvantages cited in the report.[83]

The Navy, nevertheless, was making technical progress toward a workable FBM system and it was becoming increasingly apparent that those counseling funding delays in the Navy development program would not be successful. The Air Force had long held on the shelf a proposal for a second-generation, solid fuel missile which, according to Air Force, Navy, and industry sources, grew more attractive as a direct result of the competitive pressures of the Polaris development.[84] Approved in late 1958, the Minuteman, as this missile came to be called, became the Air Force's favored system. No

81. Richard Witkin, "POLARIS Shot Opens Crucial Test Series," *New York Times* (March 28, 1960), p. 22.

82. Senate Preparedness Subcommittee, *Hearings, Inquiry into Satellite and Missile Programs,* Pt. II, January 13, 1958, pp. 1743–1744.

83. Int I-69.

84. Ints I-70, 71, 72.

longer did a solid fuel ballistic missile seem impractical to the Air Force.

With the development of the Minuteman, the Air Force had a missile system whose expected deployment dates and operational characteristics made it a direct alternative to the FBM system. In promoting the Minuteman, the Air Force stressed its relatively low costs and argued against major commitment to an FBM submarine construction program.[85] One early claim was that for the same $300 million, the United States could have either 1,600 Minuteman or 48 to 64 Polaris missiles.[86] When the Navy sought 45 FBM submarines, the Air Force thought 15 to 20 would be sufficient.[87]

Polaris partisans saw the Air Force threat everywhere. The frequent visits of retired Air Corps generals to their wartime friend in the White House were viewed as an Air Force device to pass on pro-Minuteman (and anti-Polaris) arguments directly to President Eisenhower.[88] Reporters who had made the rounds of Air Force installations always appeared to have extremely distorted opinions about the FBM system's invulnerability and technical capabilities.[89] Admiral Raborn at one point asked General Schriever, the commanding officer of the Air Force Ballistic Missile Division, to intervene with the people at the Wright Field Air Force Laboratories who were said to be spreading misinformation about the Polaris guidance equipment.[90] And, of course, the Air Force strongly argued that the operational FBM system be combined with the other strategic missiles and placed under the direct control of the Air Force's Strategic Air Command.[91]

Today, we are all the beneficiaries of the Air Force-Navy competition, for it forced both services to examine carefully the missiles and the operational doctrines that they were de-

85. An Air Force cost comparison of the major missile systems appears in *An Analysis of Management Effectiveness in Ballistic Missile Program,* BSL-68 prepared by the Ballistic Systems Division of the Air Force Systems Command (Norton Air Force Base, Calif.: 30 April 1962) (SRD Group I), pp. 68–69.

86. Jack Raymond, "500 to 5,500-Mile Missile Is Approved for Air Force," *New York Times* (February 28, 1958), p. 3.

87. Witkin, "Polaris Shot Opens Crucial Test Series," p. 22.

88. Int I-48B.

89. Int I-73.

90. Minutes of the Navy Ballistic Missile Committee Meeting, First Meeting, February 20, 1957, p. 23 (Secret).

91. Int I-74.

veloping. For example, the Special Projects Office's plan for two crews to increase the on station time of FBM submarines can be attributed to Air Force criticism that, with normal overhauls and crew scheduling, it would take three Polaris submarines to keep one within range of Soviet targets.[92] Also, the strategic value of the FBM system's invulnerability was not well appreciated until the Air Force argued strongly the comparative cost advantages of land-based missiles.[93] To those managing missile development, however, competition was a direct threat to the survival and success of their program.

In addition to Air Force opposition discussed above, the environment contained a number of other groups whose actions or inactions could easily have blocked or delayed the FBM Program. Congressional committees, the General Accounting Office, the Bureau of the Budget, White House staff groups, the Civil Service Commission, and the State Department were not bound by Department of Defense priorities and directives, yet their cooperation or neutrality was needed if the FBM Program was to be implemented. Within the Department of Defense itself there were numerous independently constituted organizations, such as review panels, audit agencies, and laboratories, who, with their own priorities and authority, controlled resources vital to the program. Although the Special Projects Office had extremely few problems working with these groups, they always stood as potential threats. Failure to consider them as such could have added substantially to the difficulties that the FBM Program encountered.

FOUR STRATEGIES IN BUREAUCRATIC POLITICS

The basic objective of the Polaris proponents was to gain the organizational autonomy required to deploy a force of FBM submarines in the shortest possible time. They were concerned about Soviet developments in missiles and believed in the effectiveness of strategic deterrence. Given their basic objective, they sought to obtain the resources and authority to control independently the design, construction, and maintenance of the FBM force. Having had extensive experience in

92. Int I-69.
93. Ints I-75, 76A.

other weapon programs, the proponents were aware of the many ways in which projects fail because of their dependence on cooperation among government agencies, each having independent bases of power and conflicting goals and interests. For the Polaris proponents, the obstacles to success were the many agencies of government. It was to avoid dependence on the rest of government that they strove to secure their own organizational autonomy.

Official priority designations alone would not be sufficient to gain necessary organizational autonomy. Proponents of the program recognized that the power of priorities lay in reputation rather than in use. Frequent reliance on them to protect the program would only force the highest defense officials to make difficult choices at a pace they could not long sustain. Behind each of the enforceable priorities had to be support that could be effectively mobilized without the participation of any particular keeper of the national priorities, whether he be the President of the United States or the Secretary of Defense.

Nor would the marshaling of widespread support for the Polaris FBM alone have been sufficient to gain the necessary organizational autonomy. The uncertainty surrounding FBM development was so great that many of those converted to Polaris would have been tempted to monitor and direct its progress. In times of crisis, the administrative response is more likely to be centralization rather than the delegation of authority. Recognition of a missile gap brought demands for missile czars, new review panels, emergency planning agencies, and congressional inquiries, all of which were implemented. With America threatened, those officials with the greatest responsibility for its safety were reminded of their power to manage the national defense. To gain the autonomy the Polaris proponents sought, they needed to have those officials believe they were capable of managing the nation's highest priority program.

The proponents then had two distinct and only partially complementary subobjectives. First, they wanted to attract a broad base of support for the Polaris both inside and outside the Navy. Second, they wanted to prevent the rest of the Navy and the rest of the government from interfering in the management of the Polaris program. To gain the first subobjective, a unique demand for the FBM system had to be established; to gain the second, confidence in the unique management abilities of the Special Projects Office had to be established. Both were achieved.

The means by which they were achieved can be summarized best by describing four bureaucratic strategies. These strategies were not codified in any particular program document; nor were they necessarily followed consciously by the Polaris proponents. Rather, I argue that an examination of the many actions taken by Admiral Raborn and his staff to control potential threats to the program reveals patterns of decision making consistent with the four strategies outlined.

Two of the strategies, differentiation and co-optation, served primarily to develop a unique demand for the FBM; the other two strategies, moderation and managerial innovation, served primarily to protect the Special Projects Office and its contractors from outside meddlers. Not one of the strategies was tied exclusively to either of the program subobjectives. And, like the subobjectives, they could at times be contradictory.

By employing these bureaucratic strategies, FBM proponents were able to maintain the program in a difficult environment, but not without cost. The strategies modified the content of the program, influenced its development, and established long-term commitments that limit its flexibility. Yet the recognition of these constraints does not diminish the value of the bureaucratic strategies in promoting and protecting the Polaris.

Differentiation. The strategy of differentiation refers to the attempts of organizations to establish unchallengeable claims on valued resources by distinguishing their own products or programs from those of their competitors.[94] Business firms want consumers to believe that no other brand will satisfy the need for a particular product as well as their own; government agencies want congressmen, budget officials, and citizens to believe that no other program will satisfy the needs of a particular national policy as well as their own. Both types of organizations seek to avoid competition for valued resources

94. On the concept of differentiation and its relationship to organizational competition, see Harvey M. Sapolsky, "Organization Competition and Monopoly," in *Public Policy,* Vol. XVII (Cambridge, Mass.: Harvard University Press, 1968), pp. 355–376.

by creating identities that are unique and favorable in the view of those who control resource allocations.

The conceptual gymnastics involved in the initial efforts at defining the mission of the FBM system fall within this strategy. In order to gain support in the Navy and avoid substantial conflict with the Air Force, early FBM proponents often justified the weapon development in terms of potential effectiveness against tactical rather than strategic targets. Despite the fact that it was quickly evident that the FBM system would be technically unable to provide the pinpoint delivery accuracies required to eliminate tactical targets, submarine pens and port facilities were persistently mentioned in system statements as probable FBM targets. The phrase "striking targets of naval opportunity" was often used to describe the FBM objective as late as mid-1957.[95] System designers, of course, could not operationalize the phrase, but it was meant to stake out a unique Navy claim on ballistic missiles and allay the fears of naval traditionalists rather than to provide a guideline for technical development.[96]

In general, however, creating a unique and favorable identity for the FBM program was a relatively easy task because of the magnitude of the strategic threat and the unusual features embodied in the FBM system. America faced possible nuclear blackmail, but the FBM submarines could eliminate that threat by being ready to fire a missile from under the seas to targets 1,200 to 2,500 nautical miles distant. The only possible danger was that a "business as usual" complacency or a disabling skepticism would develop during the long years required to achieve the capability which seemed so vital and so intriguing. Substantial efforts were devoted to insuring that neither malady would affect the program.

To fight complacency, the program was always operated on a wartime basis. Although military officers assigned to Washington staff posts normally wear civilian clothes during work hours, naval officers attached to the Special Projects Office

95. Tactical missions for Polaris are discussed in "Navy Views POLARIS as Support Weapon," *Aviation Week*, 66 (June 17, 1957), p. 31. Note also Thomas S. Gates, Jr., *The United States Navy: Its Influence upon History* (New York: Newcomen Society in North America, 1958), p. 27.

96. Ints I-76B through H. See also Admiral Sides personal letter to Admiral Gallantin.

were "urged" to wear their uniforms, and they did. Although government-wide regulations restrict the use of overtime for civil servants, the Special Projects Office personnel were required to work an extended-hour, five-and-a-half-day-week even when the work loads were light.[97] FBM-related messages were red stamped and frequently hand carried to emphasize the need for special treatment. Polaris flags similar to Navy "E" flags used during the Second World War flew above the factories and laboratories participating in the program.

No one was allowed to think of the program in conventional terms. When a Navy field office accountant sought to apply the usual bureaucratic delays to FBM contractor requests, he was told that he would be immediately transferred to another, less desirable assignment if he attempted to do so again. "Think big or get out" was the message.[98] When the performance of the headquarters units was reviewed, branch heads were put on report if their subordinates were traveling less frequently than the office average.[99] When the Navy budget was presented to Congress, the Special Projects Office always requested a separate FBM presentation that combined the standard appropriation categories into a single FBM program total.

Every opportunity was seized to stimulate and maintain a general awareness of the program and the importance of its mission.[100] Admiral Raborn continually toured the country inspecting plants and shipyards, and at each facility the workers were assembled to hear him deliver an evangelistic Polaris rededication speech.[101] A team of Special Projects Office "tech-

97. Int I-76D.
98. Int I-76J.
99. Int I-76K.
100. The Special Projects Office public relations budget, for example, in certain years was said to be the largest in the Navy, larger even than the Navy's Public Information Office. Moreover, much of the Special Projects public relations expenditures were not clearly identified as such as they were kept hidden in administrative overheads and contractor budgets (Int I-77).
101. Edgar L. Prina in "Portrait of a Missile-Age Admiral," *Washington Sunday Star* (November 13, 1960) reports on one of Admiral Raborn's trips to a contractor's plant that had fallen behind in its scheduled deliveries. After the Admiral's speech to the workers some 250 of them "spontaneously drew up and signed a pledge to rededicate themselves to their jobs." Important deliveries were met on time from then on.

nical information officers" and the Admiral himself were ready to attend meetings of professional societies, military reserve units, and business associations to discuss the ballistic missile threat. Newly elected congressmen and newly appointed defense officials were personally visited by the Admiral and invited to special secret briefings on the program.[102] Contractors were encouraged to carry on active Polaris public relations and advertising campaigns, both in their own local areas and nationally.[103] Friendly newsmen were sought out and kept privately informed of progress. Even the families of the Special Projects Office staff were given periodic lectures on the FBM mission so that they would appreciate the personal sacrifices required of them if the program were to succeed.[104]

By design the message disseminated was kept simple and personal.[105] The theme was that everyone was threatened by Soviet ballistic missiles, but there was an effective weapon system that could be developed to nullify the threat. At the conclusion of a speech, the Admiral would often ask his audience to grasp the backs of their necks. "Those are the necks that will be saved when the Polaris is developed," he would then say.

Countering doubts about the feasibility of the system was a constant concern. Everyone could be made to fear a Soviet missile attack, but some would remain skeptical about the possibility of producing a solid-fueled missile that could be launched from a submarine in so short a time as was proposed. By nature and by necessity Admiral Raborn was optimistic. Information on the technical progress of the program was released only through his office. From this perspective, to the embarrassment of the staff, technical adversity often became a partial success and technical success, a major advance. Uncertainties were played down. The program was referred to as involving "development" efforts rather than "research" ef-

102. Int I-78.
103. Note Int I-79. See also Director, Special Projects Office Memorandum to Distribution, SPO 20-AHS:stb, 17 March 1961, subj: Briefings to Members of the Polaris industry team and their dependents: support for; and the letter with attachment from the Manager, Ordnance Division, General Electric Company, Pittsfield, Mass., to Admiral Raborn, 21 April 1961.
104. Int I-78A, B.
105. Int I-80 and Special Projects Office, "Brief Outline of Presentation Introduction" (mimeo, undated).

forts. In early 1958, the Admiral proclaimed that all remaining FBM problems were engineering in nature rather than scientific.[106]

Substantial exaggerations about technological progress were permitted to circulate. Although there was apparently no major advance in warhead technology during 1956 (there was then only the expectation of future advances), the early literature on the program invariably mentioned the 1956 warhead breakthrough that allowed the FBM system to switch from the large Jupiter missile to the smaller Polaris missile. Similarly, some promising but unverified experiments in solid propellants by the Atlantic Research Corporation became, in 1956, the single dramatic advance that demonstrated the feasibility of large-scale, solid-fueled rockets, when, in fact, they were only a step in a long series of difficult steps that led to this innovation.[107] Fortunately, technological progress often managed to catch up with technological advertising.

The efforts at differentiation have, however, had their cost. The success in providing the program with a unique identity has kept it isolated from the rest of the Navy. The question "When is Polaris going to join the Navy?" is often heard. This isolation from the mainstream of naval activities has at times, particularly in recent years, prevented senior naval officers from defending the program because they either lacked the knowledge or the will to do so. When the program's own sources of support are not sufficient for protection, it cannot draw heavily on the traditional political resources of the Navy.

Co-optation. The strategy of co-optation refers to the attempts of an organization to absorb ". . . new elements into [its] leadership or policy-determining structure . . . as a means of averting threats to its stability or existence."[108] Administratively, co-optation can involve either the actual sharing of power or simply the sharing of the burdens of power. Depending on their political strength, potentially disruptive elements

106. "The Navy Fires a Dummy Polaris from an Underwater 'Pop-Up' Launcher," *New York Times* (April 12, 1958), p. 3.

107. Ints I-42, 81, 82. The Atlantic Research discovery is also discussed in "Rockets Propellant of Aluminum Hailed," *New York Times* (July 19, 1959), p. 14.

108. Philip Selznick, "Cooptation: A Mechanism for Organization Stability," in Robert Merton, *et al.*, editors, *Reader in Bureaucracy* (Glencoe, Ill.: Free Press, 1952), p. 135.

may be given control over decisions vital to their interests in order to gain their support in other matters, or they may be given symbolic participation in decision making in order to add legitimacy to established policies.[109] For example, although the Tennessee Valley Authority had to allow the local units of the American Farm Bureau Federation covertly to determine its agricultural policies in order to overcome their opposition to government ownership of electric power in the valley, it found that soil conservation groups could be used to marshal local support without the sacrifice of any substantive policies.[110]

The Special Projects Office and the FBM Program gained some needed legitimacy within the Navy by the ostensible extensive use of existing naval facilities, expertise, and command structures. The Bureau of Ordnance, for example, had official jurisdiction over several organizations vital to the FBM Program—the Special Projects contracts office, naval plant representatives, the Naval Astronautics Group (navigation satellite), and the naval missile test unit at Cape Kennedy—but in no case could it significantly affect their operation in FBM matters since they received their technical direction exclusively from the Special Projects Office. The naval laboratories were invited to participate in the Polaris Ad Hoc Group for Long Range Research and Development, which seemingly was to guide the future of the FBM Program, but which actually had extremely limited influence on program plans. Also, the Ships Characteristics Board, a committee of senior naval officers which convened regularly to review and approve ship construction plans, was asked by the Special Projects Office to look over the plans for the FBM submarines and support ships even though these vessels were not to be subject to its directives.[111]

Systematically, potential critics of the FBM and the development effort were drawn into the program and implicated in its activities. There was sometimes a task and always some project money for any naval facility that expressed any interest at all in the development of the weapon system. As one Special Projects Office branch head put it, "We were the Medici

109. *Ibid.*, pp. 136–137.
110. *Ibid.*, pp. 138–139.
111. Ints I-83, 84.

for the rest of the Navy." The Bureau of the Budget and General Accounting Office were kept informed about the program and were asked for their ideas on its management. Any scientist who had a question on the technical plans was invited to attend a briefiing on the entire program and asked if he would be willing to contribute to the program by working on a research problem in a relevant area of technology.[112]

The support of leading scientists was thought to be particularly crucial since scientists after the Second World War years had become for many the final arbiters of whether or not a major defense project should be pursued. Faced with questions on the technical feasibility of the FBM system, Admiral Raborn apparently recognized that his own defense of the program would be severely discounted due to his lack of advanced technical training and to his deep involvement in the program's promotion. Thus, he sought wherever possible to buttress the program with the endorsements of top defense scientists. In congressional testimony and official briefings, it was always a statement from a noted weapons expert on a science advisory committee rather than one from Admiral Raborn that was used to defend the feasibility of a given technological goal.[113]

Good relations with the scientific community were relatively easy to establish. Support was cumulative and reinforcing. The NOBSKA report, which had stated that a Polaris-type missile system was both feasible and desirable, had been prepared by a committee of the National Academy of Sciences with the assistance of a number of prominent defense scientists. Other scientists, convinced of the value of the program's mission and of the competence of the NOBSKA scientists, the Special Projects Technical staff, and the program contractors could add their endorsements even though they may not have been especially conversant with the technologies involved. With the establishment in the Special Projects Office of the posts of Chief Scientist and Engineering Consultant to maintain liaison with the scientific community, there could be assurance that outside advice would be intelligently inter-

112. Ints I-85A, B, C, I-S1.
113. See, for example, U.S. Congress, House, Subcommittee on Military Appropriations of the Committee on Appropriations, *Hearings, Department of Defense Appropriations*, 86th Cong., 1st Sess. (Washington: Government Printing Office, 1959), p. 275.

preted. In order to build trust, each technical branch in the Special Projects Office always had some money set aside to follow up on the suggestions of outside scientists, no matter how relevant these suggestions were to the branch's established technical goals.

Control over the formulation of the program's technical goals and the main thrust of its development effort, however, was always retained by the Technical Director. Despite the model that existed in the Air Force missile program, no permanent board of outside scientific advisors, the members of which could have become deeply enmeshed in the direction of the development effort was tolerated.

A similar kind of costless co-optation directed toward legitimizing the program would appear to be involved in the effort to promote the nonsubmarine, nonstrategic uses of Polaris. During the late 1950s, for example, numerous plans for placing Polaris launching tubes on aircraft carriers, cruisers, and even destroyers continually circulated in the Pentagon. To be sure, these plans were partially motivated by a desire to get as many Polaris missiles as possible to sea as quickly as possible. Submarines took a long time to construct, and it was certainly necessary to ask whether other types of naval vessels could provide an interim capability. But given the fact that major operational and technological problems would make the surface ship applications of ballistic missiles considerably less valuable and more time consuming to achieve and given the fact that the technical staff of the Special Projects office never devoted significant resources to the solution of these problems after 1956, the persistent presentation of surface ship plans indicates that they may have been partially motivated by different desires. Certainly it must have been clear to Admiral Raborn and other Polaris proponents that, throughout the life of the program, the Navy's policy staffs would be dominated by carrier, cruiser, and destroyer admirals—no matter what the nation's strategic goals were. Some effort toward reconciliation had to be made. Thus, the surface ship applications plans could be interpreted as a conscious attempt to gain important support for (or at least to avoid important opposition to) Polaris within the Navy. Since the final burden of approval for these plans fell upon the Office of the Secretary of Defense and since approval never seemed likely to be given, the promotion of surface ship applications could be treated within the Special Projects Office as an aside that would have no direct impact on the FBM Program or its mission.

Other attempts to co-opt important elements in a potentially hostile environment, however, resulted in sharing decision making power. Given a national disposition to favor private as opposed to public enterprise, an effort to develop and produce a major military system completely within government facilities tends to rouse decisive opposition. Though the Army did use a private contractor, Chrysler, to produce Jupiter, the Army's reliance on its own arsenals for the development and prototype construction of missiles and for the management of the overall effort was thought by many to have been a major handicap in the competition with the Air Force (which relied heavily upon aerospace contractors in its missile program) for a share of the strategic missile mission.[114] In contrast, the National Aeronautics and Space Administration's extensive use of private contractors in its Apollo program could be viewed in part as an effort to bolster the base of political support for a politically controversial program.

The Special Projects Office, for a number of persuasive reasons—the lack of available in service facilities, the need for quick and flexible expansion of supporting staffs, and the desire to avoid a dependency upon other government agencies that could assert their autonomy—decided in the FBM Program to rely upon aerospace contractors for the bulk of the research and development effort and for management support, as well as for procurement. Consciously or unconsciously, this decision provided the program with another set of resourceful proponents who added their influence to the effort to protect the program. At the same time, however, the decision brought the contractors into the decision making processes affecting the development of the weapon system. The technical preference and orientations of the contractors of necessity affected the development process. Thus, dependence upon private contractors compensated in part for potential dependence upon government laboratories and research facilities.

The program's reliance on private contractors had an immediate payoff in the acceleration of the Polaris program. Just as some decision makers turn to prominent scientists for sup-

114. Medaris, *Countdown for Decision,* p. 148.

port in complex weapon decisions, others turn to successful businessmen. During the December 1957 period, when the fate of the Polaris acceleration proposal had to be determined, one high-level Department of the Navy official called a meeting of the presidents of all the major contractors involved in the FBM Program to discuss the feasibility of the development target dates submitted by the Special Projects Office. When, in revival meeting fashion, each president went to a blackboard and wrote the name of his firm signifying a commitment to those dates, the official was convinced that the Navy Secretariat should back the proposal. The Department of the Navy could risk its reputation if substantial firms such as General Electric, Westinghouse, Lockheed, Electric Boat, and Sperry Rand were willing to risk theirs.[115]

Peace also had to be made with the Bureau of Ships and its highly independent Nuclear Power Directorate, headed by Vice Admiral Hyman G. Rickover. The only shipyards in the United States capable of building submarines were beholden to the bureau and the only contractors in the United States capable of building submarine nuclear propulsion plants were beholden to Admiral Rickover. Important committees in the Congress often turned to the Admiral for guidance on military policy and programs. In addition, Admiral Rickover influenced the Navy in the selection and qualification of crews serving aboard nuclear submarines. If the desire to develop and deploy a fleet of FBM submarines rapidly was to be fulfilled, then the decisions determining the characteristics of the submarines, their construction scheduling, and their manning had to be shared with the bureau and the Admiral.[116] Although the Special Projects Office could with some effort get its way on the design of aspects of the submarine directly affecting the performance of the weapon system,[117] the FBM submarine development cannot be said to have been completely within its control.

Perhaps the most important accommodation that had to be made in the program was that with the submariners. Since, as the ultimate customer, their opinions would be sought both inside and outside the Navy, the early cooperation of sub-

115. Int I-85D.
116. Int I-86.
117. Ints I-87, 88, 89.

marine specialists was vital to the success of the program. Obtaining their cooperation was not an easy task for, as was noted previously, senior submariners, with very few exceptions, strongly opposed the program. One had even told junior officers on his staff that their naval careers would be finished if they had anything to do with the newly initiated FBM Program.[118]

The effort to gain the support of the submarine specialists has been continuous in the program, but a single event—the selection of sixteen as the number of missile tubes to be carried per submarine—best illustrates the nature of that effort. Sixteen has become the world standard for missile tubes per ballistic missile submarine. All forty-one of the United States FBM submarines have that number. So do the ballistic missile submarines that the French, the British, and the Russians are building.

To many, this worldwide convergence on sixteen as the most appropriate number of tubes per submarine must indicate that sixteen was the product of a careful study, if not in Britain or in France or in the Soviet Union, then certainly in the United States, the first country to select that number. It was not. In 1957, when the parameters of the FBM system were being determined, the Special Projects Office did conduct detailed trade-off studies, but these indicated that though technically any even number between four and forty-eight was feasible, thirty-two was the most practical cost/effective number of tubes per submarine.[119] A group of senior submarine officers was asked to consider the implications of these studies on submarine size; their reaction was immediately negative since thirty-two missile tubes would require a submarine much larger than they anticipated would result from the program. No submarine of such size had ever been built. Large submarines, they felt, did not handle well. Moreover, no hatch as large as six feet in diameter, which the missile tube required, had been used before on a submarine, and to place thirty-two of them on one submarine appeared much too risky.[120] Finally, thirty-two missiles just seemed like too many

118. Int I-90.
119. Int I-91.
120. Int I-92.

eggs in one basket for a strategic system.[121] The submariners intuitively decided upon sixteen as the maximum acceptable number of missile tubes.[122]

The matter came up for decision in a program planning meeting at which submariners were present. After a discussion of all arguments, an advisory vote was to be taken. When the voting began by asking for ballots starting with the highest number, thirty-two, it quickly became apparent that, while no single number would receive a majority of ballots, a majority would exist in favor of twenty-four or more tubes per submarine. The meeting was adjourned by its chairman, Captain Levering Smith, then Technical Director of the Special Projects Office, before the voting was completed. After Admiral Raborn was informed of the likely outcome and of the strong preference of the submariners, it was decided to fix the number of tubes at sixteen, regardless of any cost-effectiveness ratio. Subsequent rationales for the decision have attributed the selection of sixteen to the technical limitations of optical alignment equipment planned for the fire control subsystem on the submarines. These limitations, however, proved to be much more transitory than the goodwill that had been established with the submariners by the decision.[123]

Moderation. The strategy of moderation refers to the attempts of organizations to build long-term support for their programs by sacrificing short-term gains. Business firms are said to avoid maximizing profits in the short term so as to establish market relations that will provide long-term profits. Retail firms with an interest in maintaining a reputation for quality goods, for example, will not permit their department managers to sell shoddy merchandise even at high profits in order not to alienate customers who, except for the treatment they might receive in this instance, would otherwise continue to patronize the store. Similarly, a disciplined political faction that has some expectation of winning a primary election, but also some concern about the ability of the party to win the

121. Int I-93.
122. Int I-11S.
123. Ints I-91, 94, and S2. In 1958 and again in 1960, the desirability of increasing the number of missile launchers per submarine was raised in various meetings. No reference was made to technical limitations in these discussions.

general election, will most likely show restraint in attacking the opposing faction in the primary. The key to successfully employing a strategy of moderation is, of course, an ability to estimate and compare short-term and long-term gains (or losses).

In the early years of the FBM Program there were many instances when the proponents, particularly the Special Projects Office, had clearly the political resources to obtain certain well-recognized and desirable objectives, but failed to attempt to do so. Much of this self-imposed restraint can be attributed simply to the advantages of pursuing some other immediate objective simultaneously, and yet there remains a measure of restraint that seems to have been exercised in order to avoid an accumulation of animosity that would have hurt the program at a later date. Within the Navy there circulated in reference to the Special Projects Office the saying, "Whatever Lola wants, Lola gets."[124] Lola, however, tried to be very careful in selecting the objects of her desire.

A relatively minor example of this use of moderation is the case of facilities for the Special Projects headquarters. When the program was established, Admiral Raborn, recognizing that the main battles for its survival would be fought in the naval staffs and in the Pentagon, chose Washington for his headquarters rather than Huntsville, Alabama, where the Army Jupiter team was located, or southern California, where the Air Force ballistic missile organization and a large portion of the aerospace industry were located. The first Washington space assigned to the Special Projects Office was in Building W, a dilapidated "temporary" facility situated behind the Navy Munitions Building. With the rapid expansion of the program, the Special Projects Office obtained space in the Munitions Building itself where the headquarters of several Navy technical bureaus were located. This space, too, quickly became inadequate. The priority and funds allocated to the program would, at this point, have permitted a move to any facility that was available, or even the construction of a new building. Across the street from the Munitions Building, temptingly empty, stood a large, well-equipped building vacated when the Atomic Energy Commission moved to a new suburban Washington headquarters. Rather than flaunting wealth and

124. Int I-95.

position, however, it was decided that the Special Projects Office would stay "close to the Navy" by remaining with their less fortunate brethren in the cramped and aging Munitions Building.[125]

A more significant example of the strategy was the restraint shown in passing up the opportunity to establish an elite corps status for the FBM submarine crews. The extended patrols that these crews would undertake were expected to be both arduous and boring. In addition, most of the men needed to man the crews would have to be highly trained in specialties for which there were many attractive civilian alternatives. One important way in which the military traditionally compensates for difficult tasks and reduces the lure of civilian life is by establishing elite corps. The Air Force, for example, gives its Minuteman silo crews white helmets with bolts of lightning painted on them and white uniforms decorated with brightly colored scarfs and side arms. Faced with an ingrained Navy distaste for elite units (perhaps resulting from the Marine Corps experience) and the potential animosity of unborn generations of sailors, the FBM Program neither identified nor compensated FBM crews in any way that would have set them apart.[126] An early program-sponsored study on crew incentives that called for special uniforms and special insignia was suppressed.[127] Today, when the excitement of patrol has long since disappeared and a morale problem may be developing, the wisdom of that decision is in question.[128]

125. Int I-96.
126. Because of the two-crew arrangement for FBM submariners, special legislation had to be passed just to equalize the pay of the Polaris crews with that of other submariners. The law had read that submarine crew members were not eligible for submarine pay (hazardous duty compensation) if they were away from their boats for more than fifteen days. Such absences rarely happened with the attack boat crews, but they would be standard practice in the FBM fleet.
127. Ints I-97, A-3.
128. See Lieutenant Commander Jonathan T. Howe, USN, "POLARIS Duty: Pinnacle or Predicament?" *United States Naval Institute Proceedings*, 93 (August 1967), pp. 28–32. The resignation rate of Polaris officers has climbed dramatically in the last few years, and the Navy has been forced to establish a $15,000 bonus for the reenlistment of young officers and a special FBM insignia for all ratings. Note William Beecher, "Some Navy Men Grumble over Submarine Bonus," *New York Times* (August 15, 1969), p. 14, and Juan Cameron, "The Armed Forces' Reluctant Retrenchment," *Fortune*, 82 (November 1970), esp. p. 174; also Int I-S3.

Despite its goal of complete autonomy, the Special Projects Office did avoid seizing complete control of certain functions to which it could legitimately lay claim. For example, responsibility for the FBM communications research and development effort was shared with the Chief of Naval Communications and technical groups in the Bureau of Ships, even though the funds for this effort came exclusively from the Special Projects Office. Similarly, the official (legal) responsibility for FBM contract administration was allowed to remain with the Chiefs of Ordnance and Ships, even though the actual day-to day budgeting and administration of the contracts was exclusively under the direction of the Special Projects Office. At the time when these particular responsibilities were fixed, it was apparently assumed that financial control and the threat of appeal to higher authority would be sufficient to assure quick compliance to all requests.[129] Forcing the issue of control, though possible, seemed to be unnecessary and might ultimately antagonize enough high-ranking naval officers that a strong coalition of FBM opponents would be formed.

The Special Projects Office also carefully refrained from publicly attacking any FBM opponents or competitors. Despite frequent attacks on the feasibility of a sea-based ballistic missile system, there was an official policy of not disseminating derogatory statements about land-based Air Force systems.[130] Despite opposing claims that ICBMs alone were a sufficient deterrent, FBM proponents did not argue that a sea-based IRBM system, invulnerable as they thought it to be, should become the sole U.S. strategic deterrent.[131] In congressional testimony and official briefings, care was taken to note the contributions of the other services and the other naval commands in the effort to advance the state-of-the-art in ballistic missiles and in the management of large-scale programs.[132]

129. Contractual control is discussed in Chapter Three, and the Polaris communications research program is examined in Chapter Eight, below.

130. Int I-98.

131. See, for example, Admiral Arleigh Burke, Speech to the National Press Club, January 8, 1958, and the statements on strategic deterrence of the Under Secretary of Navy, Thomas S. Gates, Jr., in his *The United States Navy*, p. 34.

132. Note the testimony of Admiral Raborn in reference to the Air Force and Army in Senate Preparedness Subcommittee, *Hearings,*

There was to be only one recognized enemy—the Soviet Union. Competition for resources to meet the enemy threat should not be allowed to become bitter and personal, for it was thought that nothing would be achieved from such a struggle in the long run. All parts of the Navy would have to work at some time or other with the program and its product, so that today's opposition could easily become tomorrow's support. In addition, the Navy could not realistically expect to gain the dominant position in the nation's strategic force; it would only be belligerent if it were seeking more than a "fair share." Given the separate organization of the military services, Congress and the Department of Defense would inevitably be required to endorse a mixed strategic force, so there would be no long-term advantage in getting individual congressmen and defense officials to make strong public commitments to any single missile system.

Managerial innovation. This strategy was essentially an independent invention of the Special Projects Office. It can be defined as the attempt of an organization to achieve autonomy in the direction of a complex and risky program through the introduction of managerial techniques that appear to indicate unique managerial competence. High-level officials, accountable as they are for failures of subordinates, utilize a number of bureaucratic controls, such as special audits, detail reports, and staff assistants to limit the initiative of their subordinates. In extremely complex and risky programs, these officials are often tempted to limit further the independence of subordinates by intervening directly in the management of these programs. The Special Projects Office sought to avoid being required to justify in detail each decision made in the FBM Program by building official and public confidence in its general managerial abilities. Since the program involved the management of complex technological innovations, it appeared that the most effective way to build confidence was to innovate in the development of managerial techniques. Thus, the Special

---

Inquiry into Satellite and Missile Programs, Pt. 1, December 16, 1957, pp. 775–776; and in reference to the Army alone in U.S. Congress, House, Subcommittee on Government Operations, *Hearings, Systems Development and Management*, 87th Cong., 2nd Sess. (Washington: Government Printing Office, 1962), Pt. 4, August 16, 1962, p. 1462.

Projects Office actively sought and gained a reputation as an organization that was innovative in managerial techniques as well as in technology.[133]

In the early years of the program, the Special Projects Office invented and/or refined a number of managerial techniques that have gained wide notoriety. Among the famous products of this effort to innovate in the management of a large-scale technological project are Program Evaluation and Review Technique (PERT), the extension of PERT to include program costs (PERT/COST), Reliability Management Index (RMI), the concept of project management, the program management center, weekly program review meetings, and managerial graphics.

The Special Projects Office quickly became a model for the management of other development organizations, both private and public. The demand for information on management techniques became so large that fulltime personnel were assigned to handle these inquiries and a weekly briefing was scheduled for visitors.

The strategy appears to have been eminently successful, perhaps even too successful. The Special Projects Office gained an unparralleled independence within the Navy and within the Department of Defense that has only recently been eroded. In drawing general lessons from the experience of the FBM Program, defense officials have tended to emphasize the efficacy of managerial techniques and depreciate the importance of the organizational autonomy of the agency that produced both the techniques and the Polaris. Today, despite its own misgivings about the managerial value of several of the innovations, the Special Projects Office must continue to apply them all. It has a reputation to maintain, and some of the techniques are now contractual requirements imposed by the Department of Defense.

133. Although the Special Projects Office's dedication to the strategy of managerial innovation appears unique, there have been somewhat parallel efforts to emphasize management techniques in many other defense and nondefense projects. For an illuminating discussion of good fortune and skillful management in the promotion and protection of projects in less developed countries, see Albert O. Hirschman, *Development Projects Observed* (Washington: The Brookings Institution, 1967), particularly chaps. 1 and 4.

In the succeeding three chapters, the organizational structure and management practices of the Special Projects Office will be examined in detail. The role that management innovations played in the development of the Polaris can then be seen in light of the requirements of technological progress and the actual operations of the Special Projects Office.

3 | The Structure of Organizational Relationships

The establishment of the Special Projects Office was of greater consequence for the Navy than the establishment of the FBM Program. The Navy had undertaken many complex tasks prior to the FBM. It had not previously, however, formed a major subunit whose sole mission was the development of a single weapon system.

At the time the Special Projects Office was established, the Navy described itself as a bilinear organization. That is, it had two independent lines of organizational responsibility. One half of the Navy, the technical bureaus, managed the department's material resources and was responsible for the procurement of weapons; the other half, the Chief of Naval Operations and his staff, commanded the operating forces (the fleets) and was responsible for determining the Navy's weapons requirements. Responsibility for the procurement of weapons was further modified by the fact that the bureaus were independent of one another as well as of the operating forces and were organized according to distinctive technologies and functions (for example, Aeronautics, Ordnance, Ships, and Medicine).

No one in authority wanted to alter the organization of the Navy to accommodate the FBM when the program was proposed in 1955. Only a year before, the entire structure of the Navy had been reviewed and pronounced sound by a high-level panel, chaired by Under Secretary Gates.[1] Moreover,

1. Officially titled as the Committee on the Organization of the Department of the Navy, the Gates panel was convened in 1953 by the Secretary of the Navy in response to the reorganization of the Department of Defense that occurred in the same year. The committee's

reorganization in a bureaucracy as delicately balanced as the Navy always seems too politically costly to contemplate.

High-level Navy officials were aware, of course, that they were violating their own canons of organization in establishing the Special Projects Office. The new organizational unit would stand apart from the bureaus and would have the task of coordinating all naval activities required to build the FBM weapon system. It would be the first project-oriented agency to be given a rank equal to those of the functionally specialized bureaus.[2]

Their intention in creating the Special Projects Office, however, was only to settle a difficult jurisdictional dispute and not to reorganize the Navy. The Bureau of Aeronautics and the Bureau of Ordnance were competing for the control of the FBM in 1955.[3] Both apparently had important allies within the top echelons of the Navy. Aeronautics, it was said, had the backing of James H. Smith, Jr., Assistant Secretary of the Navy for Air, who was responsible for all research and devel-

---

findings are discussed in the report of a similar committee that Gates convened when he became Secretary of the Navy. *Reports of the Committee on the Organization of the Department of the Navy*, NAVEXOS P-1996 (Washington: Department of the Navy, 1959), pp. 14–15. The Gates panel recommendations, confirming and clarifying the then existing structure of the Navy, are approved in General Order No. 5, 20 November 1954.

2. The defining difference between a functionally specialized organization and a project-oriented organization lies, of course, in the tasks they are assigned. A functionally specialized organization is responsible for a particular organizational process or skill, e.g., aeronautical engineering, accounting, or typing, irrespective of the purposes to which those processes or skills are applied. A project-type organization is responsible for a particular organizational purpose, e.g., strategic retaliation, conventional warfare, or counterinsurgency, and thus ties together all the processes and skills necessary to accomplish that purpose. The classical statement on this distinction in the literature on organizations is by Luther Gulick, "Notes on the Theory of Organization," in Luther Gullick and L. Urwick, editors, *Papers on the Science of Administration* (New York: Institute of Public Administration, 1937), pp. 1–46.

3. The struggle between Ordnance and Aeronautics over missile jurisdictions had its origins in the Second World War. Note Lee M. Pearson, "Naval Administration of Guided Missile Research and Development during World War II" (unpub. paper prepared for the Seminar on Science and Public Policy, Graduate School of Public Administration, Harvard University, May 1963), and J. A. Furer, *Administration of the Navy Department in World War II* (Washington: Government Printing Office, 1959).

opment activities in the Navy and who was thought to be personally close to the Secretary.[4] Ordnance, it was said, had the support of Rear Admiral John "Savvy" Sides, the director of the missile plans section in the Office of the Chief of Naval Operations and a close friend of Admiral Burke.[5] Yet, to officials neutral in the dispute, it seemed that each of the contending bureaus was in some sense unqualified to hold the responsibility for managing a project as large and risky as the FBM. Ordnance, they recalled, had never been an enthusiastic proponent of a naval ballistic missile though its laboratories were competent in several of the relevant technologies. Aeronautics' early enthusiasium for ballistic missiles was flawed by the fact that it lacked the appropriate technical facilities and had a reputation for mismanaging major projects. The efficient as well as the politically expedient solution, therefore, was to assign the FBM to neither and to create a new unit that would be able to draw upon the competence and enthusiasm of the entire Navy.[6]

The material bureaus were not overwhelmingly pleased with the decision. Not only did Ordnance and Aeronautics each lose something they had sought, but now they and all the other bureaus had a new potential rival. To mollify them, limitations were placed on the Special Projects Office.[7] It was to be kept small. (The initial personnel authorization was only forty-five officers and an equal number of civilians.)[8] It was to rely upon the bureaus for its technical support. And it was to be disbanded with its remaining responsibilities absorbed by the bureaus upon the completion of the development phase of the FBM Program.

4. Ints II-1B, 2.
5. Ints II-1B, 3.
6. Ints II-4, 5, 6.
7. According to Robert Hunter the vague title "Special Projects Office" was selected purposely to avoid revealing to the Soviet Union *and* the Navy the true scope and nature of the FBM Program. Robert E. Hunter, "Politics and Polaris: The Special Projects Office in the Navy as a Political Phenomenon" (Senior Honors Thesis, Wesleyan University, June 1962). The "s" in Projects was said to have been added by Admiral Raborn to give the civilians in the office hope of future employment in case the FBM fell through as many observers at the time thought likely (Int II-8).
8. The personnel limitations imposed on the program led some participants to say that the FBM was a Martini Project rather than a Manhattan Project (Int II-H1).

The general expectation in 1955, then, was that the Special Projects Office would be only a minor and temporary deviation from the Navy's standard organization for the procurement of weapons. It did not turn out that way. Instead, the Special Projects Office soon came to provide the Navy with an alternative model for the organization of the weapon procurement process.

THE RELATIONSHIP WITH THE BUREAUS

Some degree of conflict was inevitable between the Special Projects Office and the bureaus. The Special Projects Office had been given the responsibility for managing all naval technologies and functions required to develop the FBM weapon system and yet each of the bureaus retained, unaltered, its responsibility for managing a specific technology or function within the Navy. The extent of the jurisdictional conflict would necessarily depend on the definition of the FBM weapon system, that is, its technological and functional boundaries.

After settling the dispuite between Ordnance and Aeronautics, high-level officials were unwilling to provide further jurisdictional guidance. Neither the order establishing the Special Projects Office, which was signed by the Secretary of the Navy, nor the FBM development requirement, which was issued by the Office of the Chief of Naval Operations, offered an unambiguous system definition.[9]

Admiral Raborn, on assuming the directorship of the Special Projects Office, recognized immediately that the FBM's boundary relationships were certain to be a cause of continuing difficulties. Without waiting for specific problems to develop, he sought the maximum definitional flexibility for the office. The Admiral asked that he be given the authority to direct all naval commands, including the bureaus, in any matter the Special Projects Office determined to be related to the FBM.[10] His request was denied. It was impossible, he was told, to centralize by fiat that much authority in an organization as

9. For example, Development Characteristic No. SC-16702-1, Op-371 M/jbc, Ser: 00118P37, 20 February 1957 (Secret), the Polaris development requirement, states on page I-1 that: "The Project Director is assigned responsibility for: (a) Technical development of the FBM system, *including* provisions for shipboard fire control, launching, storage handling, servicing and testing" [italics added].
10. Int II-8.

diverse as the Navy. The most Admiral Raborn could obtain was a letter signed by Admiral Burke stating that he, Admiral Burke (the highest ranking officer in the Navy, but himself not possessing command authority over the bureaus), wanted to be informed of any obstacles encountered in the FBM Program.[11] It was implied, however, that, if the letter had to be used often to remove obstacles, the program would fail.[12] The Special Projects Office would have to find its own way through the jurisdictional maze.

The FBM system obviously had to mean something more to the Special Projects Office than the Fleet Ballistic Missile since, in the joint Army-Navy project, the Redstone Arsenal held the assignment to develop the missile. And obviously the office had to be concerned with the design of a surface ship or submarine and with the development of specialized navigation, fire control, launching, and test equipment if the missile were to be fired at sea. A number of factors, however, led the office to define its mission and the FBM system in broader terms.

To begin with, the Navy wanted to develop a solid-fueled missile. In order to replace the liquid-fueled Jupiter with a solid-fueled missile, the Special Projects Office had to recruit personnel to direct missile design studies. The studies they sponsored, it will be recalled, showed that a solid-fueled missile would be feasible only if all missile components, including the guidance equipment and the reentry vehicle, were redesigned. After the ties with the Army were broken, the Special Projects Office came to direct the development of the missile as well as the auxiliary equipment.

Second, several officers attached to the FBM Program had previously worked on projects that in their opinion had failed to produce effective weapon systems for the fleet. They attributed these failures both to the integration problems that arose when component elements of a weapon system were the responsibility of autonomous bureaus[13] and to the sharp dis-

11. Admiral Burke Confidential Memorandum to Rear Admiral Clark and Rear Admiral Raborn (Office of the Secretary of the Navy), 2 December 1955, subj: ICBM-IRBM (Confidential).

12. Int II-8.

13. The coordination problem involved in the development of naval weapons is discussed from a historical perspective in Elting E. Morison, "Naval Administration in the United States," *United States Naval Institute Proceedings,* 62 (October 1946), pp. 1303–1313.

tinction that existed between development activities and the introduction of new weapons into the fleet. The lessons they drew from this experience were that a single organization should independently control the development of an entire weapon system and that equipment testing, crew training, and fleet support activities should be included in the definition of any weapon system.

A third factor involved the civilians in the Special Projects Office who were responsible for budgeting activities, particularly Gordon O. Pehrson. He was the head of the Plans and Program Division, and he sought to develop a concept of program management that would tie together program planning, budgeting, and performance reporting activities.[14] The experience this group had gained in other government agencies had convinced them that effective management had been frustrated by the practice of using separate systems to report financial and program performance data. Moreover, they believed that there was a tendency in government to be more concerned with the control of organizational inputs than with outputs. Moving to a new agency, especially one that was to be project oriented and was to have the highest priority, they saw the opportunity to create integrated management control systems that would focus decision making attention on program costs only in relationship to program performance. To create these systems, they sought to establish program packages that would include, in addition to the cost of military hardware, the cost of all the support facilities, such as communication installations, training centers, and supply depots required to maintain an operational unit (for example, a squadron of nine submarines) in combat readiness. Later, particularly when Charles Hitch became the Comptroller of the Department of Defense, these ideas were to be publicly identified with the RAND Corporation.[15] Their formal conceptualization and implementation, however, seems first to have occurred within the Special Projects Office.

Fourth, the Navy lacked a strategic ballistic missile force in 1955 and thus it had neither experience in determining the operational needs of a strategic ballistic missile force nor a

14. Int II-9.
15. Charles J. Hitch, *Decision-Making for Defense* (Berkeley: University of California Press, 1965).

procedure for allocating among naval commands responsibility for any support facilities that might be required by such a force. Many commands could assert jurisdiction in this area, but, since strategic ballistic missiles themselves were an innovation, no naval command could have a historical claim to a knowledge of their operational needs.

And there was a final consideration. The Special Projects Office personnel were deeply committed to the successful promotion of the FBM Program. All saw the strategic value of ballistic missiles. For the naval officers, the program provided the opportunity to make a substantial contribution to the Navy and perhaps to their own careers. For the civilians who joined the supposedly temporary Special Projects Office, the successful development of the FBM, if not the perpetuation of the Special Projects Office, was vital to their tenure in government. (The Office had been designated a separate competitive area within the department; therefore, its civil service employees could not "bump" others in the department to remain in government if the program were for any reason terminated.)[16] It was easy for them to imagine that other commands in control of FBM-related activities would treat their duties with just enough of the usual indifference to cause the program to fail. Thus, they were motivated to have the Special Projects Office gain control over all activities that could affect the success of the program.

Taken together, these factors led the Special Projects Office to view its mission as providing the Navy with a ballistic missile capability rather than with just FBM equipment. Providing such a capability would involve responsibility for all the material, personnel, and facilities necessary to maintain a strategic deterrent force at sea. The working definition of the system, then, was the broadest one possible as it included everything that might affect the operational status of the FBM

16. The designation as a separate competitive area came at the request of Admiral Raborn who was said to have wanted to protect the Special Projects Office from the bumpings of other agencies. As a result the office attracted an unusual selection of civil servants, appropriately those who were willing to risk their employment security for a project that could fail. Higher civil service ratings for civilians already in government were offered as partial compensation for this insecurity, but some individuals offered positions still refused a transfer to the Special Projects Office. The personnel that initially staffed the office were clearly the gamblers in the civil service. See also n. 4, above.

force. Moreover, since the FBM force is a strategic deterrent that has to be ready continually in order to be effective, it was thought that the FBM weapon system had to be created so that it could be operated independently of any other naval system. Thus, the Special Projects Office came to seek independent control over a significant share of naval resources so that it could accomplish a task that was largely self-generated and certainly self-defined.

Later, when the FBM force was in being, the luxury of official definitions could be afforded. The FBM weapon system now refers only to the Fleet Ballistic Missile (Polaris or Poseidon) and its specialized launching, handling, fire control, navigation, and test equipment. The term "FBM system" is used to define the FBM capability consisting of the ships (submarines, tenders, resupply vessels, floating dry docks, and test ships), missiles, military personnel, and the supporting supplies, shore facilities and services. Officially, the Special Projects Office (now the Strategic Systems Project Office) is responsible today, as it was in the late 1950's, for the development, acquisition, and support of the "FBM weapon system"; it manages the FBM weapon system.[17] Managerial responsibility for the rest of the "FBM system," however, is in perpetual dispute, despite the fact that the Special Projects Office has always assumed that it was the "FBM system manager."

In actuality, the Special Projects Office was both something more and something less than the FBM system manager. In several areas the scope of the authority it obtained exceeded its interest in the FBM mission, whereas in others, it failed to gain the authority it originally sought for that mission. It was largely responsible for the development of the FBM capability in the Navy, but it also, at least partially, was responsible for the development of other capabilities as well. It seems somewhat paradoxical that the reason for the involvement in other tasks and the reason for the failure to gain full control over the FBM task appear to be the same.

Before examining the points at which the authority obtained by the Special Projects Office exceeded or fell short of the responsibilities it had assumed for itself, however, it is important to note a point at which authority and responsibility were

17. Naval Material Command, Project Management Charter PM-1: The Strategic Systems Project Office.

matched. This was budgeting. In order that the Navy Ballistic Missile Committee, the Defense Department Ballistic Missile Committee, and the Congress would be able to review a budget for the entire FBM program and be assured that all requirements were being considered, the Special Projects Office early in the program was given authority to prepare and justify a consolidated budget that would include the financial needs of all bureaus and commands involved in the development of the FBM system. The authority to prepare the budget meant that the Special Projects Office was in a position to determine what activities affected the FBM system and to plan an integrated FBM Program. The authority to justify the budget meant that the Special Projects Office had some power to implement its plans since it could influence the funds that would be allocated to all the relevant bureaus and commands for the FBM system.

Yet budgetary influence did not give the Special Projects Office control over the entire FBM system. The Bureau of Ships had control over submarine systems and support ship designs; Admiral Rickover had control over the submarine reactors; The Bureau of Ordnance had control over certain housekeeping functions and some parts of the contract management; the Chief of Naval Communications and a subsection of the Bureau of Ships had control over communication equipment; the Atomic Energy Commission obviously had control over the warhead development; and no one apparently had control over defensive systems for the FBM submarines. The Special Projects Office planned, justified, and reported on the entire FBM system, but it did not control the development of the entire FBM system.

It has already been noted that the FBM proponents had two distinct objectives—the development of widespread support for the Polaris concept and the delegation of sufficient authority to manage the FBM Program independently—and that these objectives were only partially complementary. The conflict between these objectives appeared most sharply in the operations of the Special Projects Office. Bureaucratic strategies used to promote the Polaris could at times necessitate sharing power with other organizations, whereas strategies used to protect the independent management of the FBM Program could at times antagonize sources of important support. Whenever a conflict developed, the tendency was to trade independence for political support. To its proponents, the value of developing the FBM system exceeded the value of developing the perfect project-oriented organization. Organizational symmetry per se was expendable.

The same value calculation led the Special Projects Office to assume tasks that went beyond the FBM mission. Given its orientation toward a single development goal, one might expect that it would seek to avoid assignments that could divert resources from that goal. Most frequently it did. Nevertheless, the Special Projects Office became involved in a number of enterprises that provide services to non-FBM naval and even civilian consumers. For example, the Transit satellite navigation system, which has provided accurate navigation information for U.S. naval warships and whose services have been offered to merchantmen and naval forces of the free world,[18] has been largely financed by the Special Projects Office and has been operated by the Special Projects Office-controlled Naval Astronautics Group at Point Mugu, California. The Naval Ordnance Test Unit at Cape Kennedy, Florida, which conducts missile firings for the entire Navy, takes its techncial direction from the Special Projects Office. The construction of the naval radio facility at Cutler, Maine, the world's most poweful radio station which serves all naval units, was financed and managed by the Special Projects Office. In each of these cases, the Special Projects Office was something more than an FBM project organization. The prime motivation for the Special Projects Office's involvement was to protect its investment in the FBM system from being diluted by the actions of other naval commands, particularly the functionally specialized bureaus. Whenever the FBM system seemed likely to be forced to draw equipment and services from a common Navy source, the Special Projects Office sought to gain control of that common source. It was willing to serve others, but only to insure that the FBM system's needs were being given prime attention.[19]

The involvement of the Special Projects Office in the Deep Submergence Systems Project (DSSP) appeared to mark the greatest divergence from a single-minded focus on the FBM

18. "Navigation Satellite to Aid Civilian Ships," *New York Times* (March 9, 1963), p. 4.
19. Ints II-10, 11, 12, 13, 14.

system. In February 1964, the Deep Submergence Systems Review Group, which had been established after the loss of a U.S. nuclear submarine, the *Thresher,* in late 1963, recommended the creation of a project to improve the Navy's capabilities in the deep ocean and suggested that it be assigned to the Special Projects Office because of its proven management achievements.[20] The adoption of the recommendation by the Secretary of the Navy led to the creation of DSSP as a part of the Special Projects Office in June 1964. The scope of DSSP was later expanded to include, in addition to research on search and salvage techniques, a "Man-in-the-Sea" project and the development of a small nuclear-propelled submersible, the NR-1. By fiscal year 1966, the DSSP work had reached the $14-million level.

Even here, however, the Special Projects Office's interest in the FBM system guided its behavior. Its initial involvement in deep ocean technology came through studies on the strategic uses of the deep ocean by its Chief Scientist, Dr. John Craven, for Project Seabed. The Special Projects Office could justify its acceptance of the DSSP assignment by citing the strategic relevance of deep ocean research and the improved deep diving capabilities of submersibles. More important, at the same time DSSP was being proposed, a significant trough appeared in the Special Projects Office's development work owing to the delays in approving the Poseidon program. Since the technologies involved in deep ocean research were somewhat related to the technologies involved in the FBM system and since some Special Projects Office contractors and part of its technical staff were interested in exploring the opportunities such research presented, DSSP provided both a means to keep the FBM team together until Poseidon was approved and a possible follow-on to strategic missile work.[21] With the formal initiation of the Poseidon development, however, the conflict between FBM priorities and DSSP priorities, already severe, became

20. W. E. Wilks, "Deep Sea Effort Rivals Space Program," *Missiles and Rockets,* 18 (April 11, 1966), pp. 32ff., "Deep Submergence Project Calls for Five Year Expenditure of $200 Million . . . ," *Missiles and Rockets,* 15 (December 21, 1964), pp. 28ff; Scot MacDonald, "Background, Status and Future Goals of the Navy's Deep Submergence Program," *Armed Forces Management,* 12 (October 1965), pp. 62–71.
21. Int II-15.

impossible, and a choice had to be made.[22] In February 1966, DSSP was broken off from the Special Projects Office and established as a separate project.[23] Some key Special Projects Office personnel transferred over to the new project, and Dr. Craven was designated as the temporary DSSP Project Manager, but the integrity of the FBM team was maintained. There was to be only a single focus for the Special Projects Office.

The tenacity with which the Special Projects Office held to its FBM focus proved more detrimental to the bureaus' role in the Navy than the specific jurisdictions the bureaus lost to the Office. With but one technological objective, the Special Projects Office avoided the costly internal work assignment conflicts that plagued the bureaus and limited their efficiency. Its project orientation represented a major structural innnovation in a weapons acquisition system that had never known an alternative to functional specialization. Given the structural contrasts, its technological achievements could not help but undermine the Navy's confidence in the bureaus.

THE RELATIONSHIP WITH THE FLEET

Because the Navy in the 1950's assigned the responsibility for developing weapons and the responsibility for determining weapon requirements to separate hierarchies, it had to devise a mechanism for coordinating the interests of the development agencies and the operating forces in the acquisition of new weapons. In theory, coordination was achieved through dotted lines on the organization chart; the Chief of Naval Operations, the representative of "consumer" interests within the Navy, would designate an assistant as a program "sponsor" and, in turn, the sponsor would monitor a specific development project being managed by the bureaus, the representatives of "producer" interests within the Navy.[24] In practice, it was achieved through hard bureaucratic bargaining in endless committee meetings.

The sponsorship for the FBM Program was assigned initially

22. Int II-16.
23. NAVMATINST 5430.24, 9 February 1966, subj: Deep Submergence Systems Project, designation of.
24. *United States Government Organization Manual 1955–1956*, revised as of June 1, 1955 (Washington: Office of the Federal Register, National Archives and Records Service, 1955), pp. 150–157.

to officers in charge of the Guided Missile Division, Office of the Deputy Chief of Naval Operations for Air; a naval staff dominated by aviators naturally viewed a ballistic missile as a pilotless aircraft. As the sponsoring office, the Guided Missile Division, which was first headed by Admiral Sides and then by Admiral John Clark, had the official responsibility for preparing the operational goals for the FBM system. In addition, representatives of the Guided Missile Division and not the Special Projects Office had a seat on the Navy Ballistic Missile Committee, which officially determined the policies for the FBM Program and reviewed its process.

As might be expected, however, the Special Projects Office had more than the normal producing agency's share in determining both the performance characteristics of the FBM and overall program policies. Ballistic missiles were new in the Navy, and there was little experience upon which the small, though able, Guided Missile Division staff could draw in formulating its plans. The first operational requirements that the Guided Missile Division prepared were necessarily vague and tentative. The Special Projects Office had the resources, the contractors, and the will to establish its own firm opinions on all operational characteristics of the missile. Through the deliberations of the panels of its Steering Task Group (STG), a committee composed of senior representatives from all major naval and contractor organizations participating in the program, the Special Projects Office determined most of the actual performance goals for the FBM system. Through its own requirements staff, the Plans and Programs Branch, the Special Projects Office formulated the operational policies that were to guide FBM development.

To be sure, the Guided Missile Division had representation on the relevant STG panels and close contact with the Plans and Program Branch in the Special Projects Office. But so did the Underseas Warfare (including submarine warfare) Division of the Chief of Naval Operations' staff, and it was only to the submariners and other holders of power that the Special Projects Office was necessarily willing to make concessions. The number of missiles per submarine, as has been noted, was determined by the submariners and not by the Guided Missile Division. For a long period, the Guided Missile Division argued that the prime mode of launch should be submerged, but it was only when the Secretary of the Navy remarked that "it would look silly [to the Congress] for a nuclear submarine which can stay submerged for months at a time to come to the surface for missile firings," that the Special Projects Office gave up its preference for an initial operating capability of only surface firings.[25] And if there were a single sponsor for the FBM Program in its early years, it would have been Admiral Burke, Chief of Naval Operation, who risked the health (budget) of the Navy in initiating the program, and not the Guided Missile Division.[26]

Instead of helping to set policy, the sponsoring office's function was helping to sell policy. Although there was supposedly only one point of review for the FBM Program in the Department of the Navy, the Navy Ballistic Missile Committee, and only one point of review in the Department of Defense, the OSDBMC, numerous other boards, staff agencies, and commands were in a position to affect the program. The Guided Missile Division staff would work the corridors of the Pentagon lining up support, isolating opposition, and, in general, promoting the program. Rather than representing the fleet interests in the FBM Program, the Guided Missile Division represented FBM Program interests in the Pentagon. More than one of its officers suffered a shorter career for the vigor of his efforts.[27]

The Special Projects Office did not rely exclusively upon its sponsor for this type of political representation. Admiral Raborn had his own contacts in the Navy, in the Office of the Secretary of Defense, and in the rest of government. The Special Projects Office technical staff knew well their counterparts in the Defense Department directorates.

Official sponsorship of the FBM Program, along with that of all other missile programs, shifted to the Deputy Chief of Naval Operations for Development when the office was created in 1959.[28] By that year, however, the FBM Program was too far along to mesh well with an office oriented exclusively to-

25. Int II-17.
26. Int II-18.
27. Int II-19.
28. This organizational change in the Office of the Chief of Naval Operations was a result of a recommendation of the Franke Committee, *Report*, NAVEXOS P-1996, p. 127.

ward development problems, and the sponsorship was soon transferred over to sections in the Office of the Deputy Chief of Naval Operations for Fleet Operations and Readiness. Jurisdiction within this part of the naval staff kept shifting among sections. A satisfactory arrangement did not appear to be reached until antisubmarine activities were removed from the Undersea Warfare Division, and it was given responsibility for the FBM Program as well as all other prosubmarine programs.[29]

With responsibility for the FBM Program lodged in an office exclusively concerned with submarine warfare, it might seem that responsibility was being matched with organizational authority. Yet just as these changes were occurring, authority over strategic programs was shifting within the Department of Defense and within the Navy. In the 1960's, agencies attached to the Office of the Secretary of Defense came to have a much greater influence over program requirements than they did during the 1950's. Within the naval staff, a new office, the Director of Strategic Offensive and Defensive Systems, which would report directly to the Chief of Naval Operations, was established to coordinate naval strategic systems. The official FBM Program sponsor is still the Undersea Warfare Division, but the Special Projects Office must now look more and more to the civilians in the Office of the Secretary of Defense and the Admiral in charge of Strategic Systems in the Navy than to the submariners for new directions in strategic programs.

The Special Projects Office's relationship with the operating forces would appear to be more straightforward. Officially, development organizations such as the Special Projects Office are not supposed to control or direct any operational units. Since the FBM system became operational, command over FBM submarines has rested with the Atlantic and Pacific fleet commanders who report through the Commanders-in-Chief Atlantic and Pacific to the Joint Chiefs of Staff and the Secretary of Defense. A small number of FBM submarines are assigned to NATO. The Special Projects Office provides new equipment and supports the FBM weapons system, but the line between operating and developing responsibilities is supposed to be sharp.

29. Int II-20.

In practice, however, the Special Projects Office is deeply involved in what are usually termed operational activities. With the justification that the entire system is still in a stage of development, the Special Projects Office controls directly the ground stations for the navigational satellite system that provides the FBM force and others with vital operational information. After the fleets ran into some difficulties, the Special Projects Office assumed direction of all operational tests of the FBM missile. Through its contractors, who in this instance work also for the Joint Chiefs of Staff, it evaluates the operational readiness of the FBM submarines, and it is quick to report any suggestions that could lead to higher performance. The Special Projects Office's influence on FBM operations are most often subtle—the preparation of manuals, establishment of training courses, codification of procedures, an eagerness to do staff work—but they are all pervasive.[30]

The Special Projects Office, of course, is not tied into the command and control network through which an actual order to fire would be sent. Fleet personnel tend to depreciate its supporting role, burdened as they are with the day-to-day operations of the FBM force.[31] And yet the Special Projects Office is the single point at which all recognized problems, such as ship maintenance, equipment design, crew morale, and tactical procedures, are brought together and analyzed. Concerned as it is with the entire FBM system, the Special Projects Office seeks to become aware of and to correct all of the system's deficiencies. It is the great, if unobtrusive, protector of the FBM force.

The Special Projects Office's channels to the fleet are many. Every time an FBM submarine completes overhaul, it is subject to elaborate tests managed by the Special Projects Office. After every combat patrol, an extensive report covering all aspects of crew and ship performance is prepared for submission to the Special Projects Office. Close liaison is maintained with the staffs of the Atlantic and Pacific fleet commanders. FBM submarine captains often visit Special Projects Office headquarters on trips to Washington. Line officers in the Special Projects Office often take their sea duty with the

30. Int II-21.
31. Ints II-22, 23, 24.

FBM force. The Deputy Director of the Special Projects Office is traditionally a submariner captain who is highly rated (likely to make Admiral) and who has his own network of friends in the fleet. The FBM system is viewed as too vital by both the fleet and the Special Projects Office to let organizational regulations prevent an effective collaboration that will insure its reliability.

THE RELATIONSHIP WITH THE CONTRACTORS

Historically, the military departments developed a large portion of the weapons they used in their own production facilities or arsenals. The arsenal system, though perhaps sustained through the years for other reasons, was functional in one important sense; it permitted the military to improve weapon designs during periods of peace when private contractors would find weapons work unprofitable. Military equipment purchases from private contractors during peacetime, therefore, were normally limited to commercial products such as wagons or trucks which could be adapted for military use by the addition of a coat of paint or other minor change.

The military's relations with contractors, however, were dramatically altered as a consequence of the Second World War. This war, unlike others, was not followed by a period of near total disarmament. Instead, it was followed by a period of sustained arms purchases. Firms mobilized or created during the conflict had the opportunity to continue weapon developments with the expectation of profits on future production contracts. In addition, the war increased the technological complexity of weapon designs. Major technological advances achieved during the war created the belief that the outcome of a future conflict would be determined solely by the technological power of the weapons that the adversaries could bring to bear in its first moments. Hence, the military had a strong desire to have always in hand weapons that were, technologically, the most sophisticated imaginable.

The weapons that were produced during the postwar years differed sharply from those that preceded them. Rather than being developed piecemeal, they were developed increasingly as integrated systems. The weapon, its means of delivery, and numerous supporting equipment, each the product of a separate organization, were conceived of as integrated packages to be produced to meet an overall optimal design.[32]

System integration necessarily became the central management task in the procurement of weapons. Arsenals, it was discovered, could not be expected to perform effectively in the development of a major weapon system which required the coordination of component elements. As an independent governmental subunit, each arsenal would claim the right to determine its own program priorities. None would take direction from another. In contrast, private firms were much more pliable. Through contracts, they could easily be arranged in a variety of subordinate-superior relationships. With the promise of future production contracts, their cooperation was assured. Increasingly, the military came to rely on contractors for development of its weapons.

By the time the FBM was conceived, it was common practice to hire a single firm or "prime contractor" to manage the development of an entire weapon system. The prime contractor would subcontract with other firms for the component elements of the system and would coordinate their performance. In addition, the prime contractor as weapon system manager would supply the contracting government agency with design and management support services.[33]

32. The atomic bomb used against Hiroshima can be said to have been both the first modern weapon and the last of the old. The bomb was the first modern weapon in that it demonstrated for all the devastating impact that technological sophistication could have on warfare. But the bomb was less than modern in that it was developed apart from ancillary equipment upon which its effectiveness depended. For example, the physical size of the bomb was determined not by the limits of technology, but by the dimensions of the bomb bay doors of a B-29, an aircraft designed several years before the bomb.

33. The evolution of weapon system manager-type contracts is described in Fremont E. Kast and James E. Rosenzweig, *Management in the Space Age: An Analysis of the Concept of Weapon System Management and Its Non-Military Applications*, (New York: Exposition Press, 1962), pp. 73–87; Richard Arvid Johnson *et. al.*, *The Theory and Management of Systems* (New York: McGraw-Hill Book Co., 1957); Merton J. Peck and Frederick M. Scherer, *The Weapons Acquisitions Process: An Economic Analysis* (Boston: Harvard Graduate School of Business Administration, 1962), chap. 2; and U.S. Congress, House, Subcommittee for Special Investigations of the Committee on Armed Services, *Hearings under the Authority of House Resolution 19: Weapons System Management and Team System Concept in Government Contracting*, 86th Cong., 1st Sess. (Washington: Government Printing Office, 1959). The arsenal method, despite its longer history, is less well described. A brief outline of the method appears in Kast and

As a complex weapon system, the Polaris would certainly have been developed under the direction of a private weapon system manager if it had not been for the accident of the FBM program's ties with the Army in the Jupiter project. To be sure, the Army had contracted with Chrysler Corporation for the production of the missile and the overall management of the project. The Navy, as the Army's partner, had obligingly contracted with Chrysler for the same services. It had also required the contractors for the FBM's shipboard subsystems to become subcontractors to Chrysler. These arrangements, however, only guaranteed that the development of the Polaris would not be controlled by a weapon system contractor.

The Navy, of course, had no intention of using the liquid-fueled Jupiter as its submarine-launched missile. Rather, it was interested in developing a solid-fueled alternative and in perfecting the necessary support equipment. Since Chrysler was firmly committed both to the Army and to the Jupiter missile, it had difficulty working closely with the Special Projects Office in furthering the Navy's quest. Gradually, the contractors for the shipboard subsystems learned from the naval officers directing their work that it would be to their advantage to act as if there were no prime contractor for the FBM system.

The break with the Army, and therefore with Chrysler, did not mean that the contractor relationship in the FBM Program could be easily restructured. The program had operated nearly a year and had made substantial progress without the presence of a strong weapon system manager or central coordinator. The technical branches of the Special Projects Office (there was a branch for each major subsystem, for example, fire control, navigation, ship installation, and others) and their contractors had developed close ties that were not amenable to change.

Rosenzweig, *Management in the Space Age*, pp. 61–65. See also, Carl Kaysen, "Improving the Efficiency of Research and Development," in *Public Policy*, Vol. XII (Cambridge, Mass.: Harvard University Press, 1963); U.S. Congress, House, Subcommittee for Special Investigations, *Hearings: Weapons System Management;* Robert L. Perry, "The Atlas, Thor, Titan, and Minuteman," in Eugene M. Emme, editor, *The History of Rocket Technology: Essays on Research, Development, and Utility* (Detroit, Mich.: Wayne State University Press, 1964), pp. 142–161; and U.S. Congress, House, Subcommittee of the Committee on Government Operations, *Hearings, Systems Development and Management,* 87th Cong., 2nd Sess. (Washington: Government Printing Office, 1962).

At the start of the Polaris effort, consideration was given to contracting with another weapon system manager to replace Chrysler. Lockheed's Missile and Space Division was an obvious candidate to assume the role of FBM weapon system manager since, through its work on solid-fueled missile designs for the Special Projects Office, it was to become the Polaris missile contractor. Lockheed, however, had had no previous experience in integrating a major missile system and had had nothing to do with the nonmissile parts of the FBM system during its year's apprenticeship on the program.[34] Its experience on these particular FBM matters was easily challenged. Due to the entrenched opposition of the nonmissile branches and their contractors, Lockheed's role was not expanded, and it had to be content with developing the missile and providing some general overhead support for the Special Projects Office. The nonmissile branch heads, of course, feared that their units would be made subordinate to some larger organization working with a prime contractor to monitor the entire weapon system. Their contractors feared that a weapon system manager, once established, would become strong enough to assume responsibility for developing and manufacturing their own type of equipment.

Actually, Lockheed was not even given full control over missile development. With the initiation of the Polaris development, Lockheed was designated the missile system manager. Standard procedure at the time called for the missile system contractor to hold responsibility for the missile, missile guidance, and all missile launch, handling, and test equipment. A single firm then would become responsible for the entire missile development, coordinating the activities of any subcontractors involved in missile-related work. The Polaris development, however, was initiated after the division of labor for the Jupiter missile had been firmly imbedded into the organization. When Lockheed formally became the missile system manager, there was already a branch and contractor for missile launching and handling and another for missile instrumentation and testing, and they would not relinquish their jurisdictions.

Missile guidance had been tied to the needs of the Jupiter

34. Ints II-28A, B.

in a joint Army-Navy project. With the switch to Polaris, the Jupiter guidance concept, never pleasing to the Navy, could be abandoned. A search began for an alternative. The fire control branch discovered that a satisfactory guidance concept was being explored at M.I.T.'s Instrumentation Laboratory (IL). The Massachusetts Institute of Technology, however, as a matter of principle, would not submit to a subcontractual relationship in any program. If the Navy was to gain the services of the laboratory in the FBM Program, it would have to contract directly with the laboratory and not indirectly through another contractor. Moreover, M.I.T., although interested in participating in the program, would need some industrial support since it would not, also on principle, undertake any production of the equipment it designed. At the time, M.I.T. did not have much confidence in the abilities of Lockheed's guidance group. General Electric's Ordnance Division, the FBM fire control contractor, however, had worked in the past with M.I.T. and had gained its confidence. A relationship between M.I.T. and G.E. was possible since it was argued that the interface between guidance and fire control equipment in the FBM system was at least as crucial as that between guidance and the missile itself. Thus, the jurisdiction for guidance was assigned to the fire control branch rather than the missile branch; another part of the missile system was effectively removed from Lockheed's direct control.[35]

Finally, missile propulsion was not initially included in Lockheed's responsibilities. During the effort to develop an alternative FBM missile, the Aerojet-General Corporation had been the Special Projects Office contractor for solid propellant investigations. Lockheed and Aerojet worked together in developing a solid-fueled design, but each had a separate contract. In the first year of the Polaris program, the cooperative, but separate relationship was continued with both contractors reporting independently to the missile branch as they worked together to develop the major elements of the missile.[36]

With the demise of the Chrysler contract, other mechanisms to integrate the activities of the several subsystem contractors

35. Ints II-29, 30.
36. Much to its own dissatisfaction, Aerojet was made a Lockheed subcontractor in 1957.

were devised.[37] The post of Chief Engineer was created on the staff of the Technical Director and assigned the task of monitoring system interface relationships. Committees composed of representatives from the various technical branches and their contractors were established to provide exact agreements on subsystem boundaries. The Technical Director had to approve these agreements in detail before they could take effect. The Vitro Corporation was later hired to aid the Chief Engineer and the Technical Director in documenting and monitoring the interface relationships. The Applied Physics Laboratory of Johns Hopkins University, a Navy contract laboratory, was called in to conduct system studies (for example, suggesting subsystem boundaries) and to analyze system tests (for example, independently evaluating subsystem performance). Neither Vitro nor the Applied Physics Laboratory, however, acted as the weapon system manager for the FBM Program. Each FBM subsystem contractor was an independent contractor to the Special Projects Office; there was no prime contractor for the FBM system.

Who, then, ran the Polaris project? Contradictory opinions on the answer to this question exist both within and outside the FBM Program. Branch engineers and military officers at Special Projects headquarters claim that the FBM development was unique among major defense projects because it was managed completely by an in house staff of technically competent government personnel. Responsible officials of the major FBM contractors smile understandingly when informed of the claim of the Special Projects technical staff; in their view the Polaris program was managed directly by the FBM contractors. Accepting the position of the Special Projects technical staff, a social scientist at RAND, who has long analyzed the management of defense research and development projects, thinks that it would be most interesting to discover for what the contractors were being paid. "After all," he points out, "the contractors took no financial risks in the ballistic missile R & D projects since these risks were absorbed by the government and, in the case of the Polaris program, they

37. Negotiations for a settlement to terminate officially the Navy contract with Chrysler continued until 1960 when the matter was finally closed in the courts.

did not even bear the usual burdens of project management."[38] One high-level defense official who held a position that required the monitoring of a number of major missile projects had quite a different opinion. He thought it would be better to ask the Navy when it was going to start to manage the Polaris Program. It was his view that the Polaris was a "total buy" in which the Navy admitted it could not run the program by turning to the contractors for all the management as well as all the research involved in the Polaris development.[39]

Discerning who ran the Polaris project would be a relatively simple task if the FBM Program had employed a weapon system contractor or were an arsenal-type development. In one case, the contractor clearly dominates; in the other, the government is dominant.

Given that the answer is more complicated, perhaps the best way to approach it is to contrast the development organization the Air Force utilized in its ballistic missile programs with that which the Navy utilized. The Air Force's structure has been critically examined and thoroughly documented in a series of congressional and official reports.[40] Perhaps because of the

38. Int II-38.
39. Int II-39.
40. U.S. Congress, House, Subcommittee of the Committee on Government Operations, *Hearings, Organization and Management of Missile Programs*, 86th Cong., 1st Sess. (Washington: Government Printing Office, 1959); U.S. Congress, House, Subcommittee of the Committee on Government Operations, *Hearings, System Development . . . ;* Controller General of the United States, *Initial Report on the Review of the Administrative Management of the Ballistic Missile Program of the Department of the Air Force* (Washington: General Accounting Office, May 1960); Perry, "The Atlas, Thor, Titan, and Minuteman," pp. 142–161; Robert L. Perry, "System Development Strategies: A Comparative Study of Doctrine, Technology, and Organization in the USAF Ballistic Missile and Cruise Missile Programs, 1950–1960," (U) (RAND Report RM 4853-PR, August 1966) (Confidential). See also, Ernest G. Schwiebert, *A History of the U.S. Air Force Ballistic Missiles* (New York: Frederick A. Praeger, 1964); U.S. Congress, House, Subcommittee for Special Investigations of the Committee on Armed Services *Report, The Aerospace Corporation: A Study of Fiscal and Management Policy and Control*, 89th Cong., 1st Sess. (Washington: Government Printing Office, August 12, 1965); Air Force Regulations Numbers 375-1, 375-2, 375-3, 375-4, and 375-5; *The Extension of Special Organization Patterns and Management Techniques to Additional Weapons Systems*, a report prepared for the Assistant Secretary of Defense (Installations and Logistics) under Contract SP-92 (Cambridge: United Research Inc., January 1962); J. Stefan Dupre and W. Eric Gustafson,

pressure of outside examinations, the Air Force has developed a set of definitions that sharply delineate the functions performed by various organizations participating in the development of its ballistic missiles, especially those of the system management organizations that the Air Force employed. These definitions are helpful in exploring the government-contractor relationships that developed in the FBM program.

On the recommendation of its scientific advisors, the Air Force did not attempt in the initial acceleration of its ballistic missile programs to assign weapon system management responsibilities to an airframe contractor.[41] The job was thought too complex for a weapon system contractor, particularly the airframe manufacturers, the Air Force's weapon system managers, since they at the time were said to lack a strong scientific staff. The alternative of in house management, the arsenal method, was not thought desirable because the government would have had difficulty recruiting the professional personnel needed, and the then largest existing pool of such talent in the Air Force was at Wright Field, which was beset by its own management problems. The utilization of a university manager was considered, but the leading candidates felt the task was an inappropriate one for an educational institution to assume. It was then decided to create a special organization that could provide the Air Force with the technical assistance necessary to coordinate the weapon system development. An existing but newly formed private organization, the Ramo-Wooldridge Corporation, which had served as a staff aid to the Air Force Strategic Missile Evaluation Committee (the Von Neumann Committee) that had recommended the acceleration, was selected to fill the role as the Air Force's chosen technical management instrument for ballistic missiles.

The Ramo-Wooldridge organization, which through merger and reorganization became the Space Technological Labora-

---

"Contracting for Defense: Private Firms and the Public Interest," *Political Science Quarterly*, 77 (June 1962), pp. 161–177; USAFA-TR-65-1, Claude J. Johns, Jr., "The United States Air Force Intercontinental Ballistic Missile Program, 1954–1959: Technological Change and Organizational Innovation" (U.S. Air Force Academy, Colorado, 30 January 1965); Controller General of the United States, *Findings Resulting from Initial Review of the Ballistic Missile Programs of the Department of the Air Force* (Washington: General Accounting Office, December 1960) (Secret).

41. Perry, "Systems Development," p. 77; also Int II-40.

tory, Inc. (STL), a subsidiary of the Thompson Ramo-Wooldridge Corporation, had a charter as system manager to integrate the design and to direct the development of a series of ballistic missile weapon systems, including their test and launch facilities. The Air Force, however, retained financial control of the projects, contracting separately for the development of major missile components or subsystems with giant aerospace contractors (Boeing, Convair, Martin, Aerojet, Thiokol, Avco, and others) each of which was known as an associate contractor for a given missile project. STL, active for the Air Force in directing the development activities of the associate contractors, had line responsibility for technical management, but no direct control over the allocation of dollars or contract control over the contractors, both of which rested with the Air Force. STL, however, was at the same time acting as the Air Force's technical staff in the highly technical development effort, and, in this capacity, it obviously gained substantial influence over dollar allocations and contractor selection. Thus, in the Air Force ballistic missile program, STL directed the missile developments, advised on the formulation of development goals, and evaluated progress toward meeting the announced development goals.

To carry its burdens in the missile program, the Air Force established a team of three organizations. The Western Development Division (commanded initially by Brigadier General Bernard Schriever) of the Air Research and Development Command had responsibility both for the development effort and general coordination. The Ballistic Missile Center of the Air Material Command was concerned with contract administration and the preparation for full-scale production. And a unit of the Strategic Air Command known as SAC-MIKE directed the planning for operational deployment. The Army Corps of Engineers joined the team later to manage the construction of the launch sites for the missiles. STL reported to and advised the Western Development Division (WDD; retitled first the Ballistic Missile Division in 1957 and then Ballistic Systems Division in 1961). As the Air Force was involved in developing simultaneously several major ballistic missile systems, none of these organizations, including STL, was internally organized exclusively on a project basis.

Two key phrases governed STL's relationships with the Air

Force and the associate contractors. STL's functions in the ballistic missile programs have often been described as "general systems engineering" and "technical direction." Officially general systems engineering is defined as: "that portion of system engineering dealing with the overall integration of a system, design compromise among subsystems, definitions of interfaces, analysis of subsystems, and supervision of system testing, all to the extent required to assure that system concept and objectives are being met in an economical and timely manner . . . ,"[42] whereas technical direction is defined as: "that process by which a contractor's work is reviewed, information on progress and problems is exchanged, plans for future work are discussed, and, where it will better achieve Air Force objectives, the contractor's technical effort is modified, realigned or redirected."[43]

Analytically, "systems engineering" can be said to involve the identification of explicit trade-offs between component values of a system (for example, the x miles of range that will be sacrificed by the addition of y pounds of weight), "general systems engineering" to involve the integration of alternative combinations of system values into coherent system design proposals, and "technical direction" to involve a choice among alternative system design proposals in terms of some objective or subjective preference function. Based on interviews and a review of the record, it appears that STL and the associate contractors shared system engineering duties, but that general systems engineering and technical direction activities were largely reserved for STL. On occasion the Air Force's Western Development Division would assume for itself the technical direction activity by overruling STL,[44] but this must have been difficult for the division to do since it had no independent technical capability of its own. STL served as its technical advisor.

These functions or activities existed in the Polaris program. The FBM system involved the identification of trade-offs be-

42. Aerospace Corporation, *Partners in Progress* (El Segundo, Calif.: Aerospace Corporation, n.d.), p. 7.
43. *Ibid.* The definitions are taken from the Aerospace Corporation's basic contract with the Air Force, a contract derived from the STL-Air Force relationship that preceded the establishment of the Aerospace Corporation.
44. Ints II-41A, B, C, D, E, and 42.

tween component values, the integration of design alternatives, and the selection of values to be maximized. But the functions were neither as carefully defined nor as neatly assigned among participating organizations as they apparently were in the Air Force's program.

Indications of the government-contractor relationship and the distribution of technical functions in the FBM Program come from contacts with outside organizations. In 1957, the Air Force and the Navy held a joint meeting to exchange general technical information and to report on the progress of their respective ballistic missile programs. Aside from introductory greetings provided by military officers, the Air Force presentations were all made by nongovernment civilians, specifically STL (then Ramo-Wooldridge) engineers. The presentations for the Navy in each technical area were made by the naval officers who headed the appropriate technical branches in the Special Projects Office. Supplementing their work were the contributions of the civil service branch engineers.[45] The Special Projects Office then could at least hold its own in technical discussions without relying on its contractors.

Yet a somewhat different impression develops from the British experience with the Special Projects Office. Since 1964 there has been a Joint US-UK Polaris Project. Prior to that time the Royal Navy had been informally monitoring the operations of the Special Projects Office and were of the opinion that, similar to their own weapons programs, the Polaris program was being managed exclusively by the in house naval technical staff. With the initiation of the joint projects, they have discovered that, beyond a general design philosophy, all detailed questions about the technology of the Polaris system have to be directed to the FBM contractors, who are in fact the repositories of information on the FBM system.[46] Lacking this level of knowledge, the Special Projects Office staff, whose key members have been with the program since at least 1957, could not have itself managed the Polaris development. It would seem then that the in house naval staff

45. Agenda of the USAF-USN Ballistic Missile Meeting held at the Western Development Division of the Air Research and Development Command, Inglewood, Calif., April 23, 1957.
46. Ints II-43A, B, C.

(composed of officers and civil service engineers) was certainly somewhat more involved in the technology than was the Air Force staff, but that it could not have matched the technical involvement of STL.

Personnel limitations alone would have prevented the Special Projects Office from performing the functions in the Polaris program that STL performed in the Air Force ballistic missile programs. The Special Projects Office initial staff authorization, as has been noted, was only forty-five officers and forty-five civilians. Although the personnel authorization has expanded over time, the in house technical staff was not much larger than a hundred or so during the period when the basic system design decisions were made.[47] Except for one or two skill areas, the Special Projects Office has had no design or study capability of its own. Work of this type has had generally to be contracted out. Even today, when the headquarters staff complement has grown to several hundred persons, the staff is small relative to its tasks and its contractors. In the navigation branch, for example, there are about thirty-five officers and civilians supervising the development of new navigation equipment and the logistical support for several deployed systems. The navigation system contractor, however, has a separate nonmanufacturing staff of approximately a thousand persons whose job it is to provide management support for the navigation branch.[48]

Moreover, among the Special Projects Office civilian engineers and technical officers there were apparently only a few really outstanding engineers. The widely discussed limitations of government employment gave business and university contractors, at least in the early years of the program, the edge in hiring technically competent personnel. Increases in the numbers of government personnel alone would not have made up the difference. When FBM contractors were individually asked in confidence where within their own organization they would

47. There were a total of 160 persons, including secretaries, messengers, and security officers assigned to the Special Projects Office headquarters on July 1, 1957. The number grew to 325 in December 1960 and now is approximately 500. The field office complement was 134 on July 1, 1957. It now exceeds 1,800 persons scattered from Bremerton, Washington, and Sunnyvale, California, to Syosset, New York, and London, England.
48. Int II-44.

place the Special Projects branch personnel (civilian and military) if these engineers were to be hired, they unanimously replied that, except for one or two easily recognizable individuals, none would be given project leadership responsibility. In fact, some of the contractors stated that, politics aside, they would not want to hire any of them.[49] Publicly, of course, they claim that if laws and opportunities permitted, they would eagerly hire the Special Projects staff away and give every person on it a high position. Even applying a discount for the arrogance of contractors, these are telling comments. The Special Projects Office was, for a government agency, a very unusual organization, but by itself it could not have created the Polaris.

In terms of the general systems engineering and technical direction functions that were almost exclusively STL's in the Air Force programs, the most that could be claimed for the Special Projects staff was that it held the technical direction function in the Polaris program. The various subsystem contractors necessarily had to provide the subsystem designs and the trade-off studies between component values in the subsystem. General systems engineering studies that integrated subsystem designs into development alternatives necessarily had to come from the Applied Physics Laboratory, Lockheed (the largest subsystem manager), committees of subsystem contractors, and outside naval research laboratories and engineering facilities. Since the technical direction function is largely limited to a choice among alternatives presented, the contractors, as the generators of alternatives, had an influence throughout the program.

But the fact that the Special Projects staff held the technical direction function was not trivial. The Special Projects Office's technical competence was always sufficient to insure that it understood the technical implications of the alternatives presented by the contractors. Because of this, it always had the technical self-confidence to dominate the Polaris development. It was largely the Special Projects Office's design values (or those of the naval, governmental, and private organizations whose support it thought was needed to keep the program politically viable) that were maximized and not those of an outside technical organization. And it was largely the Special

49. Ints II-45A, B, C, D, E.

Projects Office's preferences and not the contractors' that guided the trade-offs among time, cost, and performance variables.[50]

The crucial factor that permitted the Special Projects Office to dominate the Polaris development was its use of a number of competing organizations to generate design alternatives in each subsystem and in the FBM system as a whole. In the Polaris program, unlike the Air Force's missile programs, the technical alternatives were not the product of a single organization, nor were they filtered through a single organization. The Special Projects Office dominated because it was dependent technically on many contractors, not one.

Internal decentralization in the Special Projects Office both hindered and helped the maintenance of government control over the FBM system. On the one hand, decentralization allowed the contractors to gain great influence on the design of particular subsystems of the FBM. Early in the program the branches were encouraged (both by the lack of an overall weapon system contractor and by the specific orders of the Technical Director)[51] to designate one of their contractors as the subsystem prime contractor. These contractors in turn developed specialized organizations whose technical competence and depth could easily exceed that of the counterpart Special Projects technical branch and its other contractors. Although there were exceptions in areas in which the technical competence of the branch civilian personnel was unusually high or where more than one contractor provided design support, the technical initiative in most FBM subsystems came to be held by the subsystem prime contractor. On the other hand, decentralization meant that each subsystem was championed by a technically articulate and aggressive organization. Fighting to gain a larger share of the work, each of these organizations would prepare independent technical presentations for each major program decision. Always in the boundary areas between subsystems, but often also within subsystems, the Special Projects Office branches and, most importantly, the Technical Director, had the opportunity to compare competing

50. For specific examples of the Special Projects Office role in providing technical direction for the Polaris project, see Chapter Five, below.
51. Int II-46.

proposals. A set of consultants and systems analysis organizations serving the Technical Director gave added assurance that decisions were based on the Special Projects Office's own perceptions of the political and technical requirements since the biases of the branch contractors could always be challenged by contractors at the Technical Director's level.

One other element in the Special Projects Office's contractor relationships should be noted. From the first days of the FBM Program, the Special Projects Office has insisted with a significant degree of success that all of its major contractors reorganize their internal structure so that an independent project-type organization is responsible for FBM work and FBM work alone within the company.[52] It was felt that this type of organization would prevent part-time involvement in the program and would protect FBM-trained talent from becoming dissipated on new business, particularly Air Force business.[53] Isolation from other company activities in turn would lead the project organization to become an advocate of FBM activities in debates over the allocation of resources within the firms.[54] It also meant that a major unit in several large firms would become dependent upon the health of the national FBM Program for its own organizational health.

Since these relationships have been important in the success of the FBM Program, they will be specified further in Chapter Five, where the techniques used to manage the FBM technical development are examined in detail. It is sufficient here to stress the fact that the FBM development required the cooperation of both the contractors and the Special Projects Office, and, in the course of the development effort, they became closely intertwined.

Figure 3 outlines the network of major contractors for the FBM, a network which has remained almost unchanged since the initiation of the Polaris program. The Westinghouse Electric Corporation of Sunnyvale, California, has acted as the FBM launcher and handling system contractor, though Lockheed and several naval laboratories and engineering facilities have provided design support. The Ordnance Division of General Electric Company at Pittsfield, Massachusetts, has pro-

52. Hunter, "Politics and Polaris," p. 71; also, Ints II-47A, B, C, D.
53. Int II-47A.
54. Int II-48.

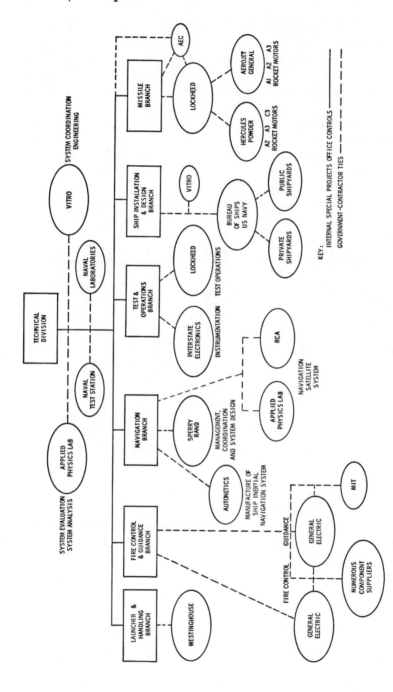

Figure 3. Major contractor network for the Fleet Ballistic Missile Program

vided systems design and manufacturing support in the fire control area, whereas in the guidance area General Electric has acted as a manufacturing agent together with IL, which has acted as the guidance design agent. The guidance branch also has maintained independent contracts with several firms for second-source manufacturing of major components and with naval facilities and business organizations for special equipment designs. The Sperry Systems Management Division of Syosett, Long Island, has been the navigation system manager. It is through this Sperry Division that most navigation contracts have flowed. Separate contracts, however, have covered the manufacture of the Ship Inertial Navigation System equipment and the development work involved in producing the navigation satellite. Interstate Electronics Corporation of Anaheim, California, has been the contractor for test instrumentation, but Lockheed has provided test operations support at Cape Kennedy. The Bureau of Ships (now Naval Ship Systems Command) can be described as the ship system contractor. The Vitro Corporation, Silver Spring, Maryland, however, has been the weapon system installation and checkout coordinator for FBM submarine new construction and overhaul. Lockheed Missile and Space Division, Sunnyvale, California, has been the missile system prime contractor. Aerojet-General, Sacramento, California, and Hercules Power Company, Wilmington, Delaware, have served separately and together as the rocket motor contractors. The Lawrence Radiation Laboratory, Livermore, California, an Atomic Energy Commission installation, has been the warhead design agent. The Lawrence Laboratory and Lockheed have worked closely with the Navy in the design of reentry vehicles. The Applied Physics Laboratory, Vitro, and several naval organizations have assisted the Technical Director with systems evaluations.

4 | PERT and the Myth of Managerial Effectiveness

The Special Projects Office has gained an international reputation for the innovativeness and effectiveness of the management control system it has employed in the development of the FBM weapon system. PERT, a computerized R&D planning, scheduling, and control technique developed initially in the FBM Program, has been extensively used in numerous private and public organizations. Its adopters frequently note that PERT originated in the successful development of the Polaris. Similarly, management concepts and techniques such as project management, program budget, management control centers, and charting—all highly regarded by management analysts—are often acknowledged to have been developed or perfected by the Special Projects Office. The demand for information on the management control system of the FBM Program has long been extensive. The Special Projects Office, and more generally the Polaris development, has become synonymous with progressive management.

Acquired quite early in the FBM Program, this reputation for managerial innovativeness and effectiveness seems to have aided greatly the effort to develop the Polaris. Expensive and risky technological ventures such as the FBM are regularly disrupted and demoralized by the intervention of high-level officials in day-to-day program management and by frequent outside reviews of program progress. Each Soviet success in missilery or space increased the general vulnerability of the FBM Program to crippling supervision by increasing the pressures for intervention and review. But since the Special Projects Office was thought to be a uniquely competent management organization, it was protected from much of this type of interference and thus was able to concentrate its management resources on the solution of technical problems rather than on the continuous justification of particular program decisions.

As will be shown in this chapter, the Special Projects Office's reputation seems not only to have been beneficial, but also to have been in large part contrived. Certainly aware they were operating in a period when the nation and its leaders were deeply concerned about the management of the major U.S. technological programs, at least some of the FBM proponents saw a competitive advantage in having the Special Projects Office perceived as possessing an extraordinarily effective management system. Their strategy apparently was to have the Special Projects Office involved in the development of innovative management techniques and then to present these innovations as being both crucial to the technical effort and effective management techniques in any large-scale and risky undertaking. Clearly, the receptivity of the Special Projects Office to managerial innovations of all descriptions and all degrees of effectiveness was facilitated and encouraged by men who recognized that management systems could have political as well as operational benefits.

Management systems are, of course, the means by which the highest-level officials, presumably the most responsible officials, in an organization monitor and control the behavior of their subordinates.[1] Even in programs that do not involve the technological uncertainties of the Polaris, there is a concern on the part of the organizational leadership that the lower-level participants in the organization are not dedicated to their work or honest in their reporting. For programs that consume enormous amounts of resources and are subject to external review, the pressure to develop management techniques that warn early of operational weaknesses and that control deviations from established goals is considerable. The management of any large-scale organization, including the Special Projects Office, thus always has an interest in discovering new mechanisms to relieve their anxiety about the behavior of organizational participants. This interest must also be included as one of the possible motivations for managerial innovation in the Polaris program.

1. Anthony Downs, *Inside Bureaucracy* (Boston: Little, Brown, 1967).

The personnel actually involved in developing the managerial innovations introduced in the program need not have had, however, the same motivation as their immediate superiors. To them, the rapid increases in the scale and complexity of programs to develop weapons in the cold war period could seem to have required the invention of new managerial methods. Certainly, the traditional means of controlling the costs, schedules, and quality of technological projects—experience, bargaining skills, and double-entry ledgers—were being depicted in numerous congressional and executive reports as being patently inadequate.[2] In particular, the failure at that time of many large-scale technological projects to meet their cost and schedule projections was being attributed to deficiencies in management methods. Throughout government and industry there was an unmet demand for the development of management techniques that could pace the development of technology. Participation in a project to develop a major weapon system provided an enormous personal challenge and opportunity to those who were inclined to speculate on the evolution of management systems. Substantial personal rewards appeared to await the pioneers in modern management methods.

Irrespective of the motivations that underlay the introduction of management innovations into the Polaris program and the success of the innovations in meeting those needs stands the question of the efficacy of the innovations in actually controlling the development of the weapon. The element most subject to generalization in the Polaris undertaking would appear to be the methods devised to manage the large-scale technological project. The wisdom of officially promoting the diffusion of the Polaris management innovations should, it would seem, depend upon their value in managing the Polaris

2. U.S. Congress, House, Subcommittee of the Committee on Government Operations, *Hearings, Organization and Management of Missile Programs,* 86th Cong., 1st Sess. (Washington: Government Printing Office, 1959); U.S. Congress, House, Subcommittee of the Committee on Government Operations, *Hearings, Systems Development and Management,* 87th Cong., 2nd Sess., 4 pts. (Washington: Government Printing Office, 1962), U.S. Congress, House, Subcommittee for Special Investigations of the Committee on Armed Services, *Hearings, Weapons System Management and Team System Concept in Government Contracting,* 86th Cong., 1st Sess., 5 pts. (Washington: Government Printing Office, 1959).

program. Despite the profusion of information on the various managerial innovations introduced during the course of the program, there has yet to appear a thorough analysis of the contribution the innovations made to the early attainment of the program's technological goals. Methodologically, of course, it is extremely difficult to assign precise values to the contribution of any particular innovation or the entire set of innovations. The procedure needed to make such a calculation has not been developed. It is impossible, for example, to re-create the development of the Polaris without managerial innovations. Nevertheless, it is useful in a subjective assessment to describe accurately the actual use of each innovation in the Polaris program and to report fully the opinions of the management-level personnel that the innovations were designed to serve.

THE POLARIS MANAGEMENT SYSTEM

The repertoire of management techniques that comprise the current Polaris management system has remained largely unchanged for at least a half-dozen years. Components of the system were devised sequentially from a basic concept during the initial years of the Polaris program. By 1961, however, either the desired reputation for managerial effectiveness had been established, or the optimum level of managerial efficiency had been reached, or the innovators had left the program, for the management system has been frozen since then and innovation in management techniques essentially ceased within the Special Projects Office. The only major component of the management system added after that year was independently conceived and presented fully developed to the Special Projects Office by one of the larger Polaris contractors. A concern, then, with the development of the Polaris management system must focus mainly on the years 1956 to 1961.

Although he could not have known its final composition, Admiral Raborn was interested from the very beginning of the program in building an innovative management system for the Special Projects Office. In early 1956 he directed the head of the Plans and Programs Division to survey the management methods of the leading public and private organizations in the country which had gained a reputation for managerial effectiveness. A small team of naval officers and civil servants set out to tour the board rooms, presidential offices, and computer facilities of such organizations as Chrysler, General Motors, and DuPont to receive hastily arranged briefings on the management of large-scale programs. Practically nothing of value could be gleaned from the tour and the Special Projects team returned to the program convinced that the reputations for management effectiveness were unearned.[3] A few years later these and other major organizations would be sending representatives to the Special Projects Office for more carefully planned presentations on the virtues of the Polaris management system.

Pressured to prepare frequent justifications for the program's existence, the Plans and Programs Division did little at the time to build its own innovative management system. With the assistance of a contractor, a management graphics capability was established, but this capability was probably introduced more to meet the needs of the day than as a part of the long-term development of a new management system. The naval officers who initially led the division did not perceive their career interest to lay in the area of developing management systems. Their colleagues who headed the technical branches in the Special Projects Office had even less patience with the development of management techniques. To them, the central organizational problem was gaining approval for the development of a viable FBM system and not experimentation in management methods.

In the summer of 1956, Gordon Pehrson, a civil servant with considerable experience in both Navy and Army procurement organizations, was persuaded by Admiral Raborn to join the Special Projects Office as the director of the Plans and Programs Division. Pehrson, as was noted previously, had a deep personal interest in developing innovative management control systems, and his service in the FBM Program soon reflected this interest. The Special Projects Office quickly divided into what was called "Special Projects North" and "Special Projects South"—the Plans and Program Division proponents of managerial innovation who were located in the northern corridor of the Munitions Building and their Technical Division opponents located in the corridors to the south. Situated

3. Int III-1.

organizationally and geographically in the middle, Admiral Raborn was the power broker and the natural ally for each of the opposing forces.

Pehrson had major personal handicaps in promoting change. He was a civilian in a military organization, a non-technical administrator in a technical agency, and a staff man in a line-oriented office.[4] Perhaps his only initial advantage, aside from his own determination and intelligence, was the Admiral's tendency to encourage competition among his subordinates in order to keep himself informed of their activities.

The basic conception for the Polaris management system was outlined in a "Memorandum for Staff" which Pehrson prepared for the Admiral's signature in January 1957.[5] This document stressed the need to develop an integrated planning and evaluation system for the entire program that would use a common format and common terms. "I must be able to reach down to any level of Special Projects Office activity and find a plan and a performance report that logically and clearly can be related to the total job we have to do."[6] Frequent internal performance reviews were to be scheduled, and they were always to identify both the effect of any program success or failure on approved plans and the recommended course of exploitative or corrective action.[7] Pehrson was assigned the responsibility for developing the management control system in detail.

Some key components of the management system were already in place when Pehrson set out to fulfill the assignment. In designing the Special Projects organization, Admiral Raborn had established a Progress Analysis Branch, later the Program Evaluation Branch, in the Plans and Programs Division. Officially, the branch's function is described as providing the Director of the Special Projects Office with an independent appraisal of overall program progress.[8] Unofficially the Admiral sought to have the branch act as an or-

4. Int III-2.
5. Admiral W. F. Raborn, Jr., Director, Special Projects Office, Memorandum to Staff, SP 10:GOP:meb, 24 January 1957, subj: Special Projects Office Management of the Fleet Ballistic Missile Program.
6. *Ibid.*
7. *Ibid.*
8. Special Projects Office, *POLARIS Management: Presentation for the National Aeronautics and Space Administration* (Washington: Department of the Navy, 29 April 1964).

ganizational "spy," reporting directly to him on the actual rather than the officially acknowledged accomplishments and failures of the technical branches.[9] This covert task was difficult to carry out, but the branch was available to serve as a staff unit that could record progress against established schedules.

Two other components of the management system were a "Management Center" and a "weekly staff meeting." The Management Center is a specially designed secure room that is described as the focal point of the Polaris Management System and the site of staff meetings, special conferences, congressional briefings, and daily "quick-look" readings of program progress.[10] The Management Center possesses extensive audiovisual facilities, a seating capacity for 110, and doors with combination locks. On its walls are hung classified charts that describe the progress and problems of the FBM system and its major component subsystems. Originally the center was to be called the "war room" or the "control room," but considerable self-restraint was apparently applied to contain this public relations impulse.[11] The weekly staff meetings are a Special Projects Office ritual that dates back to the very beginning of the FBM Program. In the precarious days of the Jupiter, Admiral Raborn used to meet in his office, every Saturday morning with his entire staff to review the progress of the previous week and to devise future plans. When the program grew, the meetings were shifted to Mondays in the Management Center, and participation was limited. A rigid format has developed in which the first presentation is that of the independent evaluator (the head of the Progress Analysis Branch), who reports on the overall program. He is followed first by the Technical Division branch heads, who report on their subsystems, and then either by representatives of the field offices or contractors who make special presentations.[12]

9. Ints III-2, 3, 4.
10. Special Projects Office, *Polaris Management: Fleet Ballistic Missile Program*, rev. ed. (Washington: Government Printing Office 1962), p. 2, and *Program Planning and Control System* (Washington: Department of the Navy, undated), p. 9.
11. Int III-5.
12. The first Monday of the month is now reserved for reports of the Plans and Programs Branch, the UK-Polaris representative, the Management and Manpower Branch, Shipyard and Field Representatives, SPINST 5050.2F, 8 August 1968.

The management system could not be fully developed until formalized planning and evaluation techniques were established. The first effort in this direction came in June 1957, with the introduction of what was called Program Management Plans (PMP). Forming a hierarchical structure in which each plan is logically tied to another, PMPs describe tasks, organizational responsibilities, and milestones (time-related goals) for the entire FBM weapon system. In PMPs, end products are identified, their component elements specified, and their sequence of accomplishments scheduled. The use of standardized symbols in the charting permits an abbreviated reporting of milestone completions and forecasts. Both short-range and long-range PMPs are prepared for each subsystem and major component as well as for the entire FBM system.

Measuring performance against approved plans was, of course, a central objective in the development of the integrated management control system. Initially, the official reporting of progress was based largely on subjective evaluations by the responsible technical branch and the Progress Analysis Branch. Only when milestones slipped or were achieved was there an accurate indication of performance relative to plans. Nevertheless, the Special Projects Office codified its subjective judgments. The status of major components or entire subsystems was reported at the weekly staff meetings using the following classifications: "Good Shape," or no immediate problems that could endanger the schedule; "Minor Weakness," or generally satisfactory progress with minor problems that can be handled by branch or contractor; "Major Weakness," or substantial problems developing which require timely action by the Special Projects Office Director; "Critical Weakness," or serious danger to program objectives that will require the Director to seek assistance outside the Special Projects Office.[13] Differences in the assessments between technical branches and the Progress Analysis Branch were relatively rare since an informal consultation developed between them in the preparation of official reports. When differences occurred, one or the

13. Special Projects Office, *Program Planning*, pp. 30–31. It is interesting to note that the definition of "Critical Weakness" is one that states reliance on others indicates a dangerous situation for the program. Implied in the definition is the problem's solution—absorb within the Special Projects Office a large share of activities relating to the FBM system.

other of the organizational subunits had to be publicly labeled as inaccurate in its judgment.

Given the technological orientation of the program, a search naturally began to provide more objective methods of indicating progress relative to plans. One standard management method useful in matching actual performance against initial objectives had been developed outside the program, but was extensively applied after October 1957. Called the Line of Balance (LOB), this method involved a charted comparison of the current output against planned or scheduled output and was most effective in measuring performance in repetitive, production-like tasks that have fixed lead-time relationships among component elements. The LOB specified the quantities of components that must be available at a particular date if the output schedule were to be met.[14] When the program shifted to the procurement of hardware, great reliance was placed on LOB reporting.

No standardized solution, however, was available to cope with the problem of accurately and objectively gauging progress in the research and development effort, the crucial first hurdle in the FBM Program. In research and development work there are, of course, substantial uncertainties involved in predicting the schedule, cost, and quality of the outcome. Moreover, since the nature of the research and development process is so uncertain, it is difficult to establish the sequential relationship and the lead times among component elements that will yield the desired outcome.[15] Pehrson, appropriately enough, initiated a research contract in late 1957 to explore the possibility of devising a management control system for research and development activity.[16]

14. Special Projects Office, *Polaris Management*, pp. 20–21; *Line of Balance Technology*, rev. ed. (Washington: Office of Naval Material, April 1962); A. C. Gehringer, "Line of Balance," *Navy Management Review*, 4 (April 1959), pp. 18–22; Roger W. Christian, "Production Gets a Crystal Ball That Works," *Factory*, 119 (July 1961), pp. 71–73; and William Bloom, "Line-of-Balance Technique Directs Decision Making," *Aerospace Management*, 4 (December 1961), pp. 51–61.

15. The state of current research and conventional wisdom on the topic is contained in Daniel D. Roman, *Research and Development Management: The Economics and Administration of Technology* (New York: Appleton-Century-Crofts, 1968).

16. The history of this contract is analyzed in Robert J. Massey, "Program Evaluation and Review Technique: Its Origins and Development" (unpub. master's thesis, School of Government and Public

The result of this research effort was the development of PERT-Time, as it is commonly called. Four features characterize PERT: a network that graphically describes the interrelationship of steps (called events) involved in developing a specific end item; three time estimates for reaching each event in the network—the most optimistic, the most likely, and the most pessimistic times for completing an activity; a formula for calculating the probability distribution of the "expected" time for completing the activity; and an identification of the longest expected time sequence through the network, which is labeled "the critical path" since the end item will not be realized until the path is completed.[17] The source of the input data for the construction of the network and the calculation of the critical path was initially intended to be the project engineers who were to perform the work. Because the networks would be complex in the Polaris development, PERT was programmed for computer usage. Full application of the system required the identification of surplus resources in noncritical paths and their reallocation to the critical path so as to insure the scheduled completion of the overall development project.

PERT, as originally conceived, had no capacity for considering dollar costs of particular activities and thus was not a very powerful tool in facilitating the reallocation of resources among project activities in a normal program. In the years during which PERT was developed, however, the major resource constraint of the Polaris program was time, not dollars. Somewhat later a PERT/COST system that included accounting records as an input was prepared with the assistance of

Administration, American University, 1963). The project is reported in D. G. Malcolm, J. H. Roseboom, C. E. Clark, and Willard P. Fazar, "Application of a Technique for Research and Development Program Evaluation," *Operations Research*, 7 (September–October 1959), pp. 646–669.

17. A flood of literature has become available to describe the PERT system. A Federal agency team, the PERT Coordinating Group that was composed of representatives of the Office of the Secretary of Defense, the Department of the Army, the Department of the Navy, the Department of the Air Force, the Atomic Energy Commission, the Bureau of the Budget, the Federal Aviation Agency, and the National Aeronautics and Space Administration, has prepared the most comprehensive technical summary. PERT Coordinating Group, *PERT Guide for Management Use* (Washington: June 1963). See citations listed below for further elaborations of PERT.

the Special Projects Office.[18] Similarly, PERT was unable to provide an evaluation of the quality of the research and development activity it was designed to report on. Because of the technological interests of the Special Projects Office, work was sponsored to devise a quality performance measure centered on the problem of hardware reliability (such as longevity of missile components). The end product of that effort, never fully successful, was called Reliability Management Index (RMI).[19] Unlike PERT and PERT/COST, it has not gained extensive application or extensive notoriety.

Control systems, of course, need something to control. In the Polaris program, the object to be controlled was the development of the FBM system. Technical goals for the FBM system were established through operational requirements, discussions of the Steering Task Group, and decisions of the Program Director and the Technical Director. In support of these goals, the Technical Division prepared detailed Technical Development Plans that outlined technical tasks, methods of approach, performance objectives, and test procedures. Financial programming and budget allocations for the Technical Development Plans were originally the responsibility of the Plans and Program Division. By 1959, this responsibility had passed to a committee called the Board of Directors, composed of the Technical Director, his deputy, the Director of the Plans and Program Division, his deputy, and the Deputy Program Director. The Board of Directors would meet periodically to relate financial resources to technical plans by reviewing the program budget in detail. Their decisions determined the FBM system that was actually to be developed, and, thus, the object of management control.

The completed control system, as outlined in numerous briefings and program documents, operated in the following manner. Program Management Plans would document the technical tasks, responsibilities, schedules, and interrelationships of the program. Performance reporting and evaluation systems such as LOB and PERT would indicate continued

18. Special Projects Office, *An Introduction to the PERT/COST System for Integrated Project Management* (Washington: Special Projects Office, 1961). Here, too, the literature is enormous.

19. See the testimony of Willard P. Fazar in U.S. Congress, House, Government Operations Subcommittee, *Hearings, Systems Development*, Pt. 2, p. 584.

progress and potential problems. Management meetings and reports of the Progress Analysis Branch would establish accountability, review progress, and indicate possible courses of action. Decisions made in response to actual or potential problems would be fed back into the system by changes in the PMPs.

The only major addition to the Special Projects Office's set of management techniques that occurred in the 1960's was the System for Projection and Analysis (SPAN). SPAN is a computer-based system that stores detailed information on FBM system interrelationships and requirements projected for ten or more years. The analysis of operational and planning information such as submarine deployment schedules, expected life of the guidance components, and site assignment capacities included in the system permit the evaluation of program changes as well as the anticipation of procurement needs. For example, if budgetary limitations are expected to delay the delivery of equipment used in submarine overhauls, through SPAN it would be possible to describe the impact of this action on target coverage, missile resupply, and crew training. SPAN reports, which outline future program requirements, are periodically prepared for use in the fleet and shore establishment. Originally developed by General Electric's Ordnance Division for use in the management support of the fire control and guidance subsystems, SPAN was adopted by the Special Projects Office in 1963 for application throughout the entire FBM Program.[20] Control over SPAN was passed to the Special Projects Office when it was realized that the system operated most effectively with cost and other proprietary data which potentially could be used for commercial advantage by the originating firm.[21]

PROGRESS EVALUATION

The not unintended impression given in the numerous briefings, official documents, and approved (or planted) newspaper

20. Int III-6, and Special Projects Office, *SPAN: System for Projection and Analysis: A New Tool for Planning Major Weapon Systems* (Washington: Special Projects Office, 1964). See also, "Management System for POLARIS Support Articulates Options for Big Decisions," *Aerospace Management*, 4 (No. 1, 1969), pp. 19–24.
21. Int III-7.

and magazine reports describing Polaris management techniques was that at last there had been devised an integrated management system which could cope with the complexities of technological development. Even two years before the USS *George Washington* launched the first Polaris, critics of Defense organization and management, such as Dr. J. Sterling Livingston of the Harvard Business School, could state that the Polaris program was unique among major weapon programs in terms of its managerial effectiveness.[22] With the successful launch of the missile in 1960, it appeared that the efficacy of Special Projects management techniques had been demonstrated. Since the technological success of the Polaris could be attributed to the Special Projects Office's management techniques, or so it seemed, Polaris became a model for the management of large-scale technological programs.

In fact, the Special Projects Office management techniques, at least as they are described, had little to do with the effectiveness of the effort to develop the Polaris. As will be shown, these techniques either were not applied on a significant scale in the operations of the Special Projects Office until after the successful test and deployment of the initial FMB submarines, or they were applied, but did not work, or they were applied and worked, but had a totally different purpose than that officially described. The existence of an integrated, uniquely effective management system was a myth originated by the Special Projects Office. The further removed it was from its source, the more embossed the myth tended to become.

It was a myth, however, that had value. For those who wanted the FBM submarines developed, but were reluctant to place their faith completely in the men assigned the task, it gave a sense of assurance. The management system, not the men, would guarantee the scheduled development of the Polaris. For those who were developing the Polaris, it removed the necessity of justifying each development decision to a

22. Transcript of the statement by Dr. J. Sterling Livingston at the Bureau of Ordnance, Special Projects Office, Washington, D.C., May 26, 1958. For Dr. Livingston's critique of defense organization and the management of other weapon systems, see J. Sterling Livingston, "Weapon System Contracting," *Harvard Business Review*, 37 (July–August 1959), p. 83; U.S. Congress, Senate, Preparedness Investigating Subcommittee of the Committee on Armed Services, *Hearings, Inquiry into Satellite and Missile Programs*, 85th Cong., 1st Sess. (Washington: Government Printing Office, 1957) Pt. 1, pp. 791–830.

higher authority. Errors of planning or execution, after all, would be quickly revealed by the management system. For those who specialized in particular components of the management system, it meant there was a ready market for their skills. Was not the Polaris developed years in advance of the original schedule? And were not PERT, LOB, and the rest used in the Polaris development?

The limited direct contribution that the management system could have made to the Polaris development is shown by an examination of its major components. The independent evaluations of the Progress Analysis Branch, for example, did not become independent in practice until 1968. Conceived officially as the Admiral's independent appraiser of Polaris progress, and unofficially as the Admiral's spy, the Progress Analysis Branch quickly became dependent upon the technical branches for its technical information and judgments. Civil servants technically competent in the areas to be assessed could not be attracted to the branch since positions requiring similar skills which were personally and organizationally more rewarding were available in the Technical Division. The use of junior-grade line officers as liaison officers (Progress Officers) between the technical branches and Progress Analysis hardly helped the information flow since these young men were outranked and outtalked by the naval officers assigned to development work. Progress Analysis personnel, organizationally isolated and embarrassed by their conflicting and frequently inaccurate evaluations of technical developments, soon began to submit their evaluations to the technical branch heads, first for comment and then for approval, before passing them to the Admiral or reporting on them in management meetings.[23] Briefings and brochures to the contrary, this unofficial practice of interbranch checking on progress evaluations became the organizational rule. Not until 1968, eight years after the first submarine launch of a Polaris missile, was a directive issued that required the "independent evaluator" to refrain from consulting the technical branches whose work was to be evaluated;[24] its impact is unknown.

Management graphics and the Management Center can also be eliminated as candidates for commendation. The brightly

23. Ints III-3A, 8A, B.
24. Int III-8, and SPINST 5050.2F, 8 August 1968.

colored classified charts that lined the Management Center normally attracted the eyes of visitors only. The Management Center itself, though the site of many conferences and the weekly meeting, was not the place to which the Admiral or his staff would go for a "quick look" at the program's progress or to handle a crisis. In the Special Projects Office up-to-date information on the status of the program was obtained by picking up a telephone and calling the relevant technical group or by ordering tickets and flying to the relevant location.[25]

The weekly management meetings seem to have worked well. The officers and civilians in charge of the branches, field officers, and other staff units which made regular presentations, prepared rigorously for the Saturday, then Monday, ordeal of reporting on their own progress to the Admiral in front of other top officials, the contractors, and their own subordinates. The pressure for honesty and self-analysis or criticism apparently was tremendous. Telling untruths to the boss may be one thing, but trying to tell them to the boss in front of your own staff and contractors seems to be something quite different. It was as one former participant put it, "management with a vengeance."[26]

Nevertheless, the weekly meetings were not the time at which the Admiral and other top Special Projects officials were normally informed of new problems or important changes in the status of the FBM development effort. Their involvement in the management of the program was such that they would have been angry if surprised by reports at the weekly meeting.[27] Moreover, the presence of important outside visitors and contractors at these sessions would have made the presentation of surprises even more awkward.[28]

Instead, the weekly meetings were, and still are, the time at which the Special Projects Office staff and its supporters rededicate themselves in a quasi-religious fashion to the task of creating and maintaining the FBM system. The review of the status of system components, system obstacles, and problems, and their impact on FBM deployment reconfirms the

25. Ints III-10A, B, C.
26. Int III-11.
27. Ints III-12, 13, 14.
28. Int III-15.

commitment of the assembled FBM team. In the early years it is said the Admiral made an evidently random weekly selection of one of the staff and subjected him to a devastating public questioning, as if the officer or civilian selected were failing in his part of the effort to build the Polaris fleet.[29] Later, presentations and discussions by returning FBM submarine captains (missionaries returned from abroad) were used to heighten the feeling of involvement. The weekly meetings "were like going to church" for the Polaris proponents.[30]

Now, after years of application and while the program proceeds at a comparatively leisurely pace, the Program Management Plans and the program milestones they contain are by all accounts clear guides for action. In the hectic years of creating the FBM system, however, they were more a source of confusion than guides for action. Designed to coordinate contractor activities by communicating the desires of the Special Projects Office, the PMPs could not perform their task because the Special Projects Office was itself never quite sure of its own desires. The scope and direction of the program were continually changing, and the formal plans could never quite keep up with the program.[31] Ambiguity plagued all documents. A contractor was never certain what plan was in effect and what the plan meant. Milestones were subject to conflicting interpretation by contending contractors. For example, a milestone stating that a computer to be used on an FBM submarine should be delivered to a specific shipyard by a certain date could be viewed differently by the computer manufacturer and by the shipyard.[32] Did the milestone mean delivery to the dock? Did it mean that the computer should be ready for installation aboard the submarine? Did it mean that the computer had to work? The PMPs by themselves could not provide the needed coordination.

But the Special Projects Office had other less heralded means than PMPs to convey program objectives and coordi-

29. In the last few years the format of the meetings was changed so that the fifth Monday of the month is a closed session which excludes contractors and visitors. The intention, of course, is to make the meetings more informal and open for an exchange of opinions. Ints III-12, 13, 14, 15.

30. Int III-16; also Ints III-17A, B.

31. Int III-18.

32. Int III-19.

nate contractor activities. Political and technological uncertainties led to frequent on site planning and coordinating meetings for all who were working on a given subsystem or technological interface. And the money for the three T's—travel, telephone, and TWX (closed teletype)—was never restricted; communication among program participants was always rapid.[33] At least in the early years of the program, there was a doctrine that there was no time to waste on formal documents or formal channels of communications.

The final evaluation of the efficacy of the Polaris management system, however, must be based in large part on the role of PERT, its most acclaimed component. Because of the management prominance the PERT system has gained, its analysis requires a separate and detailed examination.

PERT AND POLARIS

The Special Projects Office's international reputation for progressive management seems to rest at least as much on the Office's association with the development of the PERT system as it does on its association with the development of the Polaris system. Hailed initially as the first breakthrough in management science in a decade,[34] PERT was considered by many to be the forerunner of space age management techniques and as such likely to prove in the long run to have been a more important development than the Polaris weapon itself.[35] PERT's role in bringing forth the Polaris has been continually highlighted. PERT alone among the Special Projects management techniques has been widely credited with cutting at least two years off the original development schedule for the FBM.[36] PERT and no other aspect of the effort to develop

33. Ints III-18, 20, 21.
34. John A. Pettit, Director of Industrial Dynamics, Hughes Aircraft, cited in Norman C. Miller, " 'Maps' for Managers . . . ," Wall Street Journal (August 16, 1961), p. 1; also, Int III-21A, and statement of Professor Paul Cherington, Harvard Graduate School of Business Administration, cited in Aviation Daily (January 12, 1961), p. 69.
35. Int III-22; also Walter Maynes, "What's Wrong with PERT?" Aerospace Management, 5 (April 1962), p. 20.
36. John Stanley Baumgartner, Project Management (Homewood, Ill.: Richard D. Irwin, 1960), p. 37; "Shortcut for Project Planning," Business Week (July 7, 1962), p. 104; Joseph H. Oglesby, "Civil Servants in POLARIS," Civil Service Journal, 5 (July–September 1964), p. 31.

Polaris has been extensively studied in the leading schools of management such as the Harvard Graduate School of Business Administration and the Sloan School at the Massachusetts Institute of Technology.[37]

First made public in mid-1958, the PERT system immediately attracted intense interest. In the next ten months the Special Projects Office recorded approximately a hundred requests from government and private organizations for further information and detailed briefings on PERT.[38] At the time of the first missile launch from the USS *George Washington* in 1960, press coverage of PERT was said by a naval public relations officer to have been almost as great as that devoted to the Polaris.[39]

A deluge of literature diffused information concerning the innovation. By 1962 the U.S. government itself had issued, through six agencies, a total of 139 different documents and reports on it.[40] An English-language bibliography on PERT prepared in 1964 noted there were at that time nearly 1,000 books and articles on the subject.[41] And a limited survey of European management books and journals covering only the 1962–1965 period could cite 19 French, German, and Italian items on PERT.[42]

The attention focused on PERT quickly brought forth imitative and substitute systems. The Air Force, which not so privately thought the PERT idea was "a load of _____"[43] nevertheless introduced four "improved" versions of PERT (of which Program Evaluation Procedure (PEP) was the most

37. At least two courses at the Massachusetts Institute of Technology currently teach the principles of PERT.

38. Special Projects Office, "Examples of Active Interest in PERT by Agencies outside SP," SP 120-WF:eap, 19 March 1959.

39. Int III-23.

40. George Poletti, "The Diffusion of Network Techniques throughout Government Publications," *IEEE Transactions on Engineering Management*, Vol. EM-11 (March 1964), pp. 43–50. One government document, *The PERT Guide for Management Use* sold over 65,000 copies. Private communication from Carper W. Buckley, Superintendent of Documents, March 21, 1969.

41. Arch R. Dooley, "Interpretations of PERT," *Harvard Business Review*, 42 (March–April 1964), pp. 160ff.

42. Sergio Lerda-Olberg, "Letters to the Editor: Bibliography on Network-Based Project Planning and Control Techniques, 1962–1965," *Operations Research*, 14 (September–October 1966), pp. 925–931.

43. Int III-24.

prominent) and quickly became the largest government dispenser of information on PERT, issuing 90 of the 139 government documents and reports previously noted.[44] Within the government, eight different PERT systems were reported in use by 1962 in the Army, Air Force, Navy, and National Aeronautics and Space Administration.[45] Outside the government, consulting firms were established solely on their knowledge of PERT techniques and soon thirty or so versions of PERT were being sold.[46] The peak year for the introduction of private and public PERT substitutes, 1962, became known in the aerospace industry as the "Year of the Management Systems."[47]

Despite a few analyses that warned of limitations inherent in PERT,[48] American industry moved rapidly to apply the many variations that became available. For example, a survey of two hundred firms on *Fortune*'s list of the five hundred largest U.S. industrial firms, which was conducted in 1963, revealed that eighty-one of the firms had PERT-type systems in operation,[49] and an additional twenty-seven firms were planning their first application. Not all of the interest in PERT can be attributed to Defense Department contract require-

44. Poletti, "The Diffusion of Network Techniques," Table III, p. 44. See also U.S. Congress, House, Government Operations Subcommittee, *Hearings, Systems Development,* August 16, 1962, Pt. 4, p. 1461; Lawrence J. Curran, "Refined PERT System Guide Used," *Missile and Rockets,* 11 (August 6, 1962), p. 38, reported that the Air Force was working on PERT V.
45. Maynes, "What's Wrong with PERT?" p. 23.
46. "Shortcut for Project Planning," p. 106; see also, George A. W. Boehm, "Helping the Executive to Make up His Mind," *Fortune,* 65 (April 1962), p. 222.
47. Philip Geddes, "The Year of Management Systems," *Aerospace Management,* 5 (March 1962), pp. 89–91.
48. See, for example, Philip Geddes, "How Good is PERT," *Aerospace Management,* 4 (September 1961), pp. 41–43; Ross Clayton and Robert Glann, "Analysts Look at PERT Through Eyes of the Scientist and Engineer," *Navy Management Review,* 7 (October 1962), pp. 12–14; Ivars Avots, "The Management Side of PERT," *California Management Review,* 4 (Winter 1962), pp. 16–27; Martin Paskman, "Is PERT What Management Needs? NO," *Aerospace Management,* 5 (October 1962), pp. 52–58. Most initial articles and books on the subject, however, were ecstatically favorable in their evaluation of PERT.
49. Peter Paul Schoderbek, "PERT: An Evaluation and Investigation into Its Application and Extensions" (unpub. diss., University of Michigan, 1964), Tables 2 and 3, p. 59. See also his "A Study of the Applications of PERT," *Academy of Management Journal,* 8 (September 1965), pp. 199–210.

ments, since 62 percent of the system applications were in exclusively nondefense areas of operations.[50]

The larger American industrial firms led in the application of PERT,[51] but a wide variety of other users were soon reporting. A lawyer, a Broadway producer, a grocery store owner, a public relations man, an open heart surgery team, a church fund raiser, a university registrar, a personnel specialist, and a fictitious gang of bank robbers were numbered among those who could testify to having found PERT-type techniques valuable in their activities.[52] British and Swedish firms were among the first to adopt PERT.[53] NATO governments and industry requested a briefing on the system in 1962.[54] A member of the Soviet Academy of Sciences attended an industrial conference on PERT in New York that same year and reportedly stated that the Soviet Union intended to use PERT in preparing its next five-year plan.[55] It is not recorded whether or not he claimed that the Soviet Union had invented PERT.

Publicity notwithstanding, PERT had a simple beginning within the Special Projects Office. The system grew out of Gordon Pehrson's desire to build an integrated set of management controls that would permit the evaluation of technical progress against agreed upon program objectives. With the

50. Schoderbek, "PERT: An Evaluation," Table 9, p. 64. See also Steve Blickstein, "How to Put PERT into Marketing . . . ," *Printer's Ink* (October 23, 1964), p. 27, where it is stated that, while 81 percent of PERT applications in 1959 were government related, 50 percent of the applications were strictly commercial by 1963.

51. Schoderbek, "PERT: An Evaluation," p. 201.

52. Peter P. Schoderbek, "Overcoming Resistance to PERT," *Business Topics*, 14 (Spring 1966), p. 50; Lawrence L. Steinmetz, "PERT Personnel Practices," *Personnel Journal*, 44 (September 1965), p. 424; Edwin D. Smith, "PERT Pays in Planning," *Navy Management Review*, 8 (January 1963), p. 15; "Shortcut for Project Planning," p. 104; Robert L. Caleo, "PERT and You," *Administrative Management*, 23 (March 1962), pp. 13–14; Clifford Heinzel, "PERT Technique Can Aid in Annual Report Preparation," *Public Relations Journal*, 20 (April 1964), p. 64; and Oglesby, "Civil Servants in POLARIS," p. 8.

53. Laura Tatham, "The Many Ways of PERT," *Data and Control* (February 1963), pp. 30–42, and "Swedes Adopt PERT for Viggen Program," *Aviation Week*, 82 (June 14, 1965), p. 257ff.

54. The Director of the Special Projects Office and members of his staff made a trip to Paris to fulfill this request.

55. "PERT/COST: Newest Planning Technique for Business Everywhere," *International Management*, 17 (October 1962), p. 28; see also "Shortcut for Project Planning," p. 106.

actual birth of the PERT technique and its instant rise to fame, however, an acrimonious dispute arose over parentage. Given the size of the Polaris program, it is not surprising that many people would be in some way involved in the development and application of a management technique such as PERT. Many of these participants left the Polaris project or the firms they were with to become independent consultants, skilled as they were in a new management technique that was in high demand. Paternity, then, had a particular extra cash value that caused historical accuracy to be easily sacrificed in accounts of PERT's origins.[56]

Pehrson, after assuming office as Director of the Program and Plans Division, had directed the head of the Progress Analysis Branch to explore new management systems. He especially sought a system that would anticipate problems in accomplishing technical plans. The press of daily operations and the visible opposition of the technical half of the Special Projects Office, however, apparently prevented any real progress in this direction. In late 1957, over a year after he had hoped to begin the development of a new management system, Pehrson himself initiated discussions with representatives of Booz Allen & Hamilton, a management consulting firm, to develop such a system. In these exploratory discussions, including one at a Washington restaurant, the basic PERT concept of networking was sketched out and time, cost, and performance were identified as the central variables that the new management system would have to control.[57]

It was then decided that the best way to approach the problem was to consider it an operations research task and to establish an operations research team to solve it. Management

56. A useful, objective source of information on the origins of PERT is contained in the previously cited work of Massey. Much, but not all, of the PERT history discussed below is based on Massey. For an example of the extent to which claims of paternity can be exaggerated, see T. F. Morrow, "Chrysler's Redstone, Jupiter, and Explorer Programs," in Fremont E. Kast and James E. Rosenzweig, editors, *Science, Technology and Management,* Proceedings of the National Advanced Technology Management Conference, Seattle, Washington, September 4–7, 1962 (New York: McGraw-Hill, Inc., 1963), p. 133, where the origins of PERT are traced to the Navy's contract with the Chrysler corporation in the Jupiter program.

57. Int III-25.

itself in a research and development organization was to become the object of research. Booz Allen & Hamilton was invited to submit a research proposal for the development of the new management system. Lockheed, the Special Projects Office's largest contractor and one that had ambition at the time to become system manager of the FBM Program, became involved in the Booz Allen & Hamilton discussions and submitted its own proposal. The Booz Allen & Hamilton proposal incorporated the task concept that had previously been agreed upon and envisioned a project lasting about three months. Included at the suggestion of the Special Projects Office was a provision for Lockheed participation.[58] Lockheed's own proposal, noting parallel work that was being conducted within the firm on mathematical models of progress in technology and availability of case materials from the Regulus program, stated that a project of at least two years duration would be necessary. Lockheed also included a provision for Booz Allen & Hamilton's participation, apparently envisioning the consultant's role in the project as that of an impartial arbiter of results.[59] The compromise solution was to award the contract to Booz Allen & Hamilton, but to include Lockheed representation on the actual research team. The head of the Special Projects Program Evaluation Branch (earlier the Progress Analysis Branch), Willard Fazar, requested that he be assigned full time to the research team. Pehrson, it is said, by accepting Fazar's request, provided the operations research group with a Special Projects contact and relieved himself of a personnel problem that had long been brewing within the Program Evaluation Branch.[60]

The team consisting of Donal Malcolm, John Rosebloom, and Dr. Charles Clark, all from Booz Allen & Hamilton, Richard Young and Everett Lennen from Lockheed, and Fazar began its work on January 27, 1958. Since access to classified materials was a necessary part of the team's assignment, descriptive security forms had to be prepared for the contract. On one form space was provided for a project code name. After considering various combinations of letters beginning with

58. Massey, "Program Evaluation and Review Technique," p. 30.
59. *Ibid.*, pp. 31–32.
60. Ints III-26A, B, C.

PE for "program evaluation," Fazar coined the acronym PERT for "Program Evaluation Research Task."[61] PERT was considered to be "cute, catchy, and bold."[62] In later use, the words Review Technique were substituted for Research Task.

The PERT team's goals were stated in a document dated February 6, 1958. It was to develop a methodology that would "provide" the integrated evaluation of:

a. Progress to date and the progress outlook toward accomplishing the objectives of the FBM Program,
b. Changes in validity of the established plans for accomplishing the program objectives, and
c. Effects of changes proposed for established plans.[63]

In addition, the team was to establish procedures for applying the methodology to the overall FBM Program.

The initial intention was to devise a system that would quantitatively describe the optimum relationship among the three central variables—time, cost, and performance—for the FBM Program. It was quickly recognized, however, that cost and performance factors were difficult to standardize in a search and development situation, particularly one which involved the accounting system and technological skills of a number of independent private research groups, and work on them was deferred.[64] Moreover, in the period in which the PERT team was active (post-*Sputnik*), time alone—the prospect of meeting schedules—had become the most crucial concern of the FBM Program and its technical staff. By then financial restrictions on the program had been removed and the performance objectives of the FBM system had been modified in order to gain the early operational deployment of a Polaris force. Approximately three weeks after the PERT team

61. Willard P. Fazar, "The Origins of PERT," *The Controller*, 30 (December 1962), p. 4; Massey, "Program Evaluation and Review Technique," p. 34. RT in PERT sometimes stood for in Relation to Time and Reporting Technique.
62. Fazar, "The Origins of PERT," p. 4.
63. Special Projects Office, "Program Evaluation Research Task (PERT): Statement of Task, Objectives, and General Plan for Procedure," 6 February 1958. This is also reprinted in Appendix C of Massey, "Program Evaluation and Review Techniques."
64. Fazar, "The Origins of PERT," p. 5, Massey, "Program Evaluation and Review Technique," p. 44.

began its work, the goal of developing an integrated management methodology was abandoned, and attention focused exclusively on the time variable.[65]

Aside from the concept of networking, the three basic features of the PERT system developed in the FBM Program are the collection from bench engineers of estimates of the time needed to achieve specific development events, the use of a mathematical formula for determining the expected time of achieving the event, and the identification of the "critical path" or sequence of events that is expected to take the longest time to achieve. Dr. Clark, a mathematician, conceived and developed each of these features. Everyone on the team was aware that technological progress is inherently uncertain and that the managers of research and development projects in making decisions must take into account the progress projections of the scientists and engineers actually performing the work. How the information supplied by the research and development performers should be taken into account, however, was unclear since there existed no standard against which to judge the accuracy of current projections and no information about the assumptions upon which the projections were based. At best there would only be the record of the correctness of past estimates. Most often there would be nothing more than management's subjective impression (estimate) of the accuracy of the estimator, biased by management's own lack of detailed technical knowledge. Clark proposed that the scientists and engineers be asked regularly to supply three estimates, one assuming the most favorable technical conditions ("the most optimistic"), the second assuming normal or average conditions ("the most likely"), and the third assuming the most unfavorable conditions ("the most pessimistic"). He suggested then that the expected time of achieving the desired event could be calculated by assuming a beta distribution of the estimated times and solving for the mean. The formula is:

65. Massey, "Program Evaluation and Review Technique," p. 44. It appears also that the direction of the PERT team was influenced very much by a statement of Captain Smith at a meeting held in early February. At this time, he told them that the management system should be able to answer the question: "If we fire in September 1958, without any further executive action, will the probability of failure due to rocket motors exceed 0.3 percent and why?"

$$t_e = \frac{a + 4_m + b}{6}$$

where a is the most optimistic, m the most likely, and b the most pessimistic time. By recording the expected times on the network describing the interrelationship of events, Clark saw that it was possible for the Special Projects Office to determine periodically the sequence of events which would take the longest expected time to achieve—"the critical path." Calculating the variance for achieving each of the events along the critical path would give the Special Projects Office the current probability of finishing the project on schedule. Finally, it was possible to identify network paths where there was an excess of time, called "slack," in comparison with the critical path. The recognition of slack would give FBM management the opportunity to redistribute resources among tasks in order to influence the achievement of schedule goals.[66]

It should be noted that a management control system similar to the PERT system was independently developed at DuPont during the same period. The DuPont system, known as Critical Path Method (CPM), was intended for use in plant construction and differed from PERT in that it was based on only one time estimate per task and included provisions for projecting project costs.[67] Neither of the developing groups was aware of each other's existence until well after their basic concepts had been tested. A business magazine reporter surveying management methods in 1959 brought them together, but personal rivalry prevented an effective collaboration.[68] In practice, elements of PERT and CPM are often combined and

66. Int III-27; see also, Charles E. Clark, "The PERT Model for Distribution of an Activity Time," *Operations Research,* 10 (May–June 1962), pp. 405–406.

67. Int III-28, and Robert J. Brousseau, "CPM and PERT," *Bell Telephone Magazine,* 42 (Winter 1963–64), p. 12; Boehm, "Helping the Executive to Make up His Mind," p. 218, and Herbert Berman, "The Critical-Path Method for Planning and Control," *The Constructor* (September 1961), p. 25.

68. "Better Plans Come from Study of Anatomy of an Engineering Job," *Business Week* (March 21, 1959), pp. 60–67, and Int III-29. For details on the origins of CPM, see James E. Kelley and Morgan R. Walker, "Critical Path Planning and Scheduling," in *Proceedings of Eastern Computer Conference* (Boston: n.p., December 1–3, 1959), pp. 160–170.

variations of both systems are indiscriminately identified with one or the other of the acronyms.[69]

Devising PERT in the Special Projects Office was a simpler and quicker task than getting it adopted in the Special Projects Office. Four weeks after the initiation of the PERT project, the basic outline of the system had been discussed in an intra-office meeting. By July the first PERT publication had been distributed through the Government Printing Office and several interoffice presentations on the system had been held.[70] By October a Navy computer had been programmed for PERT, several large-scale tests had been run, an order by Admiral Raborn had been issued requiring its adoption in the program,[71] and the Special Projects Office had been deluged by otuside requests for PERT information and manuals. But participants recall that two years later only a small portion of the FBM Program was on the PERT system, widespread opposition to its implementation existed within the Special Projects Office, and any implementation of the system which had occurred had been directed toward outside consumption rather than internal use.

The PERT developers attributed this internal opposition to a mistaken fear on the part of technical officers that their control of the FBM Program would be lost to the civilian budgeteers who were PERT's main advocates in the office, and to a more accurate fear on the part of the contractors that their operations would be closely monitored by the new management system.[72] The PERT developers assumed that contractors would always oppose a system such as PERT since it would provide the Navy with independent knowledge of the actual problems and delays that bench scientists and engineers were encountering. They expected, however, that the technical officers would overcome their initial suspicions once these officers were aware of the management advantages that PERT would

69. J. J. O'Brien, "CPM—Status Symbol or Breadwinner?," *Building Construction*, 5 (April 1964), p. 51.

70. The publication was Special Projects Office, "Program Evaluation Task Summary Report, Phase I" (Washington: Government Printing Office, July 1958).

71. The order was labeled SPINST 7720.1, SP12-WF:aem, 16 October 1958, subj: Progress Reporting and Time Interval Estimating Procedures for the Program Evaluation System (PERT). See also, Fazar, "The Origins of PERT," p. 6.

72. Int M-III-1.

give them. One way to gain this awareness would be to have the advantages of PERT recognized outside of the Special Projects Office. Thus, the proponents consciously instigated an outside publicity campaign (including the writing of articles, the granting of interviews, and the preparation of briefings) on the virtues of the PERT system in order to apply pressure on the Special Projects Office to adopt the PERT system.[73] It was apparently thought that the implications of benefits, though not actually achieved in the Polaris development, would force the eventual achievement of those benefits in the Polaris development.

Contractor opposition was demonstrated quite early. Lockheed management, although it had representatives on the PERT development team, quickly dismissed the management system as worthless. One high-level Lockheed executive, on hearing PERT described at a Special Projects meeting, banged his fist on the table and reportedly said: "No management system is going to get me to admit that I am going to miss my scheduled delivery dates. This system is going to listen to some pessimistic Lockheed engineer say that Lockheed is likely to miss delivery but not to me. I sign the contracts; I hire and fire Lockheed engineers."[74] When told that PERT would not only help the Special Projects Office, but also would help him manage the Polaris development by supplying information on current progress, he replied: "How the hell can anyone from the outside tell me how to manage my program? I've got all the information I need in my desk."[75] Given this attitude and similar ones at other firms, it was not surprising that PERT installations in the FBM Program lagged despite the official directives and publicity to the contrary.[76]

Eventually, of course, the contractors complied with the PERT directives, but their compliance was unenthusiastic and

73. Int III-29.
74. Fazar, "The Origins of PERT," p. 6, and Int M-III-2.
75. Int M-III-2.
76. On the installation of the PERT system at Lockheed, see Geddes, "How Good is PERT?" pp. 41–43; Wyndham Miles interviews with Lt. D. W. Geri and Gordon Pehrson; Ints III-30 and M-III-2. Note also the discussion of the reception PERT received in general contained in Schoderbek, "Overcoming Resistance to PERT," and Henry B. Eyring, "Evaluation of Planning Models for Research and Development Projects" (unpub. diss., Graduate School of Business Administration, Harvard University, 1963).

subversive. The system was designed originally to gather estimates directly from the bench engineers and to process the resulting data centrally in a Navy computer. The contractors, however, had an irresistible urge to process—review and correct—the data at their own sites before releasing them to the Navy.[77] Moreover, practice soon led to the establishment in each plant of specialized PERT staffs which became responsible for the actual generation of the time estimates. The PERT staffs tended to be kept carefully isolated from both the bench engineers and the regular management control groups.[78] Government approval of these procedures gained increased contractor adoption, but not increased effectiveness for the PERT system.

The Special Projects Office technical staffs' opposition to PERT was based on somewhat different grounds. To be sure, there was a concern that PERT was designed to monitor their own performance as much as it was designed to monitor the performance of the contractors; the technical officers were held responsible for slippages in schedules and PERT highlighted expected schedule slippages. But, for the same reason, the Special Projects Office technical staffs craved information on expected contractor progress and would presumably have accepted such information from whatever source possible—threatening or not, legal or not. The Technical Division managers were no more willing than the Program and Plans Division managers to accept unquestioningly the schedule promises made by corporate-level executives. Unlike the PERT proponents, however, they were also unwilling to accept without question the pronouncements of the PERT computer. They feared less falling victim to the PERT innovators than they feared falling victim to unreliable information.[79]

All the basic features of the PERT system were challenged by the technical staff. The total reliance of the system of time estimates supplied by bench engineers was thought unwise

77. Maynes, "What's Wrong with PERT?" p. 25, discusses the industry demands for preprocessing PERT reports. Philip J. Klass, "PERT/PEP Management Tool Use Grows," *Aviation Week and Space Technology*, 73 (November 28, 1960), p. 90, implies that the Navy was unique among the Department of Defense agencies in its initial requirement that PERT information be processed centrally. The other services let the contractors process their own PERT data.

78. Int III-30.

79. Int M-III-3.

since program experience had shown that these engineers tended to be both overly optimistic about their own technical prowess and completely unable to judge the future availability of resources. The assumption that a beta distribution accurately describes the distribution of activity times in research was easily questioned since no justification other than mathematical convenience had been made to support its inclusion in the system. Though the concept of networking tended to be accepted, it was also pointed out that there was no way by which to test the validity of the selected network other than by using it. Computer processing of the networks would of course produce large reports rapidly, but it was argued that no one would have time to read them, particularly reports that would be out of date. Finally, it was noted that the system could be "jimmied." The very contractors or project groups that were most in need of monitoring would be the contractors or project group that would see to it that the system ran on false data.

When the technical officers wanted accurate data on development slippages in Plant X they would call a former Navy buddy in Quality Control, visit with the redhead who was the design group's sceretary, or wire the cooperative sales manager of Plant X's main subcontractor.[80] They did these things because either they could trust the information they received or they knew what discount to apply to the information. The PERT system, though supposedly designed to overcome one set of biases, was, in their opinion, riddled with other unintended and uncompensated biases. Thus, they were willing to advocate further research on the system, such as an effort to incorporate cost information, but they were unwilling to advocate its adoption and to become dependent upon the information it generated. (The management methods actually used to control the FBM development are discussed in detail in Chapter Five.)

The Technical Division was not beyond trying to sabotage the implementation of PERT. One officer in whose area of responsibility an early PERT test was conducted was certain that the Technical Director rigged the selection of his area for the test because the Director thought that the officer would be diplomatic and skillful enough to assure that PERT would not interfere with normal operations and would receive a quiet

80. Int III-31.

burial.[81] Much to this officer's lasting regret, however, he did not do PERT in when this might have been possible. Ignoring pessimistic PERT reports, he continually claimed that the technology the system was monitoring was on schedule. When the slippage did occur, PERT advocates had evidence of its efficacy in prediction. "If we had only said 'yes we know the September, 1958 date can't be met' we would have killed PERT," one of the officer's assistants later stated.[82]

Actually, by the time that schedule slippage occurred, it probably mattered little whether or not PERT could fulfill all of its promises. Months before this incident Admiral Raborn had begun taking firm stands supporting the PERT innovation. In the difficult spring and summer sessions with executives from the major FBM contractors and the heads of the technical branches, it was only Admiral Raborn's endorsements that prevented PERT from being scuttled.[83] The enthusiastic praise PERT received from outside the Special Projects Office during this period was evidence enough to him that the system had value.[84] At the Board of Directors meeting in October 1958 implementation of PERT throughout the FBM Program was approved and the Admiral, while he accepted the objections of his Technical Director and Deputy Director that the system would not aid the Special Projects Office in its technical management function, still cast his vote, the necessarily deciding one, on the side of the PERT proponents. There was the expectation, it seemed, that even if PERT could not help the Special Projects managers it might help the contractors.[85]

The contractors, of course, were PERT opponents and unlikely beneficiaries. In interviews with contractor executives reviewing their experience with the original PERT system, not one of them said that he had used the data generated by that system to manage his firm's portion of the FBM effort. Instead, many thought that it was the Special Projects Office technical officers and engineers that actually had used the PERT system data. The technical officers and engineers, in

81. Int III-32.
82. Int III-33.
83. Massey, "Program Evaluation and Review Technique," p. 56, and Fazar, "The Origins of PERT," p. 6.
84. Int. III-34.
85. Ints III-35A, B.

turn, denied ever using PERT data to manage their segments of the FBM Program; they thought it was the program evaluators in the Plans and Programs Division, if anyone, who made use of the PERT system. Persons who held positions in Plans and Programs, however, admitted that they themselves never used the system; rather, they thought that it was either the technical branch heads or the Special Projects plant representatives who worked with the PERT reports. The plant representatives were similar in their response: "No, it must have been someone else."[86]

The fact that no one of the participant groups claimed to have benefited directly from the installation of PERT did not prevent unanimous agreement that PERT was of great benefit to the program as a whole. "It had lots of pizzazz and that's valuable in selling a program."[87] "The real thing to be done was to build a fence to keep the rest of the Navy off of us. We discovered that PERT charts and the rest of the gibberish could do this. It showed them we were top managers."[88] "The people in DOD and the Congress had to be impressed. PERT made us OK with the people who had the money. We did it in spades—computers, the whole bit."[89]

Gradually, as it was recognized that PERT was needed by Admiral Raborn to sell and to defend the program, opposition faded.[90] It mattered not how PERT was used, only that it was in use. Technical officers who were with the program through 1960 noted that Admiral Raborn never asked them any question relating to PERT, other than whether they had implemented it in their area of operation.[91] The citation accompanying the Distinguished Service Medal that the Admiral received when the first Polaris missile was successfully launched from a submerged submarine read, in part: "For exceptionally meritorious service to the Government of the United States in a duty of great responsibility from 5 December 1955 to 20 July 1960. . . . He established a single yet forceful management system which encompassed all elements of his responsibility, implementing a totally new management tool—the Program

86. Ints III-36A, B, C, D, E.
87. Int III-37.
88. Int III-38.
89. Int III-39.
90. Int III-40.
91. In III-41.

Evaluation Review Technique. The widespread adoption of this method . . . by large sections of American industry reflects his keen perception and resourcefulness. . . ."[92] PERT did not build the Polaris, but it was extremely useful for those who did build the weapon system to have many people believe that it did.

Although a PERT network for the entire FBM system was never attempted[93]—the number of events in that system would have exceeded both the capacity of any computer and the ability of any network designer—work continued after 1960 in the Special Projects Office on extending and improving PERT. In 1961 a tentative method for incorporating cost estimates into the PERT analysis was developed, and a parallel effort to consider reliability factors was initiated. An inter-agency committee was soon formed to select from the multiplicity of control systems stimulated by PERT the standardized forms to be applied in aerospace contracts. Based largely on their apparent success in the FBM development, PERT systems became a contract requirement in Department of Defense, National Aeronautics and Space Administration, and Atomic Energy Commission programs.[94]

By the time work began on the Poseidon missile in 1965, the Special Projects Office had finally extended the use of PERT to a considerable portion of its activities. Within the FBM Program, attitudes on PERT began to mellow. Engineers and officers who had most strongly opposed its installation would grudgingly concede that the network aspect of PERT has some value. The disciplined planning forced by the network require-ment, in their opinion, usefully focused contractor attention on project interdependencies and future resource needs.[95] But

92. "Biography, Vice Admiral William F. Raborn, Jr., USN," Director, Special Projects Office (Washington: Special Projects Office, undated).

93. Avots, "The Management Side of PERT," p. 22.

94. The Navy PERT contract requirement is discussed in U.S. Congress, House, Government Operations Subcommittee, *Hearings, Systems Development*, August 16, 1962, Pt. 4, p. 1473. For Department of Defense and the National Aeronautics and Space Administration re-quirements, see Richard Mathews, "How to Implement PERT Costs," *Aerospace Management*, 6 (October 1963), pp. 18–22. PERT is now only permitted, not required.

95. The value of the network planning portion of PERT was vari-ously estimated to be between 75 and 100 percent of the total value of PERT. Ints III-42, 43, 44, 45, 46.

none of them would admit that the continuous running of PERT data had much benefit in the actual surveillance and management of the program. Concessions to its opponents and to the operational requirements of large-scale bureaucracies have led to significant changes in the basic PERT system. The three-time estimate feature has been largely replaced with a single-time estimate, thus preventing the probability modeling of PERT results. The almost exclusive use of specialized staffs to develop time and cost estimates has broken the system's direct tie to bench scientists and engineers, eliminating a valuable if biased source of information on actual project progress. And, most damaging in terms of its original concept, PERT is now used frequently to establish a schedule that is to be met rather than to discover the probabilities of meeting a previously determined schedule.[96] In other words, penalties are applied to those hapless enough to be reported as encountering obstacles. The worst place to be, organizationally, is on the critical path and thus deception is rewarded.[97]

Extensive use of PERT has revealed another problem—it is extremely costly to operate. The cost of running PERT/ TIME system on a contract ranges from a Navy estimate of 0.1 percent of the price of a large-volume contract[98] to an industry estimate of 1.1 percent.[99] The extra computer and accounting conversion charges involved in PERT/COST systems make them even more expensive. All estimates of the cost of PERT/COST are in the range of 4 to 5 percent of the contract prices.[100] Ironclad regulations that require PERT-type systems to be applied to every contract over a relatively modest dollar volume (at times, $2 million) have led to situations where PERT-related costs far exceed the reported maximum

96. Ints III-47A, B, and 48.

97. Anthony G. Oettinger, "A Bull's Eye View of Management and Engineering Systems," *Proceedings of the 19th ACM National Conference* (New York: Association for Computing Machinery, 1964), reprinted in Alan Westin, *Information Technology in a Democracy* (Cambridge, Mass.: Harvard University Press, 1971). Oettinger's paper is an early and magnificent indictment of the management systems fad.

98. Klass, "PERT-PEP Management Tool Use Grows," p. 91.

99. Wilbur Ray Ross, "Evaluating the Cost of PERT/Cost," *Management Services*, 3 (September–October 1966), p. 45.

100. *Ibid.*, p. 44; see also Int III-47, and Wilbur Ray Ross, "An Analysis of the PERT/COST Approach to Managing Complex Work Programs" (unpub. diss., University of Texas, 1965), p. 164.

of 5 percent. One shipyard confidentially revealed that PERT/ COST monitoring expenses on a $7 million development contract were likely to be about $1 million.[101]

Costs, of course, have to be related to benefits before their effectiveness can be assessed. Unfortunately, no one has been able to establish, or been interested in establishing, quantitative estimates of the benefits of PERT. The few studies that approach the subject are limited in scope and contradictory in result. A Bureau of Ships study of sixty-seven contracts reports cost overruns averaging 7 percent for the nineteen that used PERT/COST compared to overrruns averaging 23 percent for the forty-eight that did not use the control system. Contract growth (cost increases resulting from contract changes) was also substantially lower in the contracts monitored by PERT/COST.[102] Michael Hilton's study prepared at the Sloan School of Management reviewed the experience of forty-five contracts, twenty-four of which utilized a PERT-type system. He found essentially no performance differences among the users and nonusers of PERT.[103] It is clear, however, from every source that those most favorably disposed toward PERT tend to be persons in firms or agencies that have never directly applied the system.[104] As Hilton noted at the end of his survey, ". . . the nonusers recognized that their difficulties lay in scheduling, and they believed PERT would help them. The PERT users had similar problems, but their comments were disillusioned [sic]."[105]

101. Int III-48.
102. Reported in William Buschman, "PERT-COST," a paper prepared for the "Dynamics of DOD-Industry Management Relations," a symposium sponsored by the Electronics Industries Association, March 19, 1965.
103. Michael W. Hilton, "The Use of PERT in Industry" (unpub. master's thesis, Sloan School of Management, Massachusetts Institute of Technology, 1966). See also David M. Straight, Jr. "Project vs Functional Organization in the R&D Industry" (unpub. master's thesis, Sloan School of Management, 1965), pp. 28–29.
104. Ints III-49, 50, and Hilton, "The Use of PERT in Industry."
105. Hilton, "The Use of PERT in Industry," p. 58. Donald Marquis who directed Hilton and others in studies of PERT at the Sloan School provides a summary analysis of the investigations in "A Project Team + PERT = Success. Or Does It?" Innovation (No. 5, 1969), pp. 26–33. He reports that project managers who use PERT are about half again as likely to be rated excellent by their supervisors as those who do not. He points out, however, that there is no actual relationship between the supervisor's judgment about the excellence of his project manager

The Special Projects Office never has attempted to measure the effectiveness of PERT; the reputational cost of a negative finding would prove too costly for the organization to bear. Moreover, such a study would be somewhat pointless whatever its results since PERT-type systems are now a Department of Defense requirement on FBM and other weapon development contracts. Yet subjective evaluations of PERT do exist in the Special Projects Office, the birthplace of the PERT system. As one senior officer stated, "We would seek an immediate exemption for the OSD requirement but it isn't worth the fight. They apparently believe in it and they pay for it."[106]

If one needs more evidence on PERT's role in the Polaris program one need only examine the experience of CPM, the strikingly similar management system which was developed by engineering staff personnel at DuPont. CPM never gained much prominence at DuPont because, according to some of CPM's developers, it was not adopted by a line organization to promote a favored project.[107] The functional structure of DuPont apparently prevented such an internal promotional effort,[108] and tests of the system, despite later claims to the contrary, did not clearly demonstrate its engineering value.[109] Since DuPont carefully limited its activities in order not to compete with important customers, the developing division was not permitted to sell the idea as an engineering service

---

and the outcome of the project, either technically or administratively. Marquis' overall assessment of PERT seems to be that it has no effect on technical performance but that it can be valuable in preventing time and cost problems in projects undertaken with tight or limited resources since PERT focuses attention on scheduling and costs. For an analysis of the management of research contracts that also considers PERT, see Edward B. Roberts, "Facts and Folklore in Research and Development Management," *Industrial Management Review,* 8 (Spring 1967), pp. 5–18, and *The Dynamics of Research and Development* (New York: Harper and Row, 1964).

106. Int III-51. As indicated previously, PERT is no longer required in defense contracts. Regulations now call for the use of an approved information reporting system, and PERT is among several other systems certified for use. It should be noted also that not all defense officials are intoxicated by the promises of these information systems. See an address entitled "A New Look at Systems Engineering" by Rogert A. Frosch, Assistant Secretary of the Navy (R&D) given at the meetings of the Institute of Electrical and Electronics Engineers, New York City, March 26, 1969.

107. Ints III-D1, 2, 3.

108. Ints III-D4, 5, 6.

109. Ints III-D7, 8.

outside of DuPont.[110] Several of the developers did leave Du-Pont to join a consulting firm in order to commercialize their invention, but with little success. The commercialization of PERT overwhelmed them. As one said, "We had three men and a girl and PERT had Booz Allen & Hamilton and the U.S. Navy."[111] They had slides to demonstrate CPM at business meetings; the Navy had a color movie of the Polaris.[112] The very term CPM—Critical Path Method—it turns out, was borrowed in desperation from the better-known PERT system.[113] No one has gained much money or mileage from CPM.[114]

THE MYTH IN PERSPECTIVE

An alchemous combination of whirling computers, brightly colored charts, and fast-talking public relations officers gave the Special Projects Office a truly effective management system. It mattered not whether the parts of the system functioned or even existed. It mattered only that certain people for a certain period of time believed that they did. Thus, a former Secretary of the Navy was convinced that the Special Projects Office never missed a scheduled commitment (it did) and a former Chief of Naval Operations and a former Assistant Secretary of Defense were certain that PERT always caught impending errors (it did not).[115] The Special Projects Office won the battles for funds and priority. Its program was protected from the bureaucratic interference of the comptrollers and the auditors.

The success of the technological development confirmed the effectiveness of the management system. Brief surveys by Defense Department committees had only to determine that a particular management technique was part of the Special Projects management system before commending it for department-wide adoption. Management specialists searching aerospace projects for lessons had only to note the connection with

110. Ints III-D5, 9.
111. Int III-D10.
112. Int III-D11.
113. Int III-D12, and James E. Kelley, "History of CPM and Related Systems," (Fort Washington, Pa.: Mauchly Associates, 1962), processed.
114. Ints III-D13, 14, 15, 16.
115. Ints III-52, 53, 54.

the Polaris development to be certain that a given management technique would be useful in the operation of a modern business firm.[116]

The very few that took a closer look discovered the fabrication, but also its value. The British Admiralty, for example, had to examine carefully the operations of the Special Projects Office in order to construct their own FBM force. Its representatives were initially surprised that the Special Projects Office's documented management philosophy did not match its management practice. Nevertheless, they too recommended the adoption of the entire management system as advertised since they recognized the advantages in terms of organizational independence and resource support that such a system could provide.[117]

Over the years, however, the advantages for the Special Projects Office have worn thin or disappeared. Changes in the political environment and in the structure of the Department of Defense have limited the ability of weapon projects to chart their own careers. The Special Projects Office, much to its own discomfort, is now often required by fiat and reputation to apply management practices that it would happily abandon for the sake of efficiency. And the techniques that actually guided the Polaris program are ignored because they do not conform to the theories which had their origins supposedly in the very same program.

116. Donald J. Smalter and Rudy Ruggles, Jr., "Six Business Lessons from the Pentagon," *Harvard Business Review*, 44 (March–April 1966), pp. 64–75, and Boehm, "Helping the Executive to Make up His Mind."
117. Ints III-55A, B.

5 | The Synchronization of Progress in Several Technologies

The introduction of innovative management techniques by the Special Projects Office had little directly to do with the technical development of the FBM system. PERT, the Management Center, and the other management techniques discussed in the previous chapter were essential to the Polaris Program, but only as major components of an externally oriented strategy of managerial innovation. This strategy, along with the strategies of differentiation, cooptation, and moderation, was devised for a political purpose—to gain control over the organizational and financial resources thought necessary for the successful development of the FBM system. The effective use of the resources obtained and the actual development of the FBM system, however, were necessarily the result of other factors.

Important among these factors was the quality of the leadership provided by the Technical Director of the Special Projects Office. With a technical philosophy formulated in numerous policy decisions and official directives, Admiral Levering Smith established guidelines that facilitated the rapid, sharply focused, and coordinated technological progress required to bring forth the FBM system. The complexity of the technical effort clearly prevents the assessment of individual contributions. Yet the very recognition of this complexity highlights the importance of decisions regarding the selection and integration of component elements of the system. During the entire history of the Polaris Program, Admiral Smith has either made those decisions or determined the criteria used in making them.

A second factor was the organizational structure of the

131

Special Projects Office and the FBM Program. Best described as decentralized and competitive, this structure facilitated a rapid and synchronized advance in all the technologies that comprised the FBM system. Structural decentralization, a product of the frustrations of the joint venture with the Army, prevented an enormous burden of detailed management from being placed on the Technical Director's staff by stimulating subunit initiative. Intraprogram competition, the result of the pressures of accelerated schedules and the normal ambitions of business firms and naval officers, assured the leadership of the program, particularly Admirals Raborn and Smith, that there would always be both a range of alternatives for each major decision and sufficient information upon which to base a wise choice among the alternatives. Taken together, decentralization and competition provided nearly self-regulating control over the Polaris development and its developers.

A third factor was the esprit de corps generated within the Special Projects Office and the Polaris program by Admiral Raborn. The structural arrangements were potentially quite divisive. Subunit independence and intraprogram competition could easily have created suspicions that could have disrupted the high degree of cooperative behavior required to complete the intricate FBM system. Admiral Raborn, aware of this danger, stimulated a dedication to program goals and a personal loyalty to himself that built a unified organization out of what could have been a set of warring bureaucracies. Conscious also of the limits of economic incentives in motivating men to participate in an uncertain undertaking, the Admiral effectively employed appeals to patriotism and camaraderie to push the development effort forward. His commitment to the development of the FBM system was extraordinary, and, because of it, so was the commitment of all whose contributions were a necessity.

THE TECHNOLOGICAL CHALLENGE

Thus far, the significance of the technological advance represented by the FBM system has been asserted frequently. Some observers, however, argue that the development of an FBM system was, in fact, not a particularly outstanding technological challenge.[1] In order to appreciate the value of the factors that facilitated the development of the system, the complexity of the technological challenge must first be appreciated.

Those who take the position that creating an FBM system was not an unusually difficult task base their argument on the amount of relevant technological knowledge available to the Polaris developers. The program, they point out, was initiated a decade after the United States had begun to fund research in ballistic missiles and two years after work in this area received the highest national priority. The design of the Polaris, therefore, could incorporate the experience gained from a substantial amount of prior research. They note that important advances in reentry physics, electronic controls, and inertial guidance, crucial to the success of the Polaris, had occurred earlier in connection with other missile projects in other services. Although the Polaris was the first solid-fueled ballistic missile to be deployed, they view this achievement as simply the culmination of a history of solid propellant research which stretches back to the years before the Second World War.[2] Similarly, they note that significant work in nonmissile components of the system such as that in nuclear propulsion, deep ocean navigation, and underwater communications, preceded the start of the FBM Program. Clearly, the Navy had many well-advanced development projects available for transfer to the jurisdiction of the Special Projects Office when the decision to start the program was made. There were no technological breakthroughs, they claim, in the development of the FBM.

It is not surprising to find that many who argue thus have had a connection with the Air Force ballistic missile program; nor is it surprising to find those who most vehemently deny the argument have had a connection with the FBM Program. The contest for current prestige and budgets predictably biases the recording of history and the identification of its heroes.[3]

1. Ints IV-1, 2.
2. *Management Factors Affecting Research and Exploratory Development* (Cambridge: Arthur D. Little, Inc., April 1965), pp. III-10, 11, 12, 18.
3. For example, see comments made by General White, Air Force Chief of Staff, on the history of solid propulsion research in U.S. Congress, House, Committee on Armed Services, *Hearings, Military*

Obviously the FBM Program benefited from previous defense research investments. Project Hindsight, the Department of Defense study which sought to trace the science origins of major weapon systems (including the Polaris weapon system), has shown the great interdependency of applied defense research.[4] Fortuitous as well as planned connections tie research and development efforts together. Thus, the Special Projects Office acquired a team highly experienced in guidance and navigation technology when the Air Force canceled its Navaho cruise missile contract with North American Aviation,[5] but the FBM Program was conceived as directly capitalizing on the success of the USS *Nautilus*, the first nuclear submarine. Shifts in financial allocations also place one service or one subdivision of a service in debt to another. The Instrumentation Laboratory at M.I.T., which played a vital role in the design of the Polaris guidance equipment, was originally supported with Navy funds, but, when the first Navy contracts ran out, the laboratory was kept together by Air Force funds until the Polaris Program began.[6] And, of course, data generated in studies of reentry physics initiated by the Air Force and the Army were a national resource upon which all missile or space programs could draw.[7] The FBM system, like other major advances in weapon system designs, can be said to owe part of its success to work that preceded it, work often undertaken without future significance being recognized.

Borrowing alone, however, could not build the FBM system. In each of the component subsystems there were major technical problems that had to be solved in order to complete the program. For political reasons, these problems were always

Posture Briefings (No. 9), 87th Cong., 1st Sess. (Washington: Government Printing Office, 1961), p. 1097. See also General Schriever's testimony, U.S. Congress, Senate, Preparedness Investigating Subcommittee of the Committee on Armed Services, *Hearings, Inquiry into Satellite and Missile Programs*, 85th Cong., 1st and 2nd Sess. (Washington: Government Printing Office, 1958), p. 1654.

4. Chalmers W. Sherwin and Raymond S. Isenson, "Project Hindsight: A Defense Department Study of the Utility of Research," *Science*, 156 (June 23, 1967), pp. 1571–1577; Chalmers W. Sherwin and Raymond S. Isenson, *First Interim Report on Project Hindsight* (No. AD 642-400; Springfield, Va.: Clearinghouse for Federal Scientific and Technical Information, June 30, 1966, rev. October 13, 1966). The Polaris study is reported in *Management Factors*.

5. Int IV-3.

6. Ints IV-4, 5, 6A, B, C.

7. Ints I-4, IV-7, 8, 9.

described to defense officials and congressional committees as straightforward engineering problems that could be handled easily with the allocation of sufficient resources. To the system designers, however, they represented areas of uncertainty which had to be eliminated if a weapon were to be produced. Those who would later seek to build other weapon systems would find these efforts to eliminate uncertainties just as valuable, since success opened up new areas of technology for exploitation.

Take, for example, the work the Special Projects Office sponsored in the development of solid propellant motors. Investigations to improve propellant binders and additives completed prior to the initiation of the Polaris program gave the promise of motors powerful enough to launch ballistic missiles. The actual development of such motors, however, required the introduction of a number of design and production innovations. Specialized materials had to be developed in order to obtain lightweight and durable pressure vessels and control surfaces. Thrust vector control and thrust termination devices had to be invented in order to gain precise control over the range and direction performance of solid-fueled motors. New processes had to be devised in order to ensure the production of reliable, safe, and consistent propellants and bonds in large-lot orders.[8] Today, the main line of the nation's missile force uses solid propellant rockets.

Or consider the effort to develop a reentry vehicle for the Polaris. A solid-fueled missile required a reentry vehicle including warhead that weighed much less than those previously designed. The data on reentry heating existing in the mid-1950s were helpful, but not sufficient in themselves to lead to improvements in structural designs that would have provided the needed weight reduction. The Special Projects Office had to establish a unique arrangement between the Lawrence Radiation Laboratory, the warhead designer, and Lockheed, the system manager for the Polaris missile, in order to obtain simultaneous consideration of warhead shielding and support designs for the reentry vehicle. The resulting reentry package met the system weight-yield specifications, thus permitting the use of solid-fueled motors.[9] The success of this venture

8. Int IV-10.
9. Ints IV-11, 12, 13, 14.

stimulated the consideration of similar types of collaboration in other programs.

Or examine the FBM submarine navigation problem. Prior to the initiation of the program, the Navy was seeking to improve its navigation capability, but its needs in this field were not pressing. Positioning errors of several miles could occur regularly without impeding naval operations even under combat conditions. The FBM submarine on patrol, however, would have to obtain extremely accurate navigation information in order to fire a missile that could hit targets a thousand plus miles distant. A navigation error of only a very few miles could result in the failure to destroy targets despite flawless performances by the missiles and appropriately timed nuclear detonations by the warheads. Moreover, navigation information for the submarines had to be obtained without frequent exposure of even their periscopes if the invulnerability of the deterrent was to be maintained. Borrowing from the then existing navigation research projects could not solve the problem since no advanced navigation concept had been proven. A dozen or more alternative technologies had to be explored without the guarantee that any of them would succeed or be sufficient. In the years before deployment, the navigation subsystem was expected to be the weakest element in the FBM system. Yet the performance of the navigation equipment installed aboard the initial and subsequent classes of submarines exceeded minimum standards by so much that the target specifications imposed on the entire system could be tightened.[10]

However, if breakthrough means a substantial and unanticipated advance in the state-of-the-art, there were, it is true, no technological breakthroughs in solid propellant motors, reentry vehicles, submarine navigation, or any of the other FBM subsystems. In every subsystem the trend of technology could be identified at the initiation of the program and remained essentially unchanged during its duration. In every subsystem, progress came through a multitude of small steps and not through a dramatic leap. To be sure, each advance had to be won with patience, skill, and good fortune. And, of course, the Special Projects Office had at its disposal enormous financial and scientific resources in the effort to develop the FBM system. But the development of the FBM system was achieved

10. Int IV-15.

without any unusual scientific or engineering accomplishments of the type that become textbook classics.[11]

The technical challenge and breakthrough in the FBM Program was the early development of the system itself.[12] The deployment of the Polaris submarines required the synchronized development of a dozen different technologies. Advances in each of the component technologies could be anticipated, and it was not unprecedented to commit resources to projects based on the promise of one or two technologies. To build a system that involved interdependent progress in a dozen technologies was, however, unprecedented. Such a system represents a substantial and historically unanticipated advance in the arts of technological planning and program management.

The labels which have been attached to them notwithstanding, the military aircraft and ballistic missile projects that preceded the FBM were not integrated system developments.[13] In each instance, technological advances were added sequentially and opportunistically to a basic design which incorporated technological progress in only one or two system dimensions. Crucial system elements, such as crew training and logistical support, were inevitably omitted until deployment was imminent.[14] Neither the various model designations which typically have followed an aircraft number (for example, F-86D or B-52H) nor the high degree of component substitution and interchange which occurred among the first generation of ballistic missiles indicate a tightly executed

11. Int IV-15.
12. Int IV-16.
13. Robert L. Perry, *System Development Strategies: A Comparative Study of Doctrine, Technology, and Organization in the USAF Ballistic and Cruise Missile Programs, 1950–1960* (U) (RAND Corp., BM 4853-PR, August 1966) (Confidential). The size of the first atomic bombs was limited by the dimensions of the B-29 bomb bay, although the B-29 itself was designed to carry high explosives. See Harold Brown, "Management of Defense Research and Development," in Fremont E. Kast and James E. Rosenzweig, editors, *Science Technology and Management*, Proceedings of the National Advanced-Technology Management Conference, Seattle, Washington, September 4–7, 1962 (New York: McGraw-Hill, Inc., 1963), p. 50.
14. *An Analysis of Management Effectiveness in the Ballistic Missile Program*, BSL-68, Prepared by the Ballistic Systems Division of the Air Force Systems Command (Norton Air Force Base, Calif.: n.p., April 30, 1962) (SRD Group I) has a discussion of the omission of training needs for the initial conception of the first generation of ballistic missiles.

integration of technologies.[15] In the FBM Program the inter-relation of all factors affecting the technical performance and operational deployment of the weapon were considered from the very initiation of the development. The FBM Program in this sense was precedent setting. Most major missile projects in the three services which followed it adopted the more comprehensive systems approach to the weapon devlopment that it first established.

Herman Kahn and Anthony J. Wiener, speculating on society to the year 2000, cite two types of technological advances: (1) unexpected discoveries or applications, which they call "serendipitous" and (2) cooperative, interactive effects, which they call "synergistic."[16] The Polaris system, in their view, was a prime example of a synergistic development since it embodied and tied together surprising, that is, serendipitous, progress in a number of technical areas.[17] The Polaris developers themselves do not claim that progress in any particular FBM technology was surprising or serendipitous since the trend of technology could be confidently forecast in each area.[18] They would agree with Kahn and Wiener, however, when they point out that the product of the development, the early deployment of the FBM submarine, was a greater and more uncertain achievement than the sum of its parts would lead one to believe. It was the synergistic effort or the tying together of progress in diverse technologies on a compressed schedule that was both the challenge and the breakthrough in the FBM Program and not the progress in any of its component elements.

THE POLARIS TECHNICAL PHILOSOPHY

Since Admiral Smith served for the initial eight years of the Polaris development as the Technical Director of the Special Projects Office, the burden of directing the synergistic effort was largely his. The Admiral's task was complicated in four

15. Ints IV-17, 18.
16. Herman Kahn and Anthony J. Wiener, *The Year 2000: A Framework for Speculation on the Next Thirty Years* (New York: Macmillan Co. for the Hudson Intsitute, Inc., 1967), p. 67.
17. *Ibid.*, p. 68.
18. Int IV-19.

ways. Synergism was itself a problem. In each subsystem difficult technical problems had to be solved by narrowly focused specialists, and there was always the danger that the solution they would choose would be detrimental to the larger system. For example, there were a number of methods for launching a ballistic missile from a submerged submarine, but each was quite different in regard to crew safety and submarine detectability. Permitting the launch mode decision to be made solely in terms of launch efficiency could, of course, jeopardize the value of the entire system.

There was also the uncertainty inherent in technological progress, and the existence of agreed-upon projections for the rate and direction of technological progress within each subsystem did not eliminate uncertainties for the sequence of development still had to be specified. Progress in an area could be projected and the various relevant technical options could be identified, but it was frequently difficult to predict how and when a particular technique would fit into the projection. Thus, there could be a tendency to set high subsystem development goals and confidently tie them into a larger system just because the projection of technology indicates it is possible, when, in fact, a simple error in the selection of subsystem options could cause the whole system to fail.

Then there was the organizational legacy inherited from the Jupiter project. At the start of the Polaris program, the technical branches had a well-established independence from centralized control and had officially recognized ties to specific contractors. It was not possible to consider either major shifts in organizational responsibility or the immediate elimination of contractor teams.

There was, finally, the pressure of accelerated and expanding schedules. When the Polaris program was initiated, the deployment target was 1963. Within a year the Sputnik crisis had occurred, and the deployment target was moved up to 1960. Similarly, the program began with a somewhat vague notion about the size of the fleet it was to build—three, perhaps six boats. At the first glimmer of technical success, that number rapidly advanced from six to nine to twenty-seven to forty-one, and there was talk of even more. Planning under such changing circumstances would, not surprisingly, be quite difficult.

One important factor worked to the Admiral's advantage. The physical constraints imposed by the submarine facilitated the establishment of program discipline.[19] Unlike the Air Force missiles, which prior to the selection of the silo deployment scheme were prey to continuous design improvements and configuration changes, the Polaris system had from its initiation tight physical boundaries.[20] Moreover, since the submarine design had to be determined early owing to the need to procure long lead-time items, the first and most confining decisions within the program had to be those that outlined the system's basic dimensions and interrelationships. The Polaris had to begin life as an integrated system that fit into the limited space of a submarine.

Admiral Smith, in approaching his managerial task, established certain maxims. Some were codified in directives; others simply remained guides for the Admiral's own actions. All were aimed at simplifying the synergistic effort.

One of the maxims was that the performance requirements for the system should be set by the Technical Director in conjunction with others involved in the program who were knowledgeable in the relevant technologies. This operational guideline is contrary to standard practice, which permits technological goals to be established in the form of military requirements by headquarters staff officers often not conversant with the technologies. To be sure, all operational requirements for the FBM system originated officially with the program sponsors in the naval staffs, but the initial drafts for the documents and the final approval for their content came from within the Special Projects Office.[21] Moreover, as was noted previously, the first set of operational requirements was not issued until the basic design of the system had already been firmly established and the wording of the requirements was consciously made too vague to influence the development of the system.[22]

Control over the performance goals of the FBM system gave Admiral Smith flexibility. A standard technical strategy in priority research and development programs is to run parallel

19. Int IV-21.
20. Int IV-22.
21. Ints IV-23, 24.
22. See Chapter Three, above.

or backup projects in areas where major uncertainties exist.[23]
The failure, then, of one team pursuing a particular approach
in solving a problem does not necessarily jeopardize the entire program since a second or third team using different
approaches to solve the same problem may reach the required
solution. Backup strategy was, of course, extensively employed
in the FBM Program. In the launch area, for example, eleven
different methods of ejecting a missile from a submerged submarine were said to have been simultaneously considered.[24]
Similarly, in the navigation area at least two teams approached
the problem of developing an inertial navigation system and
several substitute navigation schemes were also being explored.[25] Having control over the performance goals, however,
provided the Admiral with the alternative of curtailing goals as
well as trying parallel approaches to build a viable system.
Instead of just employing a backup strategy, he could also
employ what could be called a fallback strategy. Thus, if none
of the underwater launching techniques appeared likely to
succeed within a given time, a surface launch would have
been acceptable. Similarly, if the inertial system could not
produce a particular navigation accuracy, a lower navigation
goal would have been acceptable. Even in areas in which no
backups were attempted, such as the warhead or the missile,
the alternative of lower performance goals were always available.[26] Performance was a manipulatable variable in the
Polaris program.

Closely tied to the first maxim and to the constraints imposed by the submarine environment and the accelerated
schedule was a maxim which stated that the program's objective was the construction of a deployable system and not the
advancement of technology.[27] Advance research projects and
engineering development projects were undertaken concur-

23. The backup system in the Air Force Atlas program became the
Titan missile. Robert L. Perry, "The Atlas, Thor, Titan, and Minuteman," in Eugene M. Emme, editor, *The History of Rocket Technology:
Essays on Research, Development and Utility* (Detroit, Mich.: Wayne
State University Press, 1964), p. 145.
24. Ints IV-25, 26. See Wyndham Miles, "The Polaris," in Emme,
editor, *The History of Rocket Technology*, p. 171.
25. Ints IV-27, 28.
26. Ints IV-28, 29, 30.
27. Int IV-31.

rently, but internal priorities were invariably assigned to engineering development rather than to advance research. Systems designs were frozen and tightly controlled. Improvements in subsystems were encouraged, but not allowed to interfere with the object of meeting ship deployment schedules. A good example of this maxim's application is in the missile test flight program. As a solid-fueled missile, Polaris required relatively little in the way of prefiring preparation, so it was possible to schedule up to eight test flights per month during the development period. The large number of firings permitted the assignment of only a few test objectives per flight. When a flight failure occurred, as was frequent in the first years of the program, the rule was to maintain the test schedule by moving on to the next flight without an elaborate investigation to determine the precise cause of the failure. For instance, if test instrumentation indicated that probable cause of failure was an igniter, all igniters would be replaced and the housings made to withstand greater vibration without a research effort to determine which particular igniter failed or why.[28] The objectives of the next test flight would not be altered by the failure. No delays in the program occurred for the examination of new problems.[29] The test program was designed to develop a missile system and not to research its components.[30]

This system focus, of course, was facilitated by the fact that the program was conceived as a progression of systems. The potentials of the technologies were recognized from the beginning, but so were the requirements for timely integration. With the acceleration of the program in 1957, the initial system goals were postponed, and an interim system was devised. The initial system became the A-2 missile, and the interim system the A-1. The potential improvements identified during the development of both systems were to be incorporated in the A-3 missile. There was no compulsion to make the first system the ideal. Development schedules did not have to be altered to accommodate improvements in performance since these improvements could be accumulated for integra-

28. Int IV-32.
29. Ints IV-33, 34.
30. Ints IV-32, 35.

tion in the next system that was being prepared almost parallel with the system being readied for deployment.[31]

A corollary to the maxim that called for program attention to focus on systems development rather than technical advancement was one which stated that all technological tasks other than those contributing directly to the deployment of a submarine-launched ballistic missile should be avoided. In the political maneuvering to promote Polaris, Admiral Raborn was continually stimulating suggestions for new applications of the system. Proposals such as the land-based Polaris and the surface ship Polaris were in large part the product of this effort. The technical half of the Special Projects Office, however, was discouraged from becoming involved in either the generation or the elaboration of such proposals. Admiral Smith, to indicate his displeasure, would mark papers containing suggestions for new applications with the word "noted" rather than the word "approved" when they passed through his office on the way to the technical branches.[32] Conflicts developed between the Plans and Program Branch, Admiral Raborn's home for the incubation of Polaris application ideas, and the Technical Director over the failure of the technical branches to become enthusiastic about what were considered opportunities for program growth. Admiral Smith, however, was adamant in his desire to prevent any deflection of the program's technical resources from the mission of creating the submarine-launched ballistic missile system.[33]

Of course, the principle could not be applied unyieldingly. The requirements of politics and hierarchy did on occasion force the Technical Director to allow the technical branches to produce feasibility and cost studies of certain new applications. In these situations, Admiral Smith would insist that the studies be scrupulously done. He would not sign the final reports for release until he was convinced that they accurately

31. Ints IV-36, 37, 38. The discussion of the Polaris A-3 dimensions by the Steering Task Group raised the question of optimal system design and came to this conclusion. *Proceedings of the Special Projects Office Steering Task Group, Task II—Monitor and Sponsor the Fleet Ballistic Missile Development Program,* 14th Meeting, 3 September 1959. (SRD).

32. Int IV-39.

33. Int IV-40.

portrayed the technical difficulties and dollar costs likely to be involved in each development effort. Such honesty was invariably sufficient to guarantee that the proposals would not gain Department of Defense approval.[34]

What was perhaps a more important drain on the program's technical resources stemmed from the concessions that had to be made to outside scientists. With the program oriented toward development rather than research activities, scientists were not automatically involved in its daily operations. In fact, there was a conscious effort to exclude them from such an involvement since scientists were thought likely to propose continually a number of changes in the system.[35] Nevertheless, scientists periodically had to be invited in to review and approve the program's technological progress. Their favorable reviews served two functions: they enhanced the program's standing with defense officials who looked to scientists for advice,[36] and they bolstered the self-confidence of engineers engaged in the very uncertain effort of developing several technologies.[37] In exchange for these services the Special Projects Office apparently was obligated to pursue some of the scientists' suggestions, even though it was known the suggestions often would not contribute directly to achieving the program's narrowly defined objectives. Investigations of unstable combustion conditions, research in the deflammation-detonation transition (known as DDT), and the continued develop-

34. Int IV-41.
35. Scientists could be a source of new ideas, but the continuous introduction of new ideas on the organizational agenda would not increase the likelihood that organization could meet its objectives or even implement the proposals since the independence of the scientists would weaken hierarchical authority. What the program leaders intuitively sensed has been elaborated in a theory of organizational innovation. See James Q. Wilson, "Organizational Innovation: Notes Toward a Theory," in James D. Thompson, editor, *Approaches to Organizational Design* (Pittsburgh, Pa.: University of Pittburgh Press, 1966), pp. 193-218.
36. The role of science advisory committees in technological projects has not been sufficiently examined. There is, however, a strong belief that they serve at least in part to add prestige and endorsements to major undertakings. See Paul Cherington, Merton J. Peck, and Frederic M. Scherer, "Organization and Research and Development Decision Making in a Government Department," in Universities-National Bureau Committee for Economic Research, *The Rate and Direction of Inventive Activity* (Princeton, N.J.: Princeton University Press, 1962), pp. 402–405.
37. Int IV-42.

ment of a radiometric sextant have been cited as examples of cases in which resources were invested only to satisfy the demands of visiting scientists.[78]

A fourth maxim was that naval laboratories were not to be used in the development effort unless they possessed a technical competence unavailable in private organizations.[79] Although to some this program guideline may seem to have been based on political pressure, it appears to have had a much less sinister, but equally distressing, origin. Naval laboratories were considered too unresponsive to program priorities to be used unless there was no alternative. The laboratories, unlike private contractors, were subject to government-wide cutbacks in staff and facilities. Because of this vulnerability to economy drives, it was impossible to predict the ability of a laboratory to meet its program commitments, even though the program had the highest national priority. Moreover, since the laboratories held charters from higher authorities (for example, Congress, the Secretary of the Navy) that allowed them to operate independently of their clients, their behavior could not be controlled as easily as that of the private contractor. The lure of follow-on contracts and high profits could not be used to get them to shift technological orientations to meet the demands of the Special Projects Office. Many naval laboratories did, of course, participate in the FBM program, and their contribution to the successful development of the Polaris was said to be significant.[40] The opportunity to make that contribution was always, however, the result of necessity rather than choice.[41]

In a program as complex and large as the FBM, knowing what to control would seem to be as important as having the power to control. Early in his tenure as Technical Director, Admiral Smith began to focus his attention and that of his

38. Ints IV-42, 43.
39. Ints IV-44, 45, 46, 47, 48.
40. A record of their involvement is contained in a Special Projects Office report: *Contributions of the In-House Navy Laboratories and Facilities to the Fleet Ballistic Missile Program* (U) (Washington, n.d.) (Secret).
41. For an evaluation of the use of in house defense laboratories in other project offices which has similar conclusions, see William V. Gudaitis, "Use of In-House R&D Laboratories by DOD Project Managers" (unpub. master's thesis, Sloan School of Management, Massachusetts Institute of Technology, June 1966).

staff on the system interfaces rather than on the details of particular subsystems. It became a maxim of the program that the interface specifications would be fixed early and monitored tightly.[42] To be sure, the concern with system interfaces was facilitated by the organizational independence that each of the technical branches had established during the Jupiter project. It appears, however, also to have been a conscious decision since the Polaris segment of the program began with a close review of branch actions by the central staff.[43] A focus on subsystem interrelationships prevented the central staff from being buried in technical minutiae as the pace of the development effort accelerated. It also allowed the program to benefit from the initiative and energy of the technical branches and their contractors.[44]

The mechanisms for control were the coordination drawings maintained by Vitro Laboratories for the Technical Director.[45] At meetings among system contractors, the branches, and the central staff, the characteristics and outputs of the subsystems (usually in the form of electronic signals and the like) would be specified and recorded in drawings. From that point on, all work within the subsystem was the responsibility of the subsystem contractor and the relevant branch, but all changes affecting system interfaces were considered fundamental and required formal approval.[46] For a long period, Admiral Smith himself signed ("authenticated") all coordination drawings and reviewed all deviations.[47] Nothing appears to symbolize the Admiral's deep involvement in guiding the FBM system development more than the attention he paid to controlling the coordination drawings.

Admiral Smith, however, was also aware that the program ran on money as well as on engineering designs. After having some development contracts delayed because the program's

42. Ints IV-49, 50.
43. Int IV-32.
44. Int IV-51.
45. Ints II-32, IV-52.
46. Ints IV-53, 54, 55, 56. See Director, Special Projects Office letter to Lockheed Aircraft Corporation via Bureau of Naval Weapons representative, Sunnyvale, California, SP20-LS:pp XII-2/1 of 15 December 1959, subj: Polaris Missile Design and Process Change Control Policy.
47. Int II-32.

financial office miscalculated the need, he made it his policy to gain control of internal budget allocations. At his suggestion, the Special Projects Board of Directors was established and given authority to approve the budget requests of all branches in the Office.[48] Composed of the Technical Director, his deputy, the head of the Program and Plans Division, his deputy, and the Deputy Director, the Board of Directors examines semiannually the line item budget of the entire program. Through this device the Admiral could influence the operations of any aspect of the program and could tie together technical plans with financial resources.[49]

Finally, the program took as its own measure of technical success the operational reliability of the FBM system. The Admiral, it was said, did not want to be known as having built a fleet filled with telephone poles.[50] Reliability and methods to achieve it became program fetishes. An elaborate system of technical documentation was established to insure that components matched design specifications and that discrepancies could be traced to their source. The quality control procedures in Polaris manufacturing facilities exceeded in stringency those applied in other projects. The test program included both subsystem tests and integrated system tests. Independent technical evaluations occurred at a number of points. The design of the system itself included redundancy in the navigation, fire control, launch, and ship systems components. Apparently, the only complaints about FBM's reliability are that perhaps too many resources were devoted to this end. Some have argued that too much testing may actually impair the reliability of the system. The system, it is thought, would be more reliable if it were left alone instead of constantly being examined, tested, and evaluated. Others have argued that the reliability effort became so ritualistic, expensive, and advertised that it most likely had its origins in motivations as political and opportunistic as PERT.[51] Within the program,

48. Int IV-57.
49. Ints IV-58, 59.
50. Int IV-60.
51. Ints IV-61, 62A, B. My own investigations were not thorough enough on this point to make a clear judgment. The entire area of reliability testing in weapon programs could use a searching examination.

however, it is noted with pride that no submarine patrol has been aborted due to technical failure.[52]

CONTROLLING THE DEVELOPERS

The technical philosophy articulated in the Polaris program was a necessary adjustment to the organizational legacy inherited from the joint Army-Navy Jupiter project. There was no weapon system contractor to manage the FBM system. Each technical branch had obtained independent authority to develop a particular FBM subsystem, and each had established a close relationship with its own set of specialized contractors. Thus it was no exaggeration to describe the Special Projects Office, as one observer did, as a loose federation of technical branches.[53] What were the central staffs of the Special Projects Office to do but focus on the system interfaces and attempt to manipulate resource allocations among the branches?

The decentralized structure of the Special Projects Office meant, of course, that decisions affecting the technical details of a subsystem could be made by those closest to the problem and that the energies of contractors and subordinate managers could be stimulated by the developmental challenge. These desirable organizational characteristics, often attainable only in the rhetoric of government manuals, were imbedded in the very fiber of the Special Projects Office.[54]

Still, there was a system to create. Structural arrangements posed two seemingly contradictory dangers for the FBM project. First, the various technical branches could attempt to exercise their authority in full by managing the subsystems tightly from the Washington headquarters. If the tendency to engineer the subsystems from Washington had developed unchecked, the technical talent of the contractors would have been dissipated in bureaucratic paperwork generated by the branches.[55] Second, in the construction of a complex system, there could be a tendency on the part of the branches and

52. Int IV-63.
53. Int IV-64.
54. Int IV-65. See also, Robert E. Hunter, "Politics and Polaris: The Special Projects Office of the Navy as a Political Phenomenon" (unpub. Senior Honors thesis, Wesleyan University, June 1962), pp. 49–52.
55. Ints II-32, IV-66, 67.

their contractors to hide subsystem difficulties and to push off their problems on to other subsystems. The protection of the subunit and the subsystem could be placed before the welfare of the entire organization and the entire system.[56] The burdening of the hierarchy with an enormous number of detailed decisions and the suppression of information on subsystem problems is would seem, are the twin dangers of large-scale projects in technology.

These potential weaknesses in the organizational structure were overcome on the one hand by consciously promoting increased decentralization and on the other by taking advantage of the natural competition that developed among the branches and the contractors. Increased decentralization was accomplished by giving the field offices authority independent of the technical branches to approve contractor requests and to issue technical instructions not affecting interface specifications. The field offices reported directly to Admiral Smith and Admiral Raborn. Their independence served as a check on the technical branches and assured prompt attention to local technical problems. The technical branches were simply outflanked to prevent them from controlling the contractors too tightly.[57]

The role competition played in the development of the FBM system is more complicated to explain. At the branch or subsystem level competition was an artificial mechanism used consciously to alter the cost, lead time, or performance of component equipment.[58] Competition, like increases in staff or the establishment of a new production line, was a device by which planned objectives could be met. Some branches relied upon it more than others. The Guidance Branch, for example, used competitive sources in a number of areas and ended up orchestrating an entire network of contractors in the effort to build the electronics of the guidance and fire control systems. But almost all of the branches at some point or another felt the need to have second source contractors and backup developments. Admiral Raborn encouraged them to use competition as a management device for he thought that competition was

56. Int II-32.
57. Int II-32.
58. Ints IV-68, 69, 70, 71, 72. See also Hunter, "Politics and Polaris," pp. 76–77.

an effective way ". . . to put fire under a contractor working on critical items."[59]

This form of competition apparently had some important benefits for the program. The competition between Aerojet-General Corporation and Hercules Powder Company in the production of rocket motors was said to have spurred the introduction of innovations in motor case construction, thrust vector controls, and propellant mixtures.[60] The use of multiple sources for the procurement of guidance gyros and inertial navigation equipment was thought to have been crucial in obtaining reliable units to meet the accelerated deployment schedules.[61] And the establishment of Hughes Aircraft as an alternative to General Electric in the manufacture of fire control computers was said to have resulted in significant price reductions and an improved product.[62] Introducing such competition, however, required access to substantial resources as the start-up (leaning) costs of the second or third contractor have to be absorbed—an access that other less favored projects often lack.[63]

Another, more subtle form of competition existed in the program. This competition originated in the ambitions of business firms and of naval officers. Rather than attempting to protect an existing empire and avoiding responsibility, most organizations and individuals involved in the program sought to expand their jurisdiction. For the business firm, the FBM Program and the entire missile effort represented new opportunities for industrial growth. For the naval officer, the program offered opportunities to demonstrate executive competence in an important project. In an expanding environment, each could see the rewards of action; the competition was for dominance in a new field.

In every functional area of the program, two, three, or a half-dozen organizations sought the right to operate. At each interface the branch and its subsystem contractors sought greater responsibility. No one was immune from potential competition (see Table 1). Lockheed wanted to become the

59. Int IV-73.
60. Ints IV-74, 75, 76, 77.
61. Ints IV-78, 79, 80, 81, 82.
62. Ints IV-83, 84, 85, 86.
63. Ints IV-68, 69.

TABLE 1. Jurisdictional conflict and potential competition in the Fleet Ballistic Missile Program

Functional area	Special Projects Office unit having official jurisdiction	Contractor having prime responsibility	Contractors seeking function	Navy or Special Projects Office units seeking function
Launcher Handling	SP 22	Westinghouse	Lockheed Electric Boat, Newport News	Naval Ordnance Test Station, SP 27, Bu Ships 424
Fire Control	SP 23	General Electric	Hughes	SP 27
Guidance	SP 23	General Electric	Lockheed, Raytheon, Hughes	SP 27
Navigation	SP 24	Sperry Rand, Applied Physics Laboratory, RCA[a]	MIT, Autonetics, Lockheed, Nortronics, Electric Boat	Naval Applied Sciences Laboratory, Naval Ordnance Laboratory (White Oak), Naval Ordnance Laboratory (Corona), SP 27
Test	SP 25	Lockheed[b]	Interstate Electronics	SP 27, SP 205
Ship Installation	SP 26	Interstate Electronics Bu Ships, Vitro[c]	Lockheed, Vitro Electric Boat, Lockheed	Bu Ships 424
Missile	SP 27	Lockheed	Aerojet, Boeing[d]	Naval Ordnance Test Station
Rocket Motors	SP 27	Aerojet-General[e]	Lockheed,[f] Hercules	
System Tests	SP 205	Applied Physics Laboratory	Vitro, Lockheed	SP 25, SP 27

[a] APL and RCA shared responsibility in the navigation satellite work.
[b] Lockheed responsible for flight test opeartions; Interstate responsible for instrumentation.
[c] Vitro monitors system tests at the shipyard.
[d] Boeing is only one of a number of firms outside the program which have sought to gain entrance through the proposal of new missiles.
[e] Original firm with prime responsibility since replaced by Hercules.
[f] Lockheed did gain contract responsibility for the propulsion system, but did not actually produce motors.

151

system manager of the FBM and thus threatened all the other contractors, but others also sought to gain a role in the missile subsystem. Virto thought it should be permitted to do more than documentation and the monitoring of system tests in the shipyards, but Electric Boat and the other shipyards were willing to take on part or all of Vitro's functions. General Electric worked well with the Instrumentation Laboratory in the design of the guidance equipment, but it never thought it was unable to perform the entire design task. And the IL itself saw opportunities to exercise its technological skills in both the fire control and navigation subsystems. Even naval organizations and the technical branches had expanding vistas. The Naval Ordnance Laboratory (White Oak), the Naval Ordnance Laboratory (Corona), and the Naval Applied Sciences Laboratory all sought enlarged roles in the navigation subsystem. The Naval Ordnance Test Station wanted to be assigned the launching design and management task. The Missile Branch (SP-27) supported Lockheed's often-asserted claims, particularly in the guidance and launcher areas, and wanted the Test and Instrumentation Branch's (SP-25) functions transferred to its own jurisdiction. The Bureau of Ships, the Launching and Handling Branch (SP-22), and the Ship Installation Branch (SP-26) simultaneously sought to supervise work in the shipyards whereas the Bureau of Ordnance, the Test and Instrumentation Branch, the Missile Branch, and the Assistant for Weapon System Evaluation (SP-206) presented counterclaims on the test operations at Patrick Air Force Base.[64]

To be sure, system managers were designated for each subsystem, and the jurisdictions of the naval organizations were formally recorded. The Technical Division, in fact, took pride in the sharp definitions of subsystem responsibilities and interfaces. Because of these definitions, it was possible to test the performance of each subsystem (and thus its contractors and contract managers) independently.[65] The competition referred to was basically for the production contract, the alterna-

64. Ints II-30, 31, 32, IV-62B, IV-87 through 108.
65. Ints IV-109, 110, 111. This ability to test subsystems independently apparently was quite unique among the major missile programs. Kurt R. Stehling, *Project VANGUARD* (Garden City, N.Y.: Doubleday and Co., Inc., 1961), p. 156.

tive design, and the follow-on task. Responsibilities were defined, but not fixed. Jurisdictions, at least in the initial years of the program, were uncertain.

As was noted previously, decentralization and competition within the program provided nearly self-regulating control over the Polaris development and its developers. Through decentralization, authority to act was given to those closest to the problems, yet competition assured the central staff that decisions affecting the vital needs of the entire system would be brought to their attention. Initiative was not suppressed, but neither was information on development problems and the system consequences of subsystem decisions. The rewards for effective performance were great because the program was conceived as the development of a series of systems with fixed deployment dates. If successful, the FBM would become one of the largest military procurements. The presence of actual and potential competitors guaranteed that the value of the rewards would be recognized.

Thus, a number of contractor and naval organizations, each with its own independent role in the program, would work on a particular subsystem. If there were no disagreements among them or with the organizations in adjoining subsystems, development strategies would be determined quickly and locally. If, however, one of the organizations questioned the feasibility of a design or was questioned about the impact of the design on another subsystem, the problem could be brought to the next hierarchical level, or even to the Technical Director, for a decision. The independence and competitiveness of the participating organizations would insure that development alternatives and their consequences would be revealed.

In 1958, for example, there were at least six organizations concerned with the rocket motor development. Aerojet-General had the motor development contract. Lockheed was responsible for the missile frame and therefore had to monitor the rocket motor development. It established a propulsion development section in its Sunnyvale installation and maintained a large and separate propulsion engineering unit at the Aerojet facility in Sacramento. The West Coast field office of the Special Projects Office was located in Sunnyvale where it could watch Lockheed. A subunit of the field office was placed in Sacramento to watch Aerojet (and the Lockheed office at

Aerojet). And finally, the Missile Branch at the Special Projects Office, with the aid of consultants and Navy laboratories, managed both the Lockheed and the Aerojet contracts. Each of the organizations perceived one of the other organizations as its natural rival. Each had a viewpoint on rocket motor problems. Each was willing to evaluate the technical judgments and time estimates of its rival. And each had its own access to the program's top management. Although the noise level generated by the arrangement was quite high (Aerojet's independence was later intentionally restricted by making the firm a Lockheed subcontractor), the strategic decisions involved in the design of the missile and its interaction with other subsystems were the subject of a searching analysis.[66]

Admiral Smith had many formal and informal channels of communication through which he could be kept informed of and could control the technical effort. The technical branches reported to him. The civilian branch engineers could gain access to his office without approval of the naval officers in charge of the branches.[67] The field offices, whose job in part was to cultivate personal ties with the bench engineers and technicians in the contractors facilities, reported to the Admiral independently of each other, the branches, and their contractors.[68] Coordination meetings, presided over by Admiral Smith or members of his immediate staff, brought together representatives of all contractor and naval organizations working on related technologies and subsystems. STG meetings gave top officials from the contractors an opportunity to bypass the branches in speaking to the Admiral.[69] System evaluators and monitors such as Vitro and the Applied Physics Laboratory who had no hardware interest in the program worked directly for the Admiral. For a period, the Admiral even received copies of all TWX messages that flowed through the branches.[70] And, of course, he continually visited FBM installations, reviewed the coordination drawings and their amendments, and was involved in budget allocation decisions.

But the FBM development was too important, too big for

66. Ints IV-112, 113, 114, 115.
67. Int IV-116.
68. Ints II-34, IV-117, 118.
69. Ints II-32, IV-119, 120, 121.
70. The daily TWX file was eight inches thick when the practice was stopped. Int II-32.

the Program's Director, Admiral Raborn, to rely simply on the good judgment and honesty of his Technical Director. Although giving assurance to others that the Polaris would be developed successfully and on time, he needed assurance of his own that this would be so. Thus, Admiral Raborn had to have independent sources of information through which he could check on Admiral Smith and the progress of the FBM Program. The Chief Scientist and the Engineering Consultant, men whose functions were never clearly defined or even distinguishable, but whose experience was broad and whose knowledge of the technologies was extensive, reported to Admiral Raborn on program developments and opportunities. The weekly Management Meeting, which Admiral Raborn never missed, provided another check on the Technical Director as it offered an intensive review of the program through the reports of the Program Evaluation Branch, the technical branches, the field offices, and the contractors.[71] In addition, Admiral Raborn was the beneficiary of the conflict between the Director of the Plans and Programs Division and the Director of the Technical Division over budgets since it kept him informed of the alternatives for resource allocations.[72] He also knew personally the presidents of all major contractors and traveled constantly to their plants asking questions and making inspections. Finally, with the assistance of the Naval Ordnance Laboratory, he established a special advisory committee of technical naval personnel to review independently the program's important technical decisions and test results.[73]

As Figure 4 shows, Admiral Smith monitored the technical branches and their contractors and Admiral Raborn monitored Admiral Smith. Decentralization and competition served them both. Decentralization provided independent channels of communication, and competition assured that the channels were used. It was the interdependencies among technologies and the schedules that had to be closely watched in a project as complex and urgent as the FBM. The program's structural ar-

71. Ints III-15, IV-122, 123.
72. Ints II-32, IV-124, 125, 126, 127.
73. Ints II-32, IV-128, 129, 130, 131. See also U.S. Congress, House, Subcommittee of the Committee on Appropriations, *Hearings, Department of Defense Appropriations for 1960*, 86th Cong., 1st Sess. (Washington: Government Printing Office, 1959), Pt. 5.

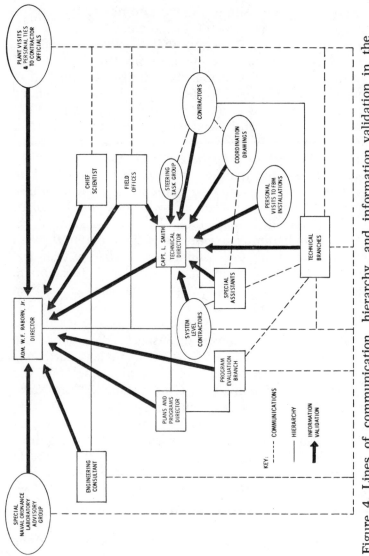

Figure 4. Lines of communication, hierarchy, and information validation in the Fleet Ballistic Missile Program

rangements helped focus attention on precisely those points.[74]

The program's structural arrangements, however, were not without critics. In the first years of the program, there were many who thought that a weapon system contractor was needed. Some highly placed defense officials, in particular, were fearful that the welter of organizational responsibilities involved in the FBM development would make the timely integration of an effective weapon system impossible. They argued that experience in large-scale weapon projects had shown that responsibility for the entire development effort should be given to a single contractor.[75] But to have done this would have forced the Special Projects Office to become dependent upon the technical judgments of one firm. It would have reduced the influence of the government's own experts in the design of the nation's major nuclear deterrent system. And, most important, it would have removed a powerful incentive for effective performance by a contractor, the fear of being overtaken by a rival.[76]

MAINTAINING THE ORGANIZATION

The program's structural arrangements, however, were potentially quite divisive. Organizations that had to cooperate with one another were encouraged to be rivals. Technological jurisdictions were not fixed. Assignments had to be won continuously. Opportunities for participating organizations to gain exoneration in failures or time in meeting schedules could

74. The arguments presented here are parallel to those that Richard Neustadt has offered in his analysis of effective presidential staff organization. The management styles of Admiral Raborn and the Presidents that Neustadt describes as effective stand in sharp contrast to the official military staffing patterns, which sharply fix responsibility and which protect high-level officials from their subordinates. See Richard Neustadt, *Presidential Power* (New York: John Wiley & Sons, 1960), and "Approaches to Staffing the Presidency: Notes on FDR and JFK," *American Political Science Review*, 57 (December 1963), pp. 855–863. The key problem with the more open style of management is the level of interpersonal and interorganizational conflict it generates. Mechanisms for controlling this conflict are discussed below.

75. J. O. Spriggs Secret Memorandum for Dr. Furnas, OASD (R&D), 9 January 1967, subj: Agenda of 26th Meeting, Ballistic Missile Committee (Secret), and Minutes of the Navy Ballistic Missile Committee Meeting of 20 February 1957, 1st Meeting, pp. 15–17 (Secret).

76. Compare Hunter, "Politics and Polaris," p. 76.

be found, but only at the expense of other organizations involved in the program.

The personal strains of independence and competition are also potentially great. Organizational uncertainty can be converted into individual uncertainty. The men involved in the Polaris program were aware that, just as their organizational unit could be replaced, so could they. Despite the personal commitment required by the program—long hours, extensive travel, separation from family—there was always the danger of summary release or reassignment. Branch heads were told they would be relieved in twenty-four hours if they slipped; the civil servants knew that they could not return to their previous assignments in the bureaus if they were forced to leave the program; contractor employees found themselves looking for another job if their customers became dissatisfied.[77]

Admiral Raborn understood these pressures well. He believed that the only way to achieve the degree of cooperation and dedication needed to make the organizational system work was to stimulate group and personal motivation.[78] The participants, he felt, had to believe in the importance of what they were trying to do and to be proud of being on the same team. A charismatic leader and an instinctive salesman, Admiral Raborn took the motivation task upon himself. His approach was evangelistic. He was quoted as saying, "Our religion was to build the Polaris."[79] No one subscribed more unquestionably to that religion than did the Admiral himself.

In violation of certain sacred norms, but with the best of intentions, Admiral Raborn insisted upon the development of personal friendships between government and contractor personnel. He required his men to go to industry-sponsored parties. He allowed them to take their wives on some trips to encourage social contact. He asked government personnel to entertain contractors at their homes during the evenings of important meetings. Here again the Admiral set the example.[80]

Using the strategy of organizational differentiation, the Admiral emphasized the eliteness of the group and rewarded

77. Int IV-132; see also Chapter Three.
78. Int IV-133.
79. Int IV-133.
80. Int IV-134.

group members accordingly. Each man was told that he was especially chosen for the Polaris project.[81] Admiral Raborn made certain that they had every possible benefit. The Polaris program traveled first class and lived first class. There was in the Special Projects Office none of the accounting clerk bickering about expenses, telephones, or office space which plagues the government.[82] The grade and rank structure was unusually high. And the Admiral was quick to recognize service to the program with a personal word, a commendation, or an award.[83]

Most important of all, Admiral Raborn made the participants fear the potential national consequences of their failure. Everyone—contractors, workers, wives, and children—was told about the urgency of the mission and was made to believe it. (The "Polaris couldn't fail because the wives wouldn't let it," said one high naval officer.)[84] No sacrifice then could be too great. It was not just another missile that was being built; it was, rather, the missile that was going to stop the Russian threat to the U.S. mainland.

The value to the program of this psychological orchestration of the program participants probably cannot be overstressed. Complementing the technical challenge of the FBM and tempering the harshness of the structural arrangement, it brought forth a degree of commitment to the program, a general willingness to make personal sacrifices for the program's success rare not only in government, but also in American society. The Polaris was devised and built by true believers.

81. Int IV-133.
82. Int IV-135.
83. Int IV-136.
84. Int IV-133.

6 | The Costs of Polaris

The proponents of a naval ballistic missile achieved their goals. The Polaris was established as a separate project within the Department of the Navy. It became one of the largest projects ever undertaken by an agency of the United States government. The Congress unquestioningly appropriated billions of dollars for its completion. For over a dozen years the Polaris held the highest defense priority rating. And the project was managed without significant external interference.

The proponents came to control all the major Polaris decisions. Consider, for example, the decision to build forty-one FBM submarines. In the late 1950's as the number of submarines authorized for construction increased rapidly, it became obvious that a final goal for the size of the FBM fleet had to be determined. The Naval staff unit monitoring the Polaris program obtained at this point a list of active Soviet targets for the Joint Strategic Targeting Agency.[1] It then calculated the number of Polaris missiles needed to eliminate those targets. Information gathered for the calculation covered the characteristics of the Polaris (range, reliability, warhead yield, and so forth), the characteristics of the submarines (patrol duration, overhaul schedule, and so forth), and the characteristics of the targets (size, dispersal, protection, and so forth). Ignored was information on the strategic systems of the other services (their costs, assignments, reliability, and so forth).[2] Given the constraint of 16 missiles per submarine,

1. Int V-1.
2. Ints V-2, 3, 4, 5, 6.

the number of Polaris missiles needed to cover all the available targets was 656 or forty-one submarines full.[3] The preferred fleet size was raised to forty-five submarines to allow for a margin of error and, as some say, the operational convenience of organizing five squadrons of nine submarines each.[4] The political backing the proponents had obtained for the Polaris was sufficient to prevent Secretary of Defense Robert Mc-Namara from doing anything more with the Navy's FBM fleet objective, when it was presented to him for review, than removing the four extra submarines.[5] The Secretary made no attempt to calculate independently the optimum size of the FBM fleet by comparing the advantages of the Polaris system with those of alternative strategic systems. The number forty-one was a product of the convictions of Polaris proponents and the realities of politics.[6]

The Special Projects Office soon earned its reputation for managerial effectiveness. The Polaris development was free from the accusations of performance slippages and cost over-runs that have plagued other weapon projects. And the huge task of constructing the fleet of forty-one submarines was completed close to the planned schedule.

Success, however, has its costs both in terms of dollars and opportunities foregone. The lessons that one draws from the Polaris experience are likely to be misleading without an appreciation of Polaris' full price and the circumstances in which it was paid.

3. Int V-7. Robert E. Kuenne in an unclassified econometric study of the optimum Polaris force concludes that a much smaller fleet would have been sufficient. Robert E. Kuenne, *The Polaris Missile Strike: A General Economic Analysis* (Columbus: Ohio State University Press, 1966).

4. Int V-4.

5. Int V-2. Naval officers responsible for the operational deployment of the present FBM fleet argue that squadrons of less than nine submarines unnecessarily complicate patrol planning. They feel that the decision to eliminate the four submarines was a mistake (Int V-8).

6. This description of the FBM force decision is confirmed in an article written by Alain C. Enthoven, the former Assistant Secretary of Defense for Systems Analysis. See his "Systems Analysis—Ground Rules for Constructive Debate," *Air Force and Space Digest*, 51 (January 1968).

THE DOLLAR COSTS

Creating the Polaris FBM involved expenditures of at least $10 billion.[7] This is the approximate net total of Polaris program funds allocated to the Special Projects Office in fiscal years 1955 through 1967. Costs not included and, short of a major accounting effort, unavailable for tabulation are those for such items as the construction of facilities, military personnel, and warhead development incurred by other naval commands and government agencies in support of the program. Despite Program Planning and Budgeting Systems and a project-oriented organization to direct the development effort, the total cost of the weapon system remains elusive.[8]

Disassembling the $10 billion by appropriation accounts reveals that research, development, testing, and evaluation costs absorbed 24 percent ($2.39 billion) of the expenditures; shipbuilding and conversion, 46 percent ($4.60 billion); missile procurement, 17 percent (1.76 billion); miscellaneous procurement categories, 6 percent ($.62 billion); and other miscellaneous categories, 7 percent ($.71 billion). As both development and ship construction obligations were then at or near their crest, the peak program year was fiscal year 1962, with nearly $2 billion allocated to Polaris. The program, however, ran at over a billion dollars or more a year from fiscal year 1959 through fiscal year 1964 (see Table 2).

Unit costs were not small; An FBM submarine cost about $110 million to construct in the early 1960's or $30 to $50 million more than the average construction cost of a nuclear-powered attack submarine. Loading the FBM submarine with a complement of missiles and an initial stock of spare parts required another $35 to $40 million. Nor have operating costs been trivial. The FBM submarines must be supplied, repaired,

7. Sources for this section are the program financial records unless otherwise noted.

8. Some have not even been able to come this far. Polaris was the only weapon system among twelve examined by Peck and Scherer in their study of weapon procurements for which useful cost data could not be obtained through official sources. In their book, Peck and Scherer do not identify the specific programs examined, but Polaris is easily recognizable to one familiar with its development. Merton J. Peck and Frederic M. Scherer, *The Weapons Acquisition Process: An Economic Analysis* (Boston: Harvard Graduate School of Business Administration, 1962), Table 16.1, p. 429.

TABLE 2. Special Projects Office Controlled Polaris System Program Allocations, Fiscal years 1956 Through 1967.

Fiscal year	Allocation
1956	$ 18,367,000
1957	89,471,000
1958	511,311,000
1959	1,025,958,000
1960	1,009,552,000
1961	1,748,316,000
1962	1,978,555,000
1963	1,764,472,000
1964	1,291,460,000
1965	564,180,000
1966	406,393,000
1967	370,167,000
Total	$10,778,202,000[a]

Source: Special Projects Office records.
[a] Includes funds not expended and subsequently returned to Navy for reallocation.

and overhauled. Their crews must be fed, trained, rotated, rested, retrained, and paid. Continuous readiness requires communication facilities, support bases, a logistics train, and realistic exercises. Estimates are that all of this adds up to between a half billion and a billion dollars a year.[9] As Figure 5 describes, the operating expenditures came to dominate even the Special Projects Office-controlled part of the program as research and development (R&D) activities declined sharply through fiscal year 1965 when the Poseidon development was initiated. The typical pattern in a weapon system with the life expectancy of an FBM submarine (twenty years) is for cumulative operating costs to almost equal the system's entire development and investment costs.[10]

The relationship between R&D and other expenditures can be seen more clearly in Figure 6, which breaks down program costs by appropriation categories and offers projections

9. Admiral Raborn used these amounts in congressional testimony quoted in Ed Rees, *The Seas and the Subs* (New York: Duell, Sloan & Pierce, Inc., 1961), p. 231.
10. Int V-27.

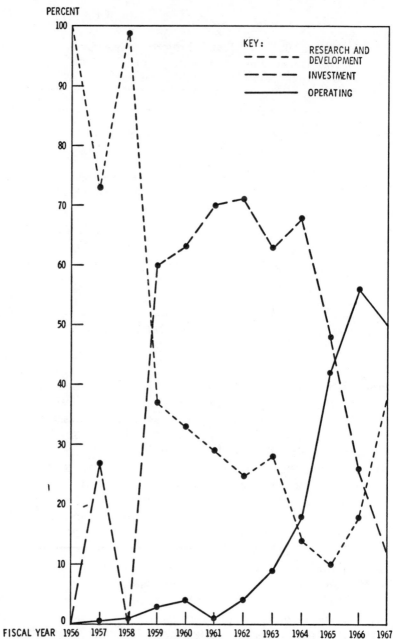

Figure 5. Fleet Ballistic Missile development, investment, and operating costs as a percentage of total Special Projects Office-monitored programs, fiscal years 1956 through 1967, from Special Projects Office records

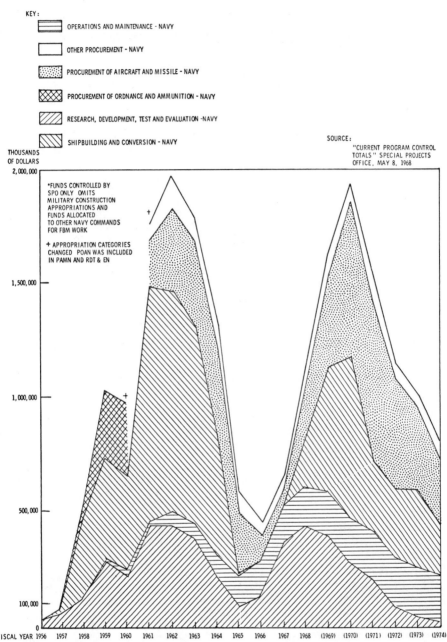

Figure 6. Fleet Ballistic Missile budget by appropriation, fiscal years 1956 through 1974

through fiscal year 1974. A deep trough occurs between the Polaris and Poseidon developments. Actually the dip in program activities may not have been as sharp as indicated due to a lag between obligation and expenditures. Moreover, problems with funding during the late 1960's probably have caused the Poseidon development to stretch out somewhat, thus changing the cost pattern from that described here. Nevertheless, R&D costs rise first and are followed quickly by investment in long-lead-time items that are needed in submarine construction. Missile and other procurements increase next and remain fairly substantial owing to the need for spares. Operational expenditures (in this case, only those controlled through the Special Projects Office are shown) climb slowly to even off at a relatively modest but steady level. Without the Poseidon development, the reduced size of the FBM Program would have made it vulnerable to absorption by other naval commands.

In creating the FBM system (and in spending $10 billion on Polaris) the Special Projects Office has relied heavily upon the assistance of private contractors. It is impossible to determine precisely what proportion of the Polaris program appropriations have gone to business firms, but there are indications that the proportion has been significant. As Table 3

TABLE 3. Conduct of military Research, Development, Test & Evaluation by commercial companies, fiscal years 1960, 1961, and 1962.

	Fiscal year 1960		Fiscal year 1961		Fiscal year 1962	
	Percent	Amount (thousands)	Percent	Amount (thousands)	Percent	Amount (thousands)
Army	57.6	$ 617,470	55.0	$ 641,437	55.4	$ 667,789
Navy[a]	57.7	747,993	59.5	814,581	60.1	779,497
Air Force	73.0	1,016,158	73.1	1,286,716	76.4	1,507,340
ARPA[b]	83.1	169,878	78.6	192,053	73.6	136,875
SPO (Polaris)	85.0	321,861	82.1	363,951	72.8	323,938

Source: Special Project Office records and U.S. Congress, Senate, Committee on Government Operations, Subcommittee on Reorganization and International Organizations, *Hearings, Federal Budgeting for Research and Development*, 87th Cong., 1st Sess. (Washington: Government Printing Office, 1961), July 26, 1961, p. 74.

[a] Includes SPO (Polaris).

[b] Advanced Research Projects Agency, Department of Defense.

shows, commercial companies received a much larger share of Polaris R&D funds than they did of Navy R&D funds. From this perspective, the Special Projects Office looked more like the Air Force and the Department of Defense's Advanced Research Projects Agency, organizations noted for their heavy use of contractors, then it did the Navy. Of the total Polaris appropriation, the five subsystem managers (Lockheed, General Electric, Sperry, Westinghouse, and Interstate Electronics) received over $5.3 billion in prime contract awards through fiscal year 1967. (Lockheed alone received $3.5 billion, but it had the rocket motor producers, Aerojet-General and Hercules Powder, as its subcontractors.) As thirty-one of the forty-one FBM submarines were built in private yards (Newport News and Electric Boat), at least another $2 billion must be added to the private sector awards. If a system contractor such as Vitro Laboratories and prime second-source contractors such as Autonetics, Hughes, and Raytheon are added, the private sector share of the $10 billion surpasses 75 percent. Finally, though no dollar figures are available, it should be noted that contractors participate to a larger than usual extent even in the operational support activities of the program. Not only does the Special Projects Office use the firms as sources of spare parts and the like, but the firms have also been used as inventory managers and performance evaluators, roles normally assigned exclusively to naval organizations.

THE OPPORTUNITY COSTS

Calculating the dollar cost of the FBM system does not reveal its true price. To determine that, the opportunity costs involved in creating the system must be considered. The $10 billion allocated to the Polaris had many alternative uses, all of which had to be sacrificed with the decision to move ahead with the system. The value of Polaris lies in the difference between the benefits obtained by building the system and those that could have been obtained by doing something else with the same resources.

Not every conceivable public use of $10 billion, however, can be considered to have been an alternative to the FBM expenditure. It may be morally fashionable to note how many classrooms, hospital beds, cancer laboratories, or housing units the $10 billion could have bought, but it is not relevant.[11] Under the political conditions prevailing in the years 1955 to 1967, the money would have been allocated to another defense project if it had not been allocated to the Polaris. To be useful, the concept of opportunity costs must refer to realistic alternatives passed over to achieve a particular end. And, during the period of the Polaris development when the nation's attention was directed toward potential military threats, significant allocations to domestic social needs were not realistic alternatives.

　· What, then, were the defense alternatives sacrificed for the Polaris? Many naval officers outside of the Special Projects Office are convinced that the FBM Program came out of the hide of the Navy, that the opportunities foregone for the Polaris were naval opportunities. Officially, only the Regulus and Triton cruise missiles and the Seamaster aircraft (a strategic seaplane) are listed as casualties of ("cancelled in favor of") the FBM development.[12] Unofficially, these naval officers claim that the program damaged the Navy severely, retarding both its maintenance and its growth. They point to the meager ship repair budgets ("Rags were tied around boiler pipe joints on destroyers because of the FBM program"), the failure to develop weapons for conventional war ("We had to cut out completely research in naval guns and gun mounts for the Polaris development") and the lack of new cruisers and hunter-killer submarines ("We paid across the board for the forty-one boats") as evidence of the program's costs.[13]

　That the initiation of the FBM Program required diversion of funds from other naval activities is clear. The historical record is replete with references to assessments placed on the bureaus to begin the FBM development. Complaints that the Secretary of Defense had promised the Navy that the ballistic missile programs would be funded independently of the regu-

11. An early analysis of this type is one done with the Apollo budget by Warren Weaver, "What a Moon Ticket Will Buy," *Saturday Review*, 45 (August 4, 1962), pp. 38–39.

12. U.S. Congress, House, Subcommittee of the Committee on Appropriations, *Hearings, Department of Defense Apporpriations for 1966*, 89th Cong., 1st Sess. (Washington: Government Printing Office, 1966), Pt. 3, p. 295.

13. Ints V-28, 29, 30, 31, 32, V-1S.

lar allocations were of no avail; the Navy had to make part of the initial investment.[14] But the long-term impact is less clear. Budgetary pressures in the federal government and in the Navy regularly require that choices be made among programs. There is never enough money to fulfill all the perceived requirements. The mere presence of scarcity during the FBM development cannot be taken as evidence of its cost.

Program officials, sensitive to the resentment toward the FBM that exists in the Navy, naturally tend to play down the possibility that the FBM development imposed significant costs on the Navy. They point out that funds reprogrammed from other naval projects to carry the first Polaris accelerations were paid back during the next budget cycle. They argue that almost from its first years the FBM competed with the Air Force for strategic weapon appropriations rather than with the rest of the Navy for general naval warfare appropriations. And they note that, at the end of the FBM deployment, the Special Projects Office turned over to the Navy a surplus of nearly

TABLE 4. Polaris program allocations as a percentage of total Navy appropriations, fiscal years 1956 through 1967.

Fiscal year	Polaris[a]	Navy[b]	Polaris percentage of Navy
1956	$ 18,367,000	$ 9,648,000,000	0.19
1957	89,471,000	10,220,000,000	0.88
1958	511,311,000	10,506,000,000	4.87
1959	1,025,958,000	11,820,000,000	8.68
1960	1,009,552,000	11,270,000,000	8.96
1961	1,748,316,000	12,431,000,000	14.06
1962	1,978,552,000	14,757,000,000	13.41
1963	1,764,472,000	15,286,000,000	11.51
1964	1,291,460,000	14,899,000,000	8.67
1965	564,180,000	14,845,000,000	3.80
1966	406,393,000	18,486,000,000	2.20
1967	370,167,000	20,710,000,000	1.79

Sources: Polaris data: Special Projects Office. Program summary 1968; Navy data: "Order of Magnitude Data on Comparative New Obligational Authority by Functional Title," Assistant Secretary of Defense (Co.mptroller) January 29, 1968.

[a] Program controlled totals only.

[b] New Obligational Authority, military functions only.

14. Int V-32.

$700 million which was used to fund programs such as the T4F trainer aircraft, Subsafe, and the 3Ts missile installations that the Navy would have found difficult to support on its own.[15] Although these officials concede that the FBM has at times been a large percentage of the total Navy budget (see Table 4), they claim the FBM appropriations, in fact, represent a bonus which the Navy would not have otherwise obtained.[16] In their view, it was the shift to strategic weapons and not the Polaris that worked against the Navy's budgetary interests.

Data contained in Figure 7 and Table 5 appear to support the program official's contention that the FBM appropriations were separate from, and in addition to, general Navy appropriations. The funds for general Navy shipbuilding and conversion rose and fell with the funds from FBM shipbuilding and conversion (Figure 7). There was no obvious competition

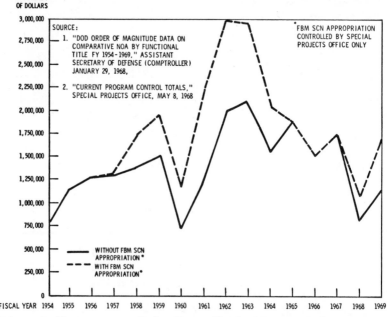

Figure 7. Department of the Navy Shipbuilding and Conversion, New Obligational Authority with and without Fleet Ballistic Missile allocations,* fiscal years 1954 through 1969

15. Ints V-33, 34, 35.
16. Minutes of the Navy Ballistic Missile Committee, August 4, 1959, p. 15 (Secret). Ints V-36, 37.

between the allocations. Similarly, the procurement of guided missiles for the non-FBM Navy seems to have been untaxed by the Polaris procurement (see Table 5). Increases in Polaris allocations did not generally come at the expense of other missile procurements. Rather, all naval missile procurements tended to move in the same direction at the same time.

Support for the opposite contention, however, comes in an examination of total naval allocations. Table 6 lists the Office of the Secretary of Defense's and the services' shares of the defense budget for fiscal years 1954 through 1967. On first glance it would seem that the Navy had the only stable claim on defense resources among the four contenders; the Air Force uniquely prospered during the Eisenhower administration, whereas the Army and agencies of the Secretary of Defense were favored by the Kennedy and Johnson defense planners. The Navy's overall position seemingly was unaffected by changes in national leadership. When the impact

TABLE 5. Department of the Navy New Obligational Authority for Guided Missile Procurement, fiscal years 1956 through 1967 (in millions of dollars).

Fiscal year	Total Navy	Polaris	Total Navy Minus Polaris
1956	238.2	.6[a]	237.6
1957	351.8	1.2[a]	350.6
1958	402.5	47.9[a]	354.6
1959	735.2	297.5[a]	437.7
1960	604.8	354.7[a]	250.1
1961	553.5	206.6	346.9
1962	878.2	354.4	523.8
1963	951.8	383.8	568.0
1964	1,107.5	378.7	728.8
1965	666.1	264.5	401.6
1966	408.0	116.7	291.3
1967	373.0	61.8	311.2

Source: Special Projects Office records and Office of the Comptroller, Department of the Navy.

[a] Estimate of Polaris missile procurement in these years is somewhat exaggerated. Appropriation category Procurement of Ordinance and Ammunition-Navy includes costs which after fiscal year 1960 were allocated to Procurement of Aircraft and Missiles-Navy and Research, Development, Test, and Evaluation-Navy.

TABLE 6. Department of Defense budget shares, fiscal years 1954 through 1967 (percentage of total DOD military functions budget).

Fiscal year	Navy with FBM	Navy without FBM	Army	Air Force	OSD[a]
1954	27.79	27.79	36.93	32.99	2.29
1955	33.20	33.20	25.22	39.42	2.16
1956	29.07	29.02[b]	22.16	46.76	2.00
1957	28.19	27.94	21.16	48.81	1.84
1958	28.59	27.20	21.03	48.25	2.11
1959	28.71	26.22	22.79	45.46	3.05
1960	27.74	25.25	23.85	45.53	2.89
1961	30.08	25.85	23.99	43.28	2.64
1962	30.84	26.70	25.38	40.78	3.00
1963	30.70	27.15	23.36	40.52	5.42
1964	29.84	27.26	25.07	38.95	6.14
1965	30.07	28.93	24.32	38.93	6.68
1966	29.57	28.92	27.98	36.24	6.20
1967	28.79	28.27	31.88	33.67	5.66

Source: See sources for Table 4 and OASD (Comptroller), Order of Magnitude Data on Comparative New Obligational Authority by functional Title FY 54–69," FAD 396, January 29, 1968.

[a] Office of Secretary of Defense Agencies and civil defense allocations combined.

[b] Fleet Ballistic Missile Program starts in fiscal year 1956.

of the FBM Program on the Navy's share of the defense budget is considered, however, this stability disappears. During the seven peak Polaris years, the non-FBM Navy suffers a relative decline. It was the popularity of the Polaris and not the Navy that accounts for the Navy Department's steady claim on the defense budget in the years between Korea and Vietnam. The FBM program caused a dip in the Navy's share that was corrected only when the program itself tapered off.

As social scientists and organizational executives know, the budgetary review process tends to be incremental.[17] The

17. For a discussion of the incremental nature of the budgeting process, see Otto A. Davis, M. A. H. Dempster, and Aaron Wildavsky, "A Theory of the Budgetary Process," *The American Political Science Review*, 60 (September 1966), pp. 529–547; Richard F. Fenno, Jr., *The Power of the Purse: Appropriations Politics in Congress* (Boston: Little, Brown and Co., 1966), chaps. 8 and 11; Charles E. Lindblom, "Decision-Making in Taxation and Expenditures," in Universities-National Bureau Committee for Economic Research, *Public Finances: Needs, Sources and Utilization* (Princeton, N.J.: Princeton University Press, 1961), pp. 295–333.

squeeze on expenditures comes in the effort to expand beyond a given base. Table 7 attempts to describe the impact of the ballistic missile programs on the incremental and total budgets of the three services. Figures for the Navy's ballistic missile program, the FBM, are readily available; those for the Air Force and Army ICBM/IRBM programs have to be, in part, estimated. Fiscal year 1955 can be taken as the base year for calculating the effect of the missile programs on the service budgets since fiscal year 1956 marks both the initiation of the FBM Program and the first budget year in which total ballistic missile appropriations exceeded a half billion dollars. In the next six budget years, fiscal years 1956 through 1961, the FBM absorbed approximately 97 percent of the total increment in the Navy budget, $4,409 billion out of an increment of $4,569 billion. Subtracting FBM appropriations for fiscal years 1956 to 1961 from the total ballistic missile appropriations of the same period gives a combined Air Force and Army ballistic missile appropriation of $9,341 billion for the period. (No service breakdown of missile expenditures by program is available.) The increments in the Air Force and Army budgets during these fiscal years totaled $38,349 billion, which means that the Air Force and Army programs absorbed only 25 percent of the increments in their combined service budgets. Even if the Air Force programs are assigned $7 billion and the Army $2 billion plus of the $9,341 billion appropriation (a not very arbitrary assignment since the ballistic missile programs were concentrated in the Air Force) both services could use substantial amounts of their increments for fiscal years 1956 to 1961 ($23 billion and $3 billion, respectively) for other activities. Only the Navy lost its entire budget increment during the first years of the ballistic missile era.

The establishment of the Program Planning and Budgeting System by Secretary McNamara and the rise in defense expenditures during the 1960's helped reduce the FBM's unique burden on its sponsoring service. Estimating that non-FBM ballistic missile program costs increased in proportion with those of FBM (this may be an overly high estimate since only the Minuteman missile among the Air Force and Army programs was extensively deployed), it becomes evident that the missile programs in the Air Force and Army absorbed about 15 percent of their services' combined increment for fiscal

TABLE 7. Budget increments and the impact of ballistic missile programs, Navy, Air Force, and Army, fiscal years 1956 through 1967 (in millions of dollars).

Fiscal year	Navy (increment over base)[a]	FBM[b]	Air Force (increment over base)[c]	Non-Navy ICBM/IRBM[d]	Army (increment over base)[e]
1956	−573	18	3,380	508	−410
1957	−1	89	5,560	1,312	−92
1958	285	511	5,595	1,639	−33
1959	1,599	1,032	6,576	1,914	1,617
1960	1,049	1,011	6,359	2,292	1,925
1961	2,210	1,748	5,474	1,676	2,125
1961 and prior	4,569	4,409	33,217	9,341	5,132
1962	4,536	1,979	7,376	N/A	4,377
1963	5,065	1,779	8,043	N/A	3,867
1964	4,678	1,303	7,309	N/A	4,799
1965	4,624	575	7,082	N/A	4,239
1966	8,265	464	10,518	N/A	9,728
1967	10,489	666	12,086	N/A	15,175
1962 through 1967	37,657	6,766	52,414	14,009	42,135
1967 and prior	42,226	11,175	85,631	23,350	47,267
Total Appropriations, 1956–1967	$164,878	$11,175	$231,274	$23,350	$135,460

Sources: See sources for Table 4 and U.S. Congress, Senate, Committee on Armed Services Preparedness Investigating Subcommittee, *Hearings, Missiles, Space and Other Major Defense Matters*, 86th Cong., 2nd Sess. (Washington: Government Printing Office, 1960), p. 509. Program data includes development and investment costs, but excludes military pay and operational costs.

[a] 1955 base, $10,221 million.
[b] Includes approximately $400 million for non-Polaris activities, i.e., Poseidon, and other programs.
[c] 1955 base, $12,137 million.
[d] Includes both Army and Air Force ballistic missile programs.
[e] 1955 base, $7,764 million.

years 1962 to 1967 ($14 billion of a $94.5 billion increment).
The FBM Program during the same period accounted for about
18 percent of the Navy's budget increment ($6.8 billion of a
$37.7 billion increase). It should be remembered that the costs
of the Vietnamese war are included in the budget increments
for this period.

Still, taking the entire time span of Polaris development, it
is clear that the Navy paid heavily for the program. One
quarter of the funds the Navy received over the 1955 base
budget during these twelve years were earmarked for FBM.
The Navy (and the Marine Corps) had only $31 billion for
expansion, pay increases, and inflation after the FBM allocations were subtracted from the increment. Even if all of the
remaining ballistic missile costs were taken from just the Air
Force's budget, which they were not, the Air Force would have
had double that amount or $62 billion for the same type of
expenditures. It is no wonder that many naval officers somewhat resent the FBM Program.

If FBM was such a financial burden, how can its apparent
lack of impact on the Navy's shipbuilding and missile procur-
ment allocations be explained? (See Figure 7 and Table 6.)
Is it not contradictory that FBM could have no effect on shipbuilding and missile procurement, the appropriation categories
where most of its own costs fall, and still be considered a
burden on the Navy? There is a rather simple explanation.
The Navy's budget requests are formulated through an internal political process that is constrained by external conditions.
During the Eisenhower administration in particular, the task
of allocating budget decreases and increases fell upon the
services after the overall defense budget was established.
Recognizing that the FBM Program would limit total naval
expenditures, senior naval officers had to choose among contending demands. Their budget strategy was apparently to
continue to procure new naval weapons (ships and missiles)
while deferring maintenance expenditures and other new
developments. Table 8 traces Navy allocations for operations
and maintenance, research and development, and certain
Marine Corps appropriations during the FBM development.
The Navy did not pay across the board for the FBM; it paid
in the maintenance of its fleets and in the development of new
equipment.

TABLE 8. Selected New Obligational Authority, Department of the Navy, fiscal years 1954 through 1967 (in millions of dollars).

Fiscal year	Operations & Maintenance Navy	Research, Development, Test, & Evaluation[a]	Procurement Marine Corps	Operations & Maintenance Marine Corps
1954	3,411	N/A	151	185
1955	2,702	378	129	154
1956[b]	2,419	379	290	181
1957	2,415	369	164	171
1958	2,537	296	0	173
1959	2,574	242	25	172
1960	2,610	384	133	175
1961	2,597	621	91	176
1962	2,896	625	264	187
1963	2,825	849	256	188
1964	2,908	985	201	191
1965	3,252	1,010	164	195
1966	3,913	1,156	685	326
1967	4,662	1,175	515	431

Source: Office of the Comptroller, Department of the Navy.
[a] RDT&E minus research and development for guided missiles.
[b] Fleet Ballistic Missile Program begins.

Some opportunity costs of the FBM are, however, unmeasurable. Observer after observer has argued that the Special Projects Office and the FBM Program stripped the Navy of its best technical talent.[18] For most of its life, the Special Projects Office has had the power to order into the program any officer it felt was needed. For most of its life, the Special Projects Office has had the incentives in the form of job classifications, overtime opportunities, and prestige to attract to the program almost any civil servant it wanted. Other technical commands were put at a disadvantage. Their most capable engineering and managerial personnel would be hired away by the FBM Program, and yet they were expected not only to meet their own schedules but to service the FBM program as well. As one retired officer put it, "The Special Projects Office would decimate a section in the Bureau of Ships and then would complain when that section was slow or inept in a response to a work request."[19] The Navy's technical talent was concentrated in the Special Projects Office, but its technical problems were not. Just how serious was the imbalance is impossible to determine. The Navy gained fame for the Polaris success and ridicule for the failure of the 3Ts (Terrier, Talos, and Tartar —ship-based missiles) during the same period. Whether or not a different distribution of personnel would have saved the 3Ts and projects like it while building the same Polaris is an unanswerable question. Many naval officers, however, are convinced they have the answer, and they oppose granting special personnel powers to any particular project.

To those who paid the price but did not make the choice, who sacrificed the organizational opportunities but did not join the program, the benefits of the FBM decision are questionable. Of course, the Navy now has some excellent navigation equipment, better shipyard test procedures, and improved training techniques,[20] and its submarines have gained more effective and more reliable hardware. Obviously these benefits could have been achieved for less than $10 billion.

There is even less point in calculating the value of the commercial and industrial gains from the FBM Program since they

18. Ints V-38, 39, 40, 41.
19. Int V-42.
20. Ints V-43, 44, 45A, B.

are at present so meager. A new blood viscosimeter was said to have been developed in the program. A manufacturer advertises his cool smoking pipe as a by-product of Polaris nose cone research. Some wire wraps used initially on FBM boats have come to be widely applied.[21] The hope is that the FBM navigational aids can be made available to commercial users. And there are, of course, PERT and the other management innovations.

The program's benefits must necessarily be found in the deployed FBM submarines and the national and organizational security they provide. In a nuclear world, national security for the major powers has come to rest on a doctrine of mutual assured retaliation. The viability of this doctrine in turn rests largely on the invulnerability of the retaliatory force. There is at present apparently no cheaper or certain way to maintain an invulnerable retaliatory force than with the FBM fleet.

For the Navy, the FBM provides, as some of its senior officers recognized, the opportunity to play an important defense role in an era when strategic missile forces have become dominant. Because of nuclear-armed missiles, the value of traditional naval units is increasingly questioned. Major reductions in force levels have occurred in several navies. The future of the aircraft carrier is again in debate. And yet nations are still striving to build submarine missile fleets similar to the U.S. Navy's FBM system. In a real sense, the FBM has become the Navy's invulnerable deterrent to strategic and technological obsolescence.

For the nation, however, the immediately apparent benefits of Polaris may hide what may ultimately prove the greatest of all costs. It is possible that the deployment of forty-one FBM submarines has generated such a sense of security in the nation that a number of potential military threats are being complacently ignored. Or, conversely, it is possible that the deployment of such a large fleet of FBM submarines has provoked the Soviet Union into taking defensive steps that could lead to a mutually fatal miscalculation. The final price of Polaris has not yet been and may never be recorded.

21. Int V-46.

ON MAKING AND MEETING ESTIMATES

The absence of significant time and cost overruns in the FBM system development effort was seen by many as reason to believe that the program held lessons for the management of technological innovation. Not only did the first FBM submarine deploy at least three years ahead of the original schedule, but the costs for the FBM system did not appear to multiply during its development and procurement. Exactly how close the actual system costs came to the estimates is not clear. An Assistant Secretary of Defense who helped set R&D and procurement policies during the McNamara era has said that the entire FBM Program came within 2 percent of meeting its cost estimate.[22] A program document, in illustrating the efficacy of the Special Projects Office's management techniques, has claimed that the actual costs for the first nine FBM submarines exceeded estimates by only 4 percent.[23] No official Department of Defense or Special Projects Office statement exists on the presence or size of the FBM Program overrun. In fact such a statement would be extremely difficult to prepare since program changes have been so numerous as almost to prevent an accurate comparison of early estimates with incurred costs.[24] Nevertheless, it is widely believed that the pro-

22. Int V-9.
23. Special Projects Office, Case Study on the Fleet Ballistic Missile Program for the Secretary of the Navy Review on Navy Management Effectiveness (U), rev. ed. (July, 1962) (Confidential), p. 104. The difference between the overrun percentages, of course, can be simply attributed to differences in data bases. The Assistant Secretary's statement presumably considered the whole program whereas that of the Special Projects Office document only referred to a nine-boat buy minus the missiles.
24. A Special Projects Office attempt to compare a 1959 estimate for the development and deployment of a full force of FBM submarines with costs incurred through 1962 and a 1962 estimate projected an overrun of 11.2 percent. The 1959 estimate of $7,077,600,000 first had to be increased by 51 percent to $10,741,900,000 since it had been based on a 45 boat program with no support vessels and only a single version of the missile; by 1962, the approved program called for a 41 boat force, several support vessels, a new missile version, and a variety of other changes. Internal Memorandum, SP 1324/DLS: 23 March 1962, subj: Comparison of Estimates Presented in WSEG Cost Study of March 1959 with Actual Costs and With Current Methods of Estimation (Confidential). It should be noted that this comparison was prepared for the report listed in the preceding footnote, but was not included. A Special Projects Office document entitled "Current Program

gram's actual costs were almost precisely on target.[25]

Meeting targets, or even coming close to them, in the acquisition of complex weapons is considered a major accomplishment. The period in which the Polaris system was developed and the years that followed have been marked by a great concern over the inability of weapon development projects to keep within their original time and cost estimates. Evidence supporting such a concern seems overwhelming. Peck and Scherer, for example, found that, in an analysis of twelve large-scale weapon projects, the average costs exceeded estimates by a factor of 3.2 and development times exceeded estimates by a factor of 1.36.[26] A RAND study of twenty-two major weapons categorized programs by their degree of technological advance. For the ten systems with the greatest advance in technology, presumably comparable to the FBM system, the actual unit production costs exceeded original estimates on the average by a factor of 4.2. Ten projects in the RAND study not categorized by the degree of technological advance exceeded time development estimates on the average by a factor of 1.5.[27] When Secretary McNamara took office, 40 per-

Control Totals" issued in May 1968 lists the total of Polaris program funds made available to the Special Projects Office through fiscal year 1967 as $10,778,182,000. This figure includes approximately $693,920,-000 which was returned to the Navy as unneeded allocations. Comparing the revised Polaris program total of $1,084,262,000 with the figure prepared in 1962 (adjusted 1959 estimate), one gets a program underrun of $657,638,000 or 6.1 percent.

25. Int V-10. Only one voice of dissent can be discovered. United Research in a study of management systems states without supporting evidence that the Polaris development exceeded original estimates by a factor of four. *The Extension of Special Organization Patterns and Management Techniques to Additional Weapons Systems*, a report prepared for the Assistant Secretary of Defense (I&L) under Contract SP-92 (Cambridge, Mass.: United Research, Inc., January 1962), pp. I-11 and I-12.

26. Merton J. Peck and Frederic M. Scherer, *The Weapons Acquisition Process: An Economic Analysis* (Boston: Harvard Graduate School of Business Administration, 1962), Table 16.1, p. 429.

27. Andrew W. Marshall and W. H. Meckling, "Predictability of the Costs, Times, and Success of Development," in Universities-National Bureau Committee for Economic Research, *The Rate and Direction of Inventive Activity* (Princeton, N.J.: Princeton University Press, 1962), pp. 461–475. See also Carl Kaysen, "Improving the Efficiency of Research and Development," in *Public Policy*, Vol. XII (Cambridge, Mass.: Harvard University Press, 1963), pp. 257–260, and Herman O. Stekler, *The Structure and Performance of the Aerospace Industry* (Berkeley, Calif.: University of California Press, 1965), pp. 171–196.

cent of development funds in Department of Defense were said to be going to pay for overruns on existing contracts.[28] A number of administrative reforms were introduced in the early and mid-1960's to correct this situation, but without much apparent success. Major aircraft projects, such as the TFX and the C5A, initiated under these reforms have been plagued with significant time and cost slippages. Even today, there exists no confidence in defense development and procurement targets; public antagonists of antiballistic missile systems, for example, commonly assume without rigorous official contradiction that the actual costs will be two or three times the estimate for a given deployment configuration.[29]

The reasons for the unjustified optimism in estimates are easy to appreciate. New weapon developments involve technological uncertainty. Overcoming obstacles in the development effort can cause considerable delays and, depending upon the program's size and priority, significant increases in cost. Contractors, anxious for the program's adoption and enthusiastic about its military advantages, naturally tend to underestimate the importance of potential obstacles. Military and civil service program monitors not only are likely to suffer from the same biases as the contractors, but they are also often poorly trained for their jobs and thus are prone to accept unquestioningly the judgments of the contractors. Finally, since the government must assume a significant share if not all of the entrepreneurial risk involved in bringing forth new weapons, the usual managerial discipline in the operation of the program is largely or entirely absent.[30]

But it is a mistake to believe that the Polaris program's

28. Statement by Charles Hitch, Comptroller, Department of Defense, in U.S. Congress, House, Subcommittee of the Committee on Government Operations, *Hearings, Systems Development and Management*, 87th Cong., 2nd Sess. (Washington: Government Printing Office, 1962), Pt. 2, p. 543.

29. "Eisenhower Gives Antimissile View," *New York Times* (January 16, 1968), p. 13; John W. Finney, "Pentagon Concedes Sentinel Would Cost More Than Estimate," *New York Times* (February 12, 1969), p. 1; "Symington Tallies $400 Billion Cost for Missile Shield," *New York Times* (March 5, 1969), p. 14.

30. Peck and Scherer, *The Weapons Acquisition Process: An Economic Analysis*, p. 443; Kaysen, "Improving the Efficiency of Research and Development," pp. 260–262; Frederic M. Scherer, *The Weapons Acquisition Process: Economic Incentives* (Boston: Harvard Graduate School of Business Administration, 1964), pp. 26–29. Ints V-10A, B.

success in meeting or perhaps even bettering its cost and time estimates provides a potential formula for reform. The Polaris program appears to have been subject to many of the same problems that beset programs with substantial overruns. Its ability to meet self-generated estimates, however, stems from its own unique advantage—overwhelming and dependable political support. The Special Projects Office and the Polaris contractors provided honest accurate estimates because they could afford to provide honest accurate estimates. After some initial uncertainty there was no doubt that Polaris would receive sufficient resources for any reasonably sized program that was conceived. With each acceleration came increased allocations to overcome the technical obstacles that the acceleration raised. Confidence in having estimates accepted permits candor in the generation of the estimates. Congress and the President wanted Polaris, and they were willing to pay for it.[31]

The initial uncertainty involved in gaining approval for the Polaris program proves the case, for it is the only point in the program's history where an important cost estimate that was optimistically biased as well as inaccurate can be detected. The Special Projects Office's 1956 request for a shift from a Jupiter-based to a Polaris-based FBM Program contained a cost estimate of a half-billion dollar saving for which there was no basis other than a recognition of the Eisenhower administration's desire to reduce defense spending.[32] The launching of Sputnik less than a year later eliminated the possibility of an embarrassing final accounting. The administration's rush to counter a storm of criticism by accelerating the development of the Polaris eradicated its memory of the estimate, and ensuing program changes made the estimate inappropriate for cost comparisons.

After Sputnik, program participants cannot recall a time when funding for the overall Polaris effort was seriously in doubt. Nor can they recall a time before the late 1960's when full employment for the Special Projects Office and it contractors did not appear certain.[33] This long period of general affluence was not without occasional moments of scarcity.

31. Int V-11.
32. Ints V-12A, B. See also James Barr and William E. Howard, *Polaris!* (New York: Harcourt, Brace and World, Inc., 1960), p. 72.
33. Ints V-13, 14, 15, 16, 17.

Passing economy drives would cause the procurement of some lead-time or support items to be delayed. An unexpected technical crisis would force internal reprogramming of funds to be undertaken. But inevitably money for all important activities was found, even if the lost time could not always be recovered.[34] Program officials learned quickly to request generous contingency appropriations. In the end, a surplus of nearly $700 million was available for allocation to other naval projects.[35]

The Special Projects Office now prides itself on the accuracy of its estimates. Admiral Smith, it is said, has always viewed a proposal which carries his endorsement as a personal contract that becomes binding on approval.[36] Thus he insists that full dollar costs be listed in order that the fulfillment of the contract obligations can be made if approval is granted. Salesmanship in the form of enticingly low estimates would result in petitioning later for supplemental funds, in failing to meet time goals, or in reducing quality standards. Admiral Smith was not required to sign the glowingly optimistic estimate that helped sell the program initially, and he has since trained the Special Projects Office team to offer only realistic estimates.[37] The FBM Program, however, must still face a long period of restricted funding for new developments, the supreme test of discipline in estimating.

MANAGING THE BILLIONS

When the allure of PERT began first to fade and then to sour, management experts apparently resolved to find some other explanation for the unusual success of the Special Projects Office and its ability to meet or surpass Polaris development targets. The simple explanation that the Special Projects Office succeeded because its proponents possessed admirable quantities of political and technological skill and were the beneficiaries of good fortune attracted no interest since such an explanation does not lend itself easily to either prescription or proscription, alternative intentions for management experts. Rather, the secret was thought to lie in some unique

34. Ints V-18, 19A, B, and 20.
35. Ints V-21, 22, 23, 24.
36. Ints V-14, V-25.
37. Int V-26.

structural or administrative feature of the Special Projects Office that heretofore had been overlooked.

In the 1960's, the attention of the management experts, both those who sought to duplicate the Special Projects Office's powers and those who sought to emasculate them, focused on financial management techniques, particularly the use of the Navy Management Fund (NMF) in the administration of Polaris allocations. The NMF was an accounting device that allowed the Special Projects Office to control Polaris funds in spite of the fact that these funds were allocated under a variety of appropriation headings. In early 1962, a study of the organizational and managerial methods employed in major missile projects concluded: "The Navy Management Fund as used on the Polaris program is perhaps the most effective single management technique used in the national urgency programs."[38] The next five or six years were spent debating whether or not the use of the NMF should be extended for the Polaris Program and to other weapon projects. It is indicative of the declining political power of the FBM proponents if not the efficacy of the NMF itself that at the end of the debate the Special Projects Office was completely denied the use of the fund in the Poseidon program and had to terminate its use of the fund in the Polaris program by the end of fiscal year 1968. Despite its high praise and its supposed role in the Polaris development, the NMF gained no further application in defense management.

Actually the NMF was more a symbol of the Special Projects Office's success than the source of its success. Never crucial to the development of the Polaris, the NMF's initial use in the Polaris program can be viewed as a victory for the Special Project's Office; its long use, as a sign of the power and independence of the office; its recent detachment, as the first defeat suffered by the office in a bureaucratic fight.

In 1955 and 1956 senior naval officers were disturbed by the financial problems the newly established FBM Program was causing in the Navy. Although the Secretary of Defense had promised that appropriations for ballistic missiles would not be taken from the regular service budget, Navy accounts were being "taxed" to initiate the Jupiter project. In order to

38. United Research, Inc., *The Extension of Special Organization Patterns*, pp. 111–117.

avoid a permanent drain on the Navy budget, several of these officers proposed that a separate appropriation independent of Navy accounts be established for the FBM Program.

The Special Projects Office itself was not pleased with the funding arrangements for the FBM, but for a different reason. The Office had been established to manage the entire FBM Program within the Navy. Its staff had sought to be independent of the Navy's functional bureau system and to prevent the fragmentation of administrative and technical direction that they thought had plagued the development of other weapon systems. The Special Projects Office administrative planners, in particular Gordon Pehrson, wanted to create an output-oriented program budget that would relate resources to development objectives in a coherent package not encumbered with the artificial boundaries of appropriation categories.[39] The funding arrangements established for FBM, however, whether or not they required the reprogramming of funds within the Navy, were tied to the traditional set of functional appropriation categories, each of which was the legal accounting responsibility of a different Navy bureau. The Special Projects Office, then, had to become involved in bureaucratic haggling with the functional bureaus over accounting definitions, bookkeeping procedures, and financial authorizations.[40] An organization conceiving of its mission as the independent development of an entire weapon system would necessarily find this haggling not to its liking. In the view of the Special Projects Office, the initial funding arrangements were "not adequately responsive to program needs" because they were not under the direct control of the Special Projects Office.[41]

Despite their dissatisfaction with the funding arrangements, FBM proponents were cautious about changing them. They knew, of course, that the necessity of reprogramming within the Navy budget had earned the animosity of many naval officers who otherwise would have been strong proponents of a naval strategic missile. With the goal being the severance of the tie to the Army and the development of a solid-fueled missile, a base of internal Navy support had to be cultivated

39. Ints V-48A, B, C.
40. Int V-49. Special Projects Office, *Polaris and the Navy Management Fund* (Washington: Department of the Navy, June 15, 1963), pp. 10–14.
41. *Ibid.*, p. 14.

rather than destroyed. But they also knew there was no certainty that new funding arrangements would provide the level of financing needed to carry out the difficult development task and that an FBM attachment to regular Navy appropriation categories provided, through possible reprogramming, a convenient if parasitic method of tapping a large source of funds. In addition, they were concerned that an FBM appropriation separate from the Navy would facilitate a possible Air Force move at some point to absorb the Navy's strategic missile.[42]

Thus, the Secretary of the Navy rejected the suggestion by the Chief of the Bureau of Ordnance that the Navy request either the establishment of a separate appropriation for the program or a separate budget activity for the program within each regular Navy appropriation.[43] The Chief of Naval Operations immediately protested the Secretary's decision, arguing that the FBM should have a separate appropriation in order to relieve other Navy programs of the budgetary pressures of the ballistic missile effort.[44] In his letter to the Secretary, Admiral Burke cited as a justification for a separate FBM appropriation the Department of Defense's failure to fulfill the promise of special funding for the FBM which would be outside the regular Navy budget. The Secretary apparently remained unmoved by the Admiral's protest, but did eventually endorse a Special Projects Office proposal that all FBM funds be consolidated in a separate subheading of the appropriation category Shipbuilding and Conversion, Navy (SCN). This proposal, if adopted, would have given the Special Projects Office the expenditure and accounting flexibility it desired without eliminating the FBM tie to the Navy and the Navy's budget.[45] With the FBM acceleration in late 1957, both the

42. *Ibid.*, pp. 15–19. Int V-37. Such a consolidation with the Air Force for the operational aspects of the FBM Program was proposed by the 1970 Fitzhugh panel on defense organization and management. *Report to the President and the Secretary of Defense on the Department of Defense* (Fitzhugh Committee) (Washington: Government Printing Office, 1970).

43. SecNav Secret Memorandum to Chief, BuOrd, 12 June 1956, subj: Jupiter Program, funding of (Secret).

44. Chief of Naval Operations Secret Memorandum to SecNav, 12 June 1956, subj: Jupiter Program, funding of (Secret).

45. Special Projects Office, *Polaris and the Navy Management Fund*, p. 17.

SCN and special appropriation concepts were taken up with Defense Department officials.

The Assistant Secretary of Defense (Comptroller) Rear Admiral Wilfred McNeil, USN (ret.), although sympathetic to the Navy's financial problems, was still the official guardian of the budgetary regulations. He felt he could not agree to asking the Congress to establish a special appropriation for the FBM without being deluged with similar special requests from all parts of the Department of Defense.[46] McNeil rejected the Special Projects Office's SCN concept as being unworkable and superfluous. Instead, he recommended to the Secretary of Defense that the Special Projects Office be permitted to use an existing budgetary device, a management fund, to gain the accounting flexibility it desired.[47] The management fund, which had been established by the National Security Act Amendments of 1949, had been used up to this point primarily for programs involving interservice financing, such as the construction of U.S. military bases in Spain, and for continuing functions in the Navy such as matériel inspection, transportation, and incentive awards;[48] now, on the initiative of Secretary McNeil, it would be used to give the Special Projects Office control over FBM appropriations within the Navy. With the granting of Navy Management Fund Charter number 22 on January 1, 1958, the Navy's budget could still be used to support the FBM Program, but the Special Projects Office was free from bureaucratic fighting over accounting procedures.

There are important misconceptions about the operations of the NMF in the Polaris program. The NMF did not permit the Special Projects Office to carry over to the next year funds that, for other agencies, would expire at the end of a fiscal year. The NMF did not permit the Special Projects Office to use funds appropriated for one purpose, say ship construction, for another purpose, say missile procurement. Although the contractors were allowed a minor convenience in that they had only to cite a single account, the NMF itself, rather than all applicable appropriation titles in their contracts, the Special

46. Ints V-50, 51.
47. Int V-52, and Special Projects Office, *Polaris and the Navy Management Fund*, p. 19.
48. Special Projects Office, *Polaris and the Navy Management Fund*, p. 9; also Int V-53.

Projects Office still had to maintain an auditable accounting for each contract by standard appropriation title. Despite the Special Projects Office's desire to comingle appropriations, the NMF permitted no such fiscal magic.[49]

The NMF even had some disadvantages. Since it was outside regular Navy operations, the Polaris NMF was often overlooked in the issuance of accounting instructions, which later required complicated adjustments. Under terms of the charter, the NMF could not anticipate and collect reimbursements from other government agencies for contract work, and thus the Special Projects Office had to avoid some types of cooperative arrangements that are commonplace in the government. Also, it seemed as if the Department of Defense required two special forms for every standard one which the Navy could not impose on the NMF.[50]

But the NMF was a useful symbol of the Special Projects Office's power and independence. By the time the fund was established it was clear that the FBM Program had enough political support within and without the Navy to make the Special Projects Office the easy victor in any petty bureaucratic fight in which it became involved. The NMF simply saved every accountant in the Navy the trouble of discovering this for himself. With the NMF there was no need for time consuming conferences, voluminous correspondence, and bothersome telephone calls to assert the Special Projects Office's control over FBM funds. The Director of the Special Projects Office was in charge of the FBM appropriations, and his interpretation of the accounting regulations would stick. The NMF formalized this power.[51]

49. Special Projects Office, *Polaris and the Navy Management Fund,* p. 26; also Ints V-54, 55. For a confirmation of the Special Projects Office desire, see the testimony of Admiral Raborn, U.S. Congress, Senate, Preparedness Investigating Subcommittee of the Committee on Armed Services, *Hearings, Inquiry into Satellite and Missile Programs,* 85th Cong., 1st Sess. (Washington: Government Printing Office, 1958), p. 777.

50. Special Projects Office, *Polaris and the Navy Management Fund,* pp. 31–33.

51. The Navy Management Fund made the Director of the Special Projects Office the manager of all FBM appropriations except Military Construction-Navy, Military Personnel-Navy, and Military Personnel-Marine Corps. Through fiscal year 1964 these appropriation categories amounted to about $473 million of the total program costs of over $10 billion.

Money flowed into the program after Sputnik. The Special Projects Office practice of never making a financial request without first presenting a briefing on the purposes of the Polaris system, the strategy of differentiation, made their requests irresistible in an era of national military concern.[52] The FBM budget began to receive special treatment from both Congress and the President. The Armed Service Appropriations Subcommittees of both houses accepted the Special Projects Office offer for a classified Polaris presentation separate from the regular Navy budget presentations. Throughout the history of Polaris effort, Congress never cut a program financial request, at times appropriating more than was asked. With this type of congressional interest in the FBM, budget examiners in the Navy, the Department of Defense, and the Bureau of the Budget found it wiser to focus on other weapon systems. None of them was eager to take the responsibility for questioning a Polaris request.[53] As an officer who served in the Special Projects Office put it, "the Polaris was never nickeled and dimed."[54]

Admiral Raborn, of course, made a point of publicly proclaiming the frugality of the program. Flaunting affluence does not win the admiration of the poor. Moderation was also the strategy. Quietly, however, he told his branch chiefs that, "they would not get medals for saving money."[55] The Special Projects Office's operational goal was getting the FBM to sea on time, rather than discovering the lowest price for the FBM system. The Polaris contractors were also perceptive enough not to be deceived by the official statement that FBM accounting was "being watched like no other Navy bureau accounting has ever been watched."[56] They and the participating Navy organizations satisfied many a long-denied need from the FBM coffers.[57] The Polaris program moved ahead without the usual financial restraints that burden government undertakings.

This is not to say that the Special Projects Office financial procedures were criminally lax. They can be more accurately

52. Int V-56A.
53. Int V-56B.
54. Int V-57.
55. Int V-58.
56. Welcoming statement of Admiral Raborn, Minutes of the Steering Task Group, 5th Meeting, 27 March 1958, p. 1.
57. Ints V-59A, B, and 60.

described as well focused. The management of money was not isolated from the management of technology, but rather was intimately related to it. The Special Projects Office budget staffs are properly praised not for their accumulation of book-keeping records, but rather for their contribution in speeding the achievement of FBM Program objectives.[58]

The General Accounting Office, like other government control agencies, learned to keep a respectful distance from the Special Projects Office during the height of its political prowess. The one critical report issued by the General Accounting Office on the Polaris, however, illustrates the gulf between program management and traditional government practice.[59] The report issued in 1965 examines the acceleration of shipbuilding schedules for five submarines in the period February 1960 through November 1960, and claims that program procedures resulted in unnecessary costs of $2.8 million. Specifically it argues that the Bureau of Ships, with the concurrence of the Special Projects Office, directed shipyards to meet ready-for-sea target dates for the submarines that were several weeks in advance of those being anticipated by other naval organizations responsible for the submarines' specialized equipment and training of the crews. The Special Projects Office countered by pointing out that the urgency of the FBM Program guided all actions. The submarine construction schedules were designed simply to force the shipyards to maintain the maximum possible effort despite slippages occurring in other aspects of the program. The objective was to have an FBM fleet, or at least parts of it, ready as soon as possible. "The General Accounting Office report [did] not recognize that advantages, over and above cost consideration, were achieved by the Bureau of Ships' establishment of earlier target dates," was the Special Projects Office's reply.[60]

With the deployment of its submarines, the program had a surplus of about $700 million, which was absorbed by other Navy projects through reallocations. These other projects were authorized by the Congress on the condition that the Navy

58. Ints V-61A, B.
59. Comptroller General, *Report to the Congress of the United States: Unnecessary Costs Incurred in Accelerating Construction of Polaris Submarines* (Washington: General Accounting Office, June 1965).
60. Department of Defense Statement for the Bureau of the Budget, in *ibid.*, p. 2.

obtain part of the necessary resources through reallocations (called recoupments in the government) from existing programs.[61] The FBM Program became a prime source for reallocations within the Navy in the mid-1960's. It was, one might say, the Navy's investment bank for new ventures during this period.

The bank existed because the program was funded for full cost plus contingencies. The contingency funds were substantial. For example, with the loss of the USS *Thresher,* a costly "Subsafe" plan was initiated to insure the safety of all other nuclear submarines. Despite unexpected costs, the Special Projects Office did not have to seek supplemental appropriations to apply Subsafe to the FBM fleet; it had only to turn to the contingency funds.[62] The surplus clearly resulted from a combination of good luck and good management. Technical obstacles were overcome with greater ease than expected, fewer of them developed than had been feared, and the program accelerations avoided the anticipated dollar penalties of inflation.[63] But the money for the surplus was there in the first place because of the great national concern for building an invulnerable deterrent. When the Navy came to collect the extra funds, Congress insisted that the Special Projects Office verify that there was no possible FBM need for the money.[64] Congress did not want the Navy to squeeze the FBM Program to meet the recoupment objectives, even though it had required in the first place that Navy programs be squeezed in order to limit new expenditures.

With maturity and success, however, the luster of the program began to fade. By the late 1960's the Special Projects Office could no longer act with its accustomed self-assurance. The symbols of its power, such as the NMF, became vulnerable when the source of its power, an overriding fear of a Soviet missile attack on the United States, lost saliency. The changing defense environment now required awkward adjustments in an organization and program that had previously caused others to make awkward adjustments.

61. NAVMAT INSTRUCTION 7130.2, MAT 123/YDM, 12 August 1965, subj: Recoupments, Reimbursements, Resources and Appropriation-wide Assessments; Naval Material Support Establishment policy on.
62. Ints V-62A, B.
63. Int V-63.
64. Int V-64.

7 | The FBM in a Changing Environment

The world did not remain static while the initial FBM force was being designed, developed, and deployed. Changes in the organization of the Department of Defense and in the course of national politics that occurred in the 1960's have significantly shaped the current FBM Program. In addition, the very success of the Polaris effort itself has had organizational and political consequences that must be understood if the past is to be appreciated and the future anticipated. This chapter, by examining changes in the defense environment and describing their impact on the FBM Program, serves as a bridge between the analysis of the Polaris development and a discussion of the program's lessons.

For expository convenience, the environmental changes are grouped into four categories—structural change, contractual change, program change, and political change—and discussed separately. The complexities involved in each require initially independent analyses even though there are obvious interactions among these changes and despite the fact that they occurred simultaneously rather than sequentially. A final section in the chapter, however, attempts to summarize the impact of the changes, describe their interrelationship, and evaluate their consequences for the Poseidon project.

DEFENSE REORGANIZATIONS

The compromises embodied in the National Security Act of 1947, upon which the Department of Defense was founded, did not clarify the role of the Secretary of Defense in either the acquisition of weapons or the command of operational forces,

192

the twin tasks of defense management. The frustrations of succeeding secretaries in controlling the policies of the three independent service departments combined with the budgetary pressures of a continuous war of technological progress led to the National Security Act amendments of 1949, 1953, and 1958 that shifted support and operational authority from the services and the Joint Chiefs of Staff to the Secretary of Defense. In eleven years, the Department of Defense changed structurally from a loose federation of independent departments, presided over by a weak executive, to a centralized organization officially subordinate in all of its activities to a single manager.[1]

When the FBM Program was established in 1955, however, the powers of the Secretary of Defense were neither fully formulated nor fully utilized. The Secretaries of Defense during the first fifty years of the FBM development preferred or felt constrained to remain the arbitrators of interservice rivalry, rather than the initiators of a coordinated defense program. Each of the services, then, despite a continual erosion of their official independence, continued to promote an independent set of interests. Programs like the FBM under the sponsorship of a service department necessarily had to marshal political resources that would first give them a favored voice within their own service and then a similarly favored voice within the Department of Defense. Thus, the FBM proponents acquiesced to the demands of the submariners, wooed the carrier admirals, and sought allies in the Congress and in industry in order to build their missile and its platform.

With the change of administration in 1961, the locus of initiative shifted dramatically. Robert McNamara, as Secretary

1. For discussions of the changing structure of the Department of Defense, see John C. Ries, *The Management of Defense: Organization and Control of the U.S. Armed Services* (Baltimore, Md.: The Johns Hopkins Press, 1964); Frederick Camp Mosher, "Old Concepts and New Problems," *Public Administration Review,* 18 (Summer 1958), pp. 169–175; Paul Y. Hammond, "Effects of Structure on Policy, *Public Administration Review,* 18 (Summer 1958), pp. 175–179; Charles J. Hitch, *Decision-Making for Defense* (Berkeley: University of California Press, 1964); A. C. Enthoven and H. S. Rowen, *An Analysis for Defense Organization* (RAND Corp. P-1640, March 17, 1959), Lawrence I. Radway, "Uniforms and Mufti: What Place in Policy?" *Public Administration Review,* 18 (Summer 1958), pp. 180–185; Eugene S. Duffield, "Organizing for Defense," *Harvard Business Review,* 31 (September–October 1953), pp. 29–42.

of Defense, was not content to observe passively the unfolding of defense policy in the organizational maneuverings of the agencies which were nominally responsible to him; he did not have to be. The independent role of the service departments in the management of defense had been severely limited in the previously enacted amendments to the National Security Act. Unified commands reporting directly to the Secretary of Defense had been given control of all operational forces, and the Department of Defense secretariat had been empowered to establish all military procurement policies. The service departments, still separately organized, were to provide matériel and training support for the operating forces, but only at the direction of the Office of the Secreatry of Defense. The much heralded "McNamara Revolution" was, then, in large part the mere exercise of authority already vested in the Secretary of Defense. Only discontinuity with past practice made the exercise of legal authority seem revolutionary.[2]

Table 9 describes aspects of the centralization that occurred in the Department of Defense under Secretary McNamara.[3] The civilian employment of the Office of the Secretary of Defense was essentially no larger in 1960 than it was in 1950, but by 1967 it had increased by one-third. In addition, about 70,000 civilian positions were consolidated during the 1960's at the Secretary of Defense level in newly established central support units such as the Defense Supply Agency and the Defense Intelligence Agency. The number of assistant secretaries and deputy assistant secretaries of defense who, in the name of the Secretary, set policies for execution by the service departments more than doubled from eighteen in 1960 to thirty-nine in 1967. Similarly, the allocations to units attached directly to the Office of the Secretary of Defense as a percentage of the total defense budget doubled in the same seven years. Clearly the burdens of defense management had been

2. Daniel Seligman, "McNamara's Management Revolution," *Fortune*, 72 (July 1965), p. 119; Hitch, *Decision-Making for Defense*, pp. 17–18. See also Harry H. Ransom, "Department of Defense: Unity or Confederation?" in Wesley W. Posvar *et. al., American Defense Policy* (Baltimore, Md.: The Johns Hopkins Press, 1965), pp. 167–182.

3. Qualitative aspects of Defense Department centralization are discussed in Paul Y. Hammond's, "A Functional Analysis of Defense Department Decision Making in the McNamara Administration," *American Political Science Review*, 62 (March 1968), pp. 57–69.

TABLE 9. Indicators of managerial centralization in the Department of Defense, 1949 through 1967.

Year	Posts with Title: Assistant Secretary of Defense	Posts with title: Deputy Assistant Secretary of Defense	Paid civilian employees of Office of the Secretary of Defense	Paid civilian Employees of Central Defense Agencies	Central level[a] budget as a percentage of total DOD budget
1949	0	0	1,530	—	—
1950	3	0	1,750	—	—
1951	4	0	2,166	—	—
1952	4	1	2,253	—	—
1953	9	3	1,986	—	—
1954	9	8	1,893	—	2.29%
1955	9	11	1,954	—	2.16
1956	9	12	1,899	—	2.00
1957	8	10	1,655	—	1.84
1958	8	9	1,646	—	2.11
1959	7	9	1,756	—	3.05
1960	7	11	1,865	—	2.89
1961	6	17	1,960	19,574	2.64
1962	7	20	1,883	27,797	3.00
1963	7	26	2,020	35,711	5.42
1964	6	27	2,085	39,981	6.14
1965	7	29	2,297	66,402	6.68
1966	7	31	2,521	76,344	6.20
1967	7	32	2,790	69,674	5.66

Source: U.S. Government Organizational Manual, 1968–69; Statistical Abstract of the United States, 1968; see also sources for Table 6.
[a] Office of Secretary of Defense and Central Defense Agencies.

195

taken up by the Secretary of Defense during McNamara's tenure.

Corresponding organizational adjustments were made all the way down the line. With no divisions of fleets under their command, the service chiefs had to become more involved in matériel support activities. With research and development policies being established by functionally specialized assistant secretaries of defense and their deputies, the service secretaries had to focus their attention on coordination and liaison tasks. Parallel reorganizations of research and procurement structures leading to greater functional specialization and centralization occurred in each of the services during the 1960's.[4] The Air Force's reorganization took place in 1961,[5] the Army's in 1962,[6] and the Navy's in two stages, 1963 and 1966.

Reorganization in this direction was particularly difficult in the Navy since decentralization was a departmental tradition.[7] For the first 17 years of its existence, the Department of the Navy was without formal structure as all units reported directly to the Secretary of the Navy. In 1815, a Board of Commissioners made up of three senior captains was formed to supervise collectively naval support activities, but control over

4. See quoted statements of Secretary of the Navy, Paul Nitze, in Jack Raymond's article, "Navy Revamping Its Management," *New York Times* (March 8, 1966), p. 1.

5. Claude Witze, "USAF's Missile Program: A Management Milestone," *Air Force and Space Digest,* 47 (May 1964), p. 173; Col. Donald H. Heaton (USAF), "Systems Management in the Air Force" (mimeo, Air Force Systems Command, n.d.), p. 2. See also the statement of Eugene M. Zuckert, Secretary of the Air Force, in U.S. Congress, House, Committee on Armed Services, *Hearings on Military Posture and H.R. 4016, to Authorize Appropriations during Fiscal Year 1966 for Procurement of Aircraft, Missiles, and Naval Vessels, and Research, Development, Test and Evaluation for the Armed Forces, and for other Purposes,* 89th Cong., 1st Sess. (Washington: Government Printing Office, 1965).

6. OSD Project 80 (Army), *Study of the Functions, Organization and Procedures of the Department of the Army* (Hoelscher Study), 7 vols. and 2 addenda (Washington: Department of the Army, October 1961). "The Case for Change," *Army,* 12 (February 1962), pp. 26ff; Lt. Gen. Frank S. Besson, Jr., "The Streamlined Concept for Timely Logistic Support," *Army Information Digest,* 17 (September 1962), pp. 2–12.

7. Elting E. Morison, "Naval Administration in the United States," *U.S. Naval Institute Proceedings,* 62 (October 1946), pp. 1303–1313. See also Vincent Davis, *The Admirals Lobby* (Chapel Hill: The University of North Carolina Press, 1967), pp. 10–47; and Ries, *The Management of Defense.*

line squadrons remained with the Secretary.[8] The Board of Commissioners was abolished in 1842 and five matériel bureaus headed by Admirals, with independent access to the Secretary, were established in its place.[9] For the next 120 years, the bureaus (with periodic deletions, alterations, and additions to reflect shifts in the Navy's technological interests) conducted their business independently of each other and independently of the operating forces. A comparative degree of formalization did not occur on the operating side of the Navy until 1915 when the post of the Chief of Naval Operations was established.[10] Even then the Chief of Naval Operations was denied full authority over the fleets by the Navy Secretariat until the Second World War. Attempts during the early 1940's to extend the control of the operational staffs over the bureaus, however, were successfully resisted by the secretariat and the bureaus.[11] Later, it became the official organizational doctrine that the Navy functioned best with a bilinear structure that separated operational command from matériel support activities. Internal organizational reviews conducted through the mid-1960's continued to confirm the validity of this doctrine and the decentralized organizational structure that it supposedly embodied.[12]

Given the ability of the bureaus to act independently of each other as well as of the operational staffs, the Navy De-

8. Robert Greenhalgh Albion and Robert Howe Connery with the collaboration of Jennie Barnes Pope, *Forrestal and the Navy* (New York: Columbia University Press, 1962), p. 42.

9. Thomas W. Ray, "The Bureaus Go on Forever . . . ," *U.S. Naval Institute Proceedings*, 94 (January 1968), pp. 50–63.

10. *Ibid.*, p. 49; Capt. R. P. Smyth (USN), "The Navy Department: The Fulcrum and the Balance," *U.S. Naval Institute Proceedings*, 93 (May 1967), p. 74.

11. Albion and Connery, *Forrestal and the Navy*, pp. 91–103; Ray, "The Bureaus Go on Forever," p. 58.

12. See, for example, *Report of the Committee on Organization of Navy* (Gates Report) (mimeo; Washington: Department of the Navy, April 16, 1954); *Report of the Committee on the Organization of the Department of the Navy* (Franke Report) NAVEXOS P-1996 (Washington: Department of the Navy, 1959), pp. 17–18; *Review of Management of the Department of the Navy* (Dillon Board) NAVEXOS P-2426A (Washington: Department of the Navy, December 15, 1962). Robert Howe Connery in *The Navy and the Industrial Mobilization in World War II* (Princeton, N.J.: Princeton University Press, 1951) provides a thorough discussion of the division of functions between operating forces and matériel support in the Navy.

partment's structure was actually multilinear rather than bi-linear in character. Inherent in this structure were competitive tensions similar to those observed in the confederation that was the Department of Defense prior to Secretary McNamara's term in office. Problems posed by weapon system developments such as that of the FBM, which involved the integration of several technologies, however, pushed the Navy to adopt mechanisms to coordinate the activities of the bureaus. The first effort at coordination was the pronouncement, in 1955, of the "lead bureau" concept whereby one bureau was to be designated as the dominant authority in a weapon project involving elements of several bureaus.[13] Next was the establishment, later in the same year, of the Special Projects Office, which was to manage the development of a single complex weapon system outside of, but utilizing, the resources of the bureaus. Then, on the recommendation of the Franke Committee in 1959, came the merger of the Bureaus of Ordnance and Aeronautics forming the Bureau of Naval Weapons which was to integrate organizationally the bureaus with the greatest interface problems.[14] All of these organizational arrangements, it should be noted, preserved the division between operations and matériel support activities, and, even if in a somewhat violated form, the independent bureau system itself.

The Navy reorganizations of the 1960's, however, were more fundamental in nature. The reorganization of 1963 eliminated the independence of the bureaus by establishing the post of Chief of Naval Material which was to stand organizationally between the matériel bureaus and the civilian secretariat and which was to direct ("supervise and command") all matériel activities in the Navy.[15] The reorganization of 1966 made the Chief of Naval Material the organizational subordinate of the Chief of Naval Operations and reformed the matériel bureaus as six systems commands (Air, Ship, Ordnance, Electronics,

13. Ray, "The Bureaus Go on Forever," p. 60.
14. Franke Report (NAVEXOS P-1996), pp. 99–106.
15. The Office of the Chief of Naval Material resulted from a 1962 recommendation of the Advisory Committee on *Review of Management of the Department of the Navy*, commonly known as the "Dillon Board." See Ray, "The Bureaus Go on Forever," pp. 61–62; "Single Executive Will Represent the Navy's 'Producer' Interest," *Navy Management Review*, 8 (July 1963), pp. 8–9.

Supply, and Facilities Engineering).[16] Thus, in three years, the Navy became first a truly bilinear organization and then a completely unitary organization. Under the current structure, operations and matériel support responsibility are combined at the top, and the bureaus, now systems commands, are third-level subunits.

Centralization within the Navy, like centralization in the Department of Defense, has led to increased functional specialization. Despite title changes, the specialized matériel bureaus still exist. With the rebirth of separate Air and Ordnance Systems Commands and the division of the old Bureau of Ships into the Electronics and Ship Systems Commands, there are now six instead of four. Their subordination to the Chief of Naval Material restricts the duplication in laboratories and programs that prevailed when the bureaus were independent organizations.[17] Parallel specialized staffs have developed in the Offices of the Chief of Naval Operations and the Chief of Naval Material to coordinate the technical tasks assigned to the systems commands.[18] The infatuation of the Department of Defense and the Navy with project management in the late 1950's and early 1960's has resulted in the establishment of a number of project managers at both the Chief of Naval Material and systems command levels, but these managers have not, with few exceptions, been given the resources and authority needed to act independently.[19] The FBM Program arrangements were not used as the model for the project management wave. Rather, project management was conceived, as it had been in the Air Force, as the staff coordination of development activities being performed by and

16. Rear Admiral Roy S. Benson, USN, "Changing Patterns in Navy Department Organization," *Navy Management Review*, 11 (June 1966), pp. 4ff; Robert W. Niblock, "Navy to Strengthen Central Authority," *Missile and Rockets*, 18 (March 14, 1966), p. 16; and Rear Admiral T. J. Rudden, USN, "How Reorganization Affects the Naval Material Command," *Navy Management Review*, 11 (May 1966), pp. 7ff.

17. Ints VI-1, 2, 3.

18. Int VI-4.

19. Ints VI-5, 6, 7, 8. See also DOD Directive 5010.14 of 4 May 1965, subj: System/Project Management; SECNAVINST 5000.21A of 8 September 1965, subj: Project Management in the Department of the Navy; NAVMAT INSTRUCTION 5000.5A of 7 December 1965, subj: Project Management in the Naval Matériel Support Establishment.

under the jurisdiction of functionally specialized line organizations.[20]

Despite the fact that they were designed in large measure to clarify responsibility in the procurement of new weapons, the structural changes in the Defense Department and the Navy have tended to cloud the responsibility for the FBM Program. In the initial years of the program, the lines of managerial responsibility were sharp and short. The Special Projects Office, as the development agent for the FBM Program, reported directly to the Secretary of the Navy (acting as the chairman of the Navy Ballistic Missile Committee) and through him to the Secretary of Defense (formally, by means of the Office of the Secretary of Defense Ballistic Missile Committee). With the centralization of defense policy making during the early 1960's, however, the Special Projects Office came to receive more and more of its direction in FBM matters immediately from the Office of the Secretary of Defense and particularly from the Director of Defense Research and Engineering (DDR&E). Because the FBM is a vital element in the U.S. strategic retaliatory force, the Defense Department Secretariat is appropriately concerned about any alterations or developments that would affect its utility. But in the 1963 reoragnization of the Navy, official jurisdiction over the Special Projects Office and the FBM Program was shifted from the Secretary of the Navy to the Chief of Naval Material. The next reorganization, of course, had the effect of moving the Special Projects Office another level lower in the Navy hierarchy, since it made the Chief of Naval Material a subordinate of the Chief of Naval Operations. Thus, as policy control over the FBM Program has moved up in the Department of Defense, the program itself has become exposed to the managerial actions of several new echelons in the Department of the Navy.

Units such as the Director of Strategic Offensive and Defensive Systems on the Chief of Naval Operations staff, the budget office in the Office of the Chief of Naval Material, and the newly reconstituted Naval Ordnance Systems Command have all attempted to assert their authority over aspects of the

20. See the special issue: "Project Management in the Navy," *Navy Management Review,* Vols. X (December 1965), and XI (January 1966). Ints VI-9, 10, 11, 12, 13.

FBM Program.[21] With the Special Projects Office located lower in the organization chart, the FBM Program now appears to be subject to normal heirarchical direction. It now seems possible to express the antagonism generated by the past aloofness and affluence of the Special Projects Office. Even the General Accounting Office has sensed the differences in organizational relationships and become more inquisitive in its reviews.[22]

The Special Projects Office has been, to be sure, a somewhat recalcitrant subordinate. Its leaders know that decision making in strategic systems rests with the Office of the Secretary of Defense. As one high-ranking officer in the Special Projects Office stated, "No service, the Navy included, has been assigned the strategic mission. What counts [with us] is what the Office of the Secretary of Defense will fund."[23] Its leaders also know that influence at the top can help tame the formal hierarchy. There are, for example, a number of persons in important positions who once were affiliated with the FBM Program. Dr. John S. Foster, the current Director of Defense Research and Engineering, served for a period on the FBM Steering Task Group when he was a project leader at Livermore. Admiral Thomas Moorer, recently Chief of Naval Operations and now Chairman of the Joint Chiefs of Staff, was the naval aide to the Assistant Secretary of the Navy (Air) during the 1956 fight for the Polaris, and, of course, Admiral I. J. Galantin, who served for several years as Chief of Naval Material, had previously succeeded Admiral Raborn in 1962 as the Director of the Special Projects Office.

Nevertheless, the Special Projects Office has had to accept the reality of its new position and, thus, the authority of functional specialists. No longer can it use the NMF to control FBM appropriations. No longer can it rely on an informal agreement with the Bureau of Ordnance to guarantee its independence in the preparation and monitoring of contracts. No longer can it use special powers to bypass the normal limitations and delays in hiring civil servants.[24]

When the Special Projects Office was transferred to the

21. Ints VI-14, 15, 16, 17, 18, 19, 20, 21A, and II-35.
22. Memorandum for the Record, SP 134/WCC:dm, 5741 (Washington, 22 June 1966) subj: Remarks of GAO Investigators Concerning Their Survey of SP 00 and SP 10; also Int VI-21B.
23. Ints VI-22, VI-23.
24. Ints VI-24, 24B, and 25.

jurisdiction of the Chief of Naval Material in 1963, a charter was issued under the signature of the Secretary of the Navy which was intended to protect the office's ability to control the FBM Program.[25] Prepared initially by the Special Projects Office itself, the charter began with a general statement which noted that the office was responsible for the entire program. The charter then legalistically went on to list in detail all the activities through which the Special Projects Office had been exercising this responsibility. As the program expanded, however, the Special Projects Office saw the need, or was asked, to become involved in new activities that had not been cited in the list and that other organizations thought were appropriately theirs. During the reorganization of 1966, the charter was acknowledged as being out of date, and the writing of another was started. For two years drafts of this document circulated for approval before one was signed.[26] Today, the FBM Program is caught in the maze of jurisdictional conflicts that the establishment of the Special Projects Office was originally meant to avoid.

That structural changes in the Department of Defense have limited the independence of the Special Projects Office may not in itself be something to lament. There are, after all, substantial costs associated with project independence. Strong project management offices drain resources away from the functional bureaucracy, that is, the agencies charged with maintaining existing weapons and capabilities in broad areas of technology. They inevitably suboptimize since their total effort is devoted to promoting the development of a single system without regard to the effect development of that system may have on total defense or national needs. Inevitably, too, they seek to perpetuate themselves, forcing technology down narrow lines of development and forming pressure groups for newer and still newer versions of the same systems.

The analysis of the FBM Program does clearly indicate that organizational independence was a crucial factor in the Polaris project. Unlike other development organizations, the Special

25. SECNAVINST 5430.64 (26 February 1964), subj: Fleet Ballistic Missile Project: Navy Department Organization and Responsibilities. for.
26. Int VI-26.

Projects Office had direct control over nearly all of the financial and technical resources needed to complete its development tasks; it did not have to wait for the concurrence of the overburdened functional bureaucracy to take advantage of technical opportunities or to solve technical problems. Thus, one could argue that all priority programs should have sufficient authority to stand autonomous.

To say this, however, is to provide very little guidance for policy since there is no formula which will uniquely identify those projects deserving priority attention and therefore independence. We do not yet know how to weigh the costs and benefits of special project arrangements other than through the political process. Priorities and project independence, as the Polaris FBM experience also illustrates well, must necessarily be won continuously with vigorous arguments and skillful bureaucratic maneuvering. If the FBM Program in general and the Poseidon development in particular are now hemmed in by jurisdictional conflicts, it may be because the arguments in their favor were not presented vigorously enough or the bureaucratic maneuvering was not executed skillfully enough. Only their proponents would then have cause for alarm.

But if, as seems to be the case, the structural changes in the Department of Defense have eliminated the opportunities for subunit initiative and innovation by centralizing decision making authority and restricting competition, there is cause for more general concern. The decentralization and competition that prevailed in the Department of Defense in the mid-1950's facilitated the rapid development of missile technologies, no small achievement given the national anguish which followed the launching of the Soviet Sputnik. Independence permitted the Bureau of Aeronautics to preserve the option of a sea-based ballistic missile at a time when there was skepticism about its value. Similarly, independence permitted the Navy to preserve the option of a solid-fueled ballistic missile at a time when there was skepticism about its feasibility. Competition within and between the services quickly revealed the weaknesses in the alternative missile concepts which were then being proposed. It also led to the rapid diffusion of the solid-fueled ballistic missile innovation when its feasibility was demonstrated in the FBM Program. In the process of gaining a solid-fueled ballistic missile, not insignificant investments in various cruise missiles and liquid-fueled ballistic missiles were necessarily abandoned. As the technological uncertainties were eliminated, so could the less effective alternatives be eliminated.

In retrospect, the costs involved in developments such as the ballistic missile may seem wasteful. Why bother, for example, with Regulus, Jupiter, Thor, Atlas, and Titan when Polaris and Minuteman provide the best systems? Looking back it is quite possible to select the "best missile proposals" (or, conversely, to point to obvious mistakes), but this can be done only because the range of alternatives and their limitations are known. At the time when initial allocations had to be made, nothing was certain. Centralizing decision making and eliminating competition (retrospectively, duplication) then would only have decreased the probability of obtaining the best system within any given time period.

Reducing the number of subunits that can generate technical alternatives can reduce the immediate costs of development by reducing the pressures for independent projects, but as it does nothing to reduce the uncertainties of development, it cannot improve the efficiency of the weapons acquisition process. Actually, such a reduction could increase the cumulative costs of development by forcing all allocation decisions to be made with less information than one might otherwise have. The money spent on the solid-fueled version of the Jupiter may seem wasteful now that we have the Polaris, but it should be remembered that the initial plans called for deploying a liquid-fueled Jupiter missile on submarines, likely a more wasteful venture.

The point is a general one which goes beyond the FBM development or even the procurement of weapons. The recent structural reforms in the Department of Defense are representative of a desire for order, quietude, and economy which is common in public administration. But this desire should not be allowed to prevent one from recognizing that the world is uncertain both technologically and politically. Based on the Polaris experience, a disciplined hierarchy seems capable of suppressing precisely the information needed to cope with such uncertainty.

THE QUEST FOR PROCUREMENT EFFICIENCY

Secretary McNamara used the reorganized structures to implement new procurement policies. In part, these policies were designed to shift weapon purchases toward items more in line with the administration's strategic doctrines, but they were also designed to increase the efficiency of the weapon procurement process itself which, in numerous programs, had demonstrated a persistent bias toward producing cost over-runs, delivery delays, and inadequate technical performance.

The quest for efficiency took two forms.[27] First, Secretary McNamara sought to improve the procedures for the evaluation of weapon development proposals in order to avoid premature commitments to projects that were technically vague though militarily attractive. Formalized as the Concept Formulation and Contract Definition phases of the development cycle, these new evaluation procedures require a rigorous and competitive analysis of the technical problems likely to be encountered in a weapon project and their cost implications before actual approval for development is given.[28] Second, Secretary McNamara sought to increase the use of incentive-type contracts which force a winning contractor to absorb at least partially the risk of his own failure to meet the development targets to which he had agreed. Incentive contracts attempt to introduce automatic market-like rewards and punishments into relationships previously governed by bureaucratic regulations and bargaining.[29]

The new procurement policies contrasted sharply with those

27. See Robert J. Art, *The TFX Decision: McNamara and the Military* (Boston: Little, Brown and Co., 1968), pp. 89–102.

28. The procedures are described in Department of Defense Directive 3200.9, subj: Initiation of Engineering and Operational Systems Development of July 1, 1965. A detailed analysis of the DOD contract system is contained in *Final Report: Study of POSEIDON C-3 Contract Definition* (U), Prepared for the Department of the Navy, Strategic Systems Project Office under Contract No. N00030-68-0242 (Boston: Harbridge House, December 23, 1968) (SRD).

29. For an elaboration on theoretical basis for incentive contracts and their effectiveness, see F. M. Scherer, *The Weapons Acquisition Process: Economic Incentives* (Boston: Harvard Graduate School of Business Administration, 1964) and F. M. Scherer, "The Theory of Contractual Incentives for Cost Reduction," *The Quarterly Journal of Economics*, 78 (May 1964), pp. 257–280.

used in the Polaris project. Most Polaris work began with a simple letter of intent that lacked both a specific work statement and a detailed estimate of costs.[30] The predominant contract form was cost-plus-fixed-fee. Incentive contracts and even fixed-price contracts were utilized for the later version of the Polaris, but only in the production phase after the prototypes had been procured and priced under cost-plus-fixed-fee arrangements. The Polaris concept itself was not clearly defined before development approval was granted. The Steering Task Group, composed largely of contractor representatives, met to outline the FBM weapon system boundaries after the Secretary of Defense had decided to allow the Navy to break its ties with the Army's Jupiter project. The rest of the FBM system definitions were filled in, not according to a formal plan, but opportunistically throughout the development period as needs arose and were recognized. The main FBM contractors, of course, were selected for the Polaris project by the Special Projects Office without formal competitions. Their incentive to perform was the opportunity to participate in a major program at a time when military procurement was shifting from aircraft to missiles, rather than the prospect of immediate profit.[31] Finally, the Special Projects Office had been directly involved in making numerous engineering trade-off decisions that affected the Polaris development, a practice that could not be allowed under incentive contracts since, in these arrangements, the contractor is held financially responsible for the projects' outcome and, thus, expects managerial independence.

Not surprisingly, there was resistance to applying the new procurement policies to the FBM Program. The veterans of the Polaris development, almost to a man, were convinced that the Polaris system could not have been built following the new DOD contracting rules.[32] Those officers and officials directing the successor developments certainly did not want to lose the

30. Int VI-27.
31. Int VI-28.
32. Ints VI-29A, B. For a published confirmation of the existence of this view, see Alain C. Enthoven, "Systems Analysis—Ground Rules for Constructive Debate," *Air Force and Space Digest*, 51 (January 1968), p. 37. One program participant claimed the new contract procedures were so complicated that they were in effect, "a form of disarmament" (Int VI-29C).

administrative flexibility that had become an integral part of the program. For a period arguments citing the indivisibility of the various models of Polaris equipments, the danger of altering the management arrangements on strategic weapons programs, and the experimental characteristics of the new rules protected the program from change. Thus, while the rest of the Department of Defense moved rapidly in the early 1960's to apply the new procurement policies, the Special Projects Office remained a bastion of the old policies.[33]

However, by the time the proposal for what became the Poseidon missile was seriously being considered in 1964, it was clear that the Department of Defense staffs were determined to have the procurement policies applied in all programs. Revised procurement instructions to that effect were just then being issued. "The only way to get it [Poseidon] approved," one Special Projects official recalls, "was to go through with it [and conform to the new policies]."[34]

Because the Poseidon was to be an important addition to the strategic offensive forces, the Special Projects Office was able to gain certain dispensations from the procurement rules.[35] The Special Projects Office, for example, was not required to open the entire Poseidon development to competition. Of all the subsystems, only the motor contract was awarded on the basis of competition; all the other contract components were sole-source awards. Thus, the Special Projects Office's dependency on the Polaris contracting team was

33. There was almost a race among the services to see which one could conform most quickly to the new procurement procedures. Each year the Department of Defense in its appropriation requests and posture statements to Congress would release statistics on the spread of incentive contracts and competitive procurements. It was claimed, for example, that in fiscal year 1965, 43.4 percent of contracts were awarded on the basis of competition as compared to only 32.9 percent in fiscal year 1961. The use of cost-plus-fixed-fee contracts dropped from 38 percent of total awards in fiscal year 1961 to 9.4 percent in fiscal year 1965. U.S. Congress, House, Subcommittee of the Commitee on Appropriations, *Hearings: Department of Defense Appropriations,* 89th Cong., 2nd Sess. (Washington: Government Printing Office, 1966), Pt. 1, pp. 193–196. The only information that was slow to be developed was that reporting on the effectiveness of the new policies in reducing inefficiencies and underestimates. Note Scherer, *The Weapons Acquisition Process: The Economic Incentives;* also Int VI-30.

34. Int VI-31.

35. The entire list of dispensations is reported in *Final Report: A Study of POSEIDON C-3 Contract Definition,* pp. II-47, II-48 (SRD).

not challenged despite the intent of procurement reforms to break such dependencies.[36] In addition, the actual development of the Poseidon was permitted to start before the writing of the final contracts had been completed. In some subsystems, as much as one-half of the design work was finished before the contracts were "definitized," a practice supposedly to be avoided under the new rules.[37] Finally, certain aspects of missile radiation hardening and guidance in the Poseidon developed, despite their importance to the success of the overall effort, were not to be included in the incentive arrangements as they were considered too risky to be developed under this type of contract.[38] The ties the Special Projects Office had established with the Office of the Director of Defense Research and Engineering (DDR&E) helped soften the transition between procurement systems.[39]

Nevertheless, the shift to the new procurement policies and, most particularly, the shift to incentive contracting marks a potential watershed in the management of the FBM Program. The development process necessarily involves trade-off decisions among time, cost, and performance variables. Under cost-plus-fixed-fee contracts, the government retains the right to specify any or all trade-off decisions during the actual development. Under cost-plus-incentive-fee contracts, even before the start of the development the government establishes certain targets denoting its preferences among the variables and indicates a structure of rewards (and penalties) for contractor achievements in relationship to those targets, but allows the contractor to determine independently any particular trade-off decision during the actual development. If the government wishes to alter its preferences in any significant way (that is, a way that would affect the contractor's rewards) while the contract is operating, then an amendment to the contract must be agreed to and the contractor appropriately

36. In the motor competition, the Aerojet-General Corporation lost to Hercules Powder Corporation. Aerojet, which had been a FBM contractor since 1956, had previously shared motor work with Hercules on the Polaris A-2 and A-3. Though Admiral Raborn joined Aerojet as a corporate executive on his retirement from the Navy, Aerojet became the first major contractor to leave the FBM Program.

37. Int VI-32.

38. Int VI-32A.

39. Int VI-33.

compensated. Clearly, an intent of the incentive contract is to heighten everyone's awareness of the dollar costs involved in changing targets and to inhibit the government from intervening frequently in the conduct of the development effort.

The technical branch engineers in the Special Projects Office, however, had been accustomed to intervening in the conduct of the development effort. They had prided themselves on their role as contract managers, choosing among technical alternatives, directing contractor staffs, and manipulating the development outcome.[40] Understandably, they were the most vehement among those involved in the FBM Program in opposing the adoption of incentive contracts for the Poseidon.

After being required to help prepare the Poseidon contracts, the branch engineers' opinions of incentives have remained entirely negative: "You can't specify enough in advance in a development project, especially one which requires system integration. Incentives put the interfaces in concrete";[41] "Incentives will cost more, involve more paperwork and give the contractors more profits."[42]

The prospect of having to refrain from direct participation in the technical management of the Poseidon program after the contracts were signed was not particularly appealing to them: "You couldn't get a GS-7 rating for the government engineer's job in a development with incentive contracts."[43] Given their past experience, it seems doubtful that they will be able to exercise the necessary restraint. "Oh, officially it's hands off but we are still in it. Money and time are involved. We are still going to have to be responsible for the end result."[44]

The FBM contractors' opposition to the new procurement system, if it ever was strong, must have waned considerably after they were certain there would be no general competition for the Poseidon definition and development awards. The contractors had long maintained that they did not need the close supervision of the technical branches in the development of

40. Int VI-34. See Chapter Three, above.
41. Int VI-35.
42. Int VI-36.
43. Int VI-36.
44. Int VI-37.

the FBM system.[45] As early as 1962, Lockheed argued that the management effectiveness of the program could be considerably improved if the Special Projects Office would only provide a clearly defined overall plan and allow its contractors to implement it.[46] From the contractors' viewpoint, the branch engineers' participation in the direction of the equipment design could easily seem to be interference.[47] The project managers at the FBM plants want the opportunity to manage their own projects.[48] Incentive contracts were intended to give them that opporunity.

To protect themselves as much from branch engineers inclined to regress back into their old behavior patterns as from major program changes, contracting firms have insisted on contracts that elaborately define their rights. One company officer confided: "We know [a Special Projects Office engineer] and how to handle him. We have a 600-page contract, so when he attempts to order technical changes he is going to pay. We're not nuts."[49]

As a result, communications between the Special Projects Office branches and the contractors that involve technical directions have become much more formal than they were in the past. Lawyers and contracting officers for both sides must now be consulted to determine whether or not an amendment to the contract is required.[50] There have, in fact, been a number of changes in some subsystem contracts, but it is too soon to assess their impact.[51] Of course, the more changes there are the more the contracts resemble cost-plus-fixed-fee arrangements rather than cost-plus-incentive-fee contracts.

The complexity of trade-off choices involved in an advanced weapon system such as the Poseidon could, it seems, easily produce situations where the interests of the government conflict with the interests of the contractor. A typical example of

45. Int VI-38A.
46. Lockheed Missile and Space Company, *Fleet Ballistic Missile Weapon System Program Management,* submitted in compliance with SPL Technical Direction 56-61 (Sunnyvale, Calif.: Lockheed, August 1, 1962), pp. 20-25.
47. Int VI-38B.
48. Int VI-39.
49. Int VI-38B.
50. Ints VI-40A, D.
51. Int VI-40B.

this conflict might be a design for a piece of equipment that facilitates long-term maintenance in the fleet versus a design for the same equipment that eases production problems at the cost of long-term maintenance but increases profits on the contract. With thousands of trade-offs to be made and with new information on operational experience being continually recorded, it is obviously difficult to specify all the desirable outcomes in advance.

The contractors are confident that they will be able to make the necessary Poseidon trade-off decisions in the "interest of the program as a whole," which they presume is the same as the government's interest. After all, the top executives of the firms point out they would be foolish "to make a fortune on the contract and kill the program."[52] The contracting firms' interest, then, may well be to maintain a good relationship with their customer and, thus, to maintain their long-term profits rather than to seek maximum advantage and profits in the short run.[53] But with incentive contracts there are objective measures of the performance of subordinate managers in the firm, the men who actually direct daily company operations. Their interests and needs are conceivably much more immediate than those of their company or its top executives. A good showing in maximizing short-term profits on the contract in their jurisdiction may seem to them to be the best strategy in gaining personal recognition as a manager. In any case, the potential for conflict is not eliminated merely by noting a long-term organizational interest in pleasing the government agency that has provided a major portion of the company's revenues.

The government's interests may even be more divided than those of the contractors.[54] In the Office of the Secretary of Defense, incentive contracts were viewed as a means of controlling the high costs of military weapon acquisitions.[55] With cost-plus-fixed-fee contracts, there was no automatic concern for dollar

52. Int VI-40C.
53. For an extensive and perceptive analysis of the defense contractor's corporate interests, see Scherer, *The Weapons Acquisition Process: Economic Incentives, passim.*
54. Scherer also analyzes internally conflicting motivations in weapon acquisitions. *Ibid., passim.*
55. Ints VI-41A, B, C, D.

costs, since the total cost of the project was not fixed and all project costs incurred by the contractor were reimbursable. The time lags and performance deficiencies produced by these contracts were also minor compared to the cost overruns they appeared to encourage. Incentive contracts, by making the total cost an explicit factor in determining the contractors' return on a project are supposed to correct a contracting imbalance and, thus, increase efficiency. The military services, however, are more concerned about time lags and performance deficiency in the procurement of weapons than about cost. To the military, a late or inoperable weapon is considerably less satisfactory than a costly weapon.[56]

. The Special Projects Office originally became involved in the complete regimen of incentive contracting to get the Poseidon project approved. Until 1964 the focus of attention in the FBM Program had been almost exclusively on surpassing schedules and meeting performance requirements. Having the responsibility of developing a deterrent system made the Special Projects Office acutely concerned about the availability dates and quality of the FBM system. Its leadership was naturally fearful that a shift to incentive contracting would result in a deterioration of the deterrent. Thus, application of incentive type contracts to the FBM Program was agreed to by the Director and his technical staff with some real if muted reluctance.

Their attitude toward incentive contracts, however, has appeared to mellow considerably with time.[57] Since the incentive contracts utilized in the Poseidon development are multiple incentive contracts, the weight assigned to the targets becomes crucial in determining the impact of the contracts on the FBM system. In the intensive effort that went into structuring the incentives, the Special Projects Office has consistently and openly placed the greatest weight on system performance targets with dilevery and cost targets usually following behind in that order.[58] With this guidance, the contractors are to be directed toward the interest of the Special Projects Office even if they seek to maximize profits in the short run. The in-

56. Int VI-41E.
57. Ints VI-42, 43, 43A.
58. Ints VI-44, 45, 46, 47, 48, 49, 50.

centive structuring, therefore, is seen mainly as a disciplined way to protect and communicate the established priorities of the FBM Program.[59] The only persistent doubt that remains is the fear that incentives will not produce the system performance desired; no similar concern exists for cost reduction.[60] Faced with the necessity of applying incentives, the Special Projects Office has sought to apply them to its own advantage.

It would seem, therefore, that the logic of incentive contracting is no match for the logic of bureaucracy. Incentive contracts are designed to increase the efficiency of the weapons acquisition process by increasing contractor rewards for meeting cost, time, and performance targets. However, because of the complexities of the issues involved, the task of establishing the targets and structuring the rewards must necessarily be left in the hands of the developing agencies and the contractors themselves. Not surprisingly, they prefer in their incentive contracts the same ranking among cost, time, and performance variables that prevailed in cost-plus contracts. Only the interests of the program participants are served in incentive contracts when the development team determines the contractual targets and rewards. As Scherer points out, we are probably even worse off because of the introduction of incentive contracts since the ranking among the variables that emphasizes performance over costs now is reinforced by the power of material incentives.[61]

Incentive contracts might not even have the advantage, in projects as large as the FBM, of forcing more accurate cost estimates. In smaller-scale projects it is possible to imagine that the contractors will be charged with any overruns attributable to their own miscalculations. But in multibillion-dollar undertakings, as the C-5A contract demonstrates, it is politically naïve to assume a contractor will be forced to absorb or will be able to absorb overruns of the size that can occur. In fact, incentive contracts are likely to have the undesirable effect of encouraging larger overruns on these contracts than would otherwise be the case since the more catastrophic the overrun the less likely it is that the contractor will be expected

59. Int VI-42.
60. Int VI-51.
61. Scherer, *The Weapons Acquisition Process*, chap. 11.

to absorb the costs. Therefore, the best strategy for a contractor approaching an overrun is to run the bill higher. All of this bodes ill for the Poseidon effort.

The Polaris experience reveals still another serious problem in incentive contracts. Unlike cost-plus contracts, the targets and their rankings in incentive contracts are supposedly fixed for the length of the contract and, thus, can reflect only the conditions that exist at the beginning of the development effort or that can be then anticipated. The assumption is that meeting fixed development and procurement targets will increase the efficiency of weapon projects. Yet, unpredictable changes in political conditions affecting major weapon acquisitions seem to require constant alterations in project targets and their rankings. In early 1956 the FBM was to have a range of 1,500 n.m. and was to be ready by 1965; a year and a half later the FBM was to have a range of 1,100 n.m. and was to be ready by 1960. In early 1960, the FBM Program called for six to nine submarines; a year and a half later, a construction plan was in effect for one submarine a month with a total of twenty-seven submarines authorized. Shortly thereafter the number of submarines authorized was raised to forty-one. It seems unrealistic to expect the development and procurement targets of major weapon systems such as the Poseidon will remain fixed. Therefore it seems wasteful to impose upon them an elaborate contracting system whose effectiveness depends upon the validity of fixed targets. Although conceived as a device to improve management performance in major projects, incentive contracts cannot possibly fulfill their promise, ignoring as they do the bureaucratic and political conditions affecting such projects.[62]

A CONTINUING PROGRAM

When it was established, the mission of the Special Projects Office was finite. Upon delivery of a submarine and a comple-

62. For excellent analyses of incentive contracts in operation, see Irving N. Fisher, *A Reappraisal of Incentive Contracting Experience* (RAND Corp. RM-5700-PR, July 1968); Frederick T. Moore, "Incentive Contracts," in Stephen Enke, editor, *Defense Management* (Englewood Cliffs, N.J.: Prentice-Hall, 1967); Oliver E. Williamson, "The Economics of Defense Contracting: Incentives and Performance," in Rowland McKean, editor, *Issues in Defense Economics* (New York: National Bureau of Economic Research, 1967).

ment of missiles to the fleet for testing and evaluation, the Special Projects Office was supposed to be disbanded, its mission fulfilled. Derivative functions such as the procurement of additional ballistic missile submarines and the support of the deployed FBM force were to be absorbed by the functional bureacracy. Plans for the transfer of responsibilities were to be prepared in conjunction with the construction of the first FBM submarine.[63]

With the actual authorization of additional submarines and improved versions of the Polaris, the early disestablishment of the Special Projects Office came to be seen as impractical. The same integration of technical skills needed for the completion of the first submarine and missile was obviously needed for the completion of later submarines and missiles. There was apparently no great dissatisfaction with the arrangements, the assumption being that the Special Projects Office necessarily had to be retained for new development work while the regular establishment could independently assume the tasks of operational support and maintenance.

In an important sense the Special Projects Office, of course, has been involved in operational support and maintenance matters from the beginning of the FBM Program. Given the high degree of reliability that is desired in a strategic deterrent, there can be little tolerance for system breakdowns. Thus, the very design of the FBM system (for example, the configuration of the submarines, the redundancy of the equipment, and the durability of the components) has determined in advance the basic support requirements of the deployed forces.[64]

Moreover, the continued existence of the Special Projects Office, based as it is on the development of new generations of FBM equipment, affects the scope of current support activities since the improved components are continuously added to the supply system. There is no standard FBM submarine nor, apparently, will there ever be one. Three classes of FBM submarines have been built. The state-of-the-art advances in many subsystems have been incorporated as they are achieved.

63. Int VI-52.
64. Admiral I. J. Gallantin, USN, "Support Lessons Learned from the POLARIS Program," a speech delivered before the Aerospace Industries Association, June 6, 1963.

Calculations of cost and strategic need as well as submarine availability have determined the extent of backfitting. Thus, according to current plans, the Poseidon will be deployed on only thirty-one of forty-one submarines, and the FBM supply system will be required to continue to support Polaris missiles and unique Polaris equipment for the foreseeable future.

After the completion of its original mission, the Special Projects Office actually gained a more direct role in operational support and maintenance activities. The office is now almost as involved in logistical activities as it is in new development work. Two factors appear to account for this expansion of mission: the failure of the established bureaucracy to carry out effectively the FBM support tasks it has been assigned, and the desire to maintain the integrity of the FBM system and its contracting team.

There are several examples of the influence of the first factor. The operational tests of the FBM system, for instance, were initially thought to be clearly the responsibility of the fleet as they had been with all other weapon systems. The Special Projects Office had warned the fleet that operational testing of the complex FBM system would require extensive instrumentation in order to determine the causes of system malfunctions, but the advice was not taken. The first FBM tests conducted by the fleet, however, turned out to be so chaotic that a special investigation was undertaken to determine what was needed to establish more effective operational test procedures. The Special Projects Office was prepared at the time to step forward with the appropriate test instrumentation equipment and staff assistance; soon it was a welcome participant in all operational tests of the FBM system.[65]

Similarly, periodic overhauls of FBM submarines were thought to be the responsibility of the regular Navy structure, the Bureau of Ships, the Type Commanders, and the Superintendents of Shipbuilding at the private yards or the commanding officers in the case of government yards. The enormity of the overhaul task on FBM submarines, crammed with complex systems, was apparently not generally appreciated by these organizations and individuals as little advance planning was initiated.[66] The result was that serious delays in

65. Int VI-53.
66. Ints VI-54A, B.

completing overhauls began to accumulate, threatening the maintenance of patrol schedules. A variety of ad hoc remedies having failed to alleviate the situation, the Special Projects Office gradually came to have a direct role in the management of the overhauls.[67] In the Poseidon conversions, it will have complete budgetary control over shipyard operations.[68]

The influence of the second factor in expanding the mission of the Special Projects Office is more subtle, but just as important as the first. Holding the responsibility to report on all aspects of the FBM system including operational and support aspects, the Special Projects Office has built up the staff resources to anticipate potential FBM system problems and to design action programs to overcome these problems.[69] Where it lacks jurisdiction, the Special Projects Office has sought to act as the coordinator for those organizations holding clear jurisdiction. The intent is at least to gain the initiative in defining problems and in presenting alternative solutions, if not to make all final decisions. From this perspective, the Special Projects Office's planning system (SPAN) can be seen as more than a useful device for projetcing future program needs; it becomes an effective method for controlling the behavior of the many independent naval organizations that participate in the operation of the FBM force.

The main threat to the integrity of the FBM system has been the growth of the functionally specialized support organizations, the product of defense reorganizations.[70] For example, in an effort to economize, responsibility for purchasing items common to the missile programs of the several armed services, such as certain types of transistors and conductors, has been consolidated in the Defense Supply Agency. In drawing from the central supply stores of the Department of Defense, however, it is often found that these standard components will not perform in the FBM equipment despite meeting Defense Department specifications.[71] Similarly, the Navy Supply Systems Command has gained responsibility for purchasing and stocking items used by FBM submarines such as

67. Ints VI-55, 56, 57.
68. Ints VI-58, 59A, B.
69. Int VI-57.
70. Int VI-60.
71. Ints VI-61, 62A, B, and 63.

the Ship Inertial Navigation System that are common to other naval units, but seems unable to meet FBM support needs. Though their normal inventory response rate of 75 percent may be satisfactory for routine naval demand, it proves inadequate for maintaining strategic targeting capability where a response rate of over 95 percent is said to be required.[72]

The Special Projects Office, therefore, has become increasingly involved in preparing the documentation necessary to prevent unique FBM components from being absorbed into the Defense Supply Agency, in devising stocking formulas for FBM-related items carried by the Naval Supply Systems Command, in organizing priority transportation networks for FBM logistics, and in establishing their contractors as FBM subsystem inventory managers.[73] Operational support and maintenance activities now form a large part of what the Special Projects Office considers to be its organizational mission.

Two consequences flow from this change in orientation. The first and most obvious consequence is that the Special Projects Office has become embroiled in numerous interorganizational disputes. An expanding interest in FBM logistics brings it into conflict with the regular logistics organizations. Each time it attempts to assert itself in FBM logistics matters, the Special Projects Office necessarily implies not only its own special competence, but also a lack of confidence in the ability of the regular organizations to do their assigned tasks.[74] Differences of opinion on system needs exist between the Special Projects Office and the regular naval units, of course, since the Special Projects Office perspective is that of a product-orineted organization whereas the established logistic network is functionally oriented.[75] But the affluence and single-minded determination with which the Special Projects Office approaches the logistics tasks seem to grate on everyone, including the operating forces in whose interest the Special Projects Office is supposedly working.[76]

The second consequence of the Special Projects Office's involvement in support activities is that it has been afflicted with

72. Ints VI-64, 65, 66, 67, 68.
73. Ints VI-69, 70, 71, 72, 73, 74, 75.
74. Int VI-76.
75. Int VI-77.
76. Int VI-78A, B, C, D.

the general boredom and loss of morale that is associated with such activities.[77] The team of skilled engineers and administrators assembled to develop a ballistic missile that can be launched from beneath the seas is hardly challenged by the problems of component repair and inventory stocking. Successively, the Apollo program, the deep submergence program, and even the poverty program have come along to attract the interest of these people, and a number of resignations have resulted. Those who remain with the FBM Program seem, at times, to question, if only tacitly, the urgency of meeting the exact overhaul completion date for the thirty-eighth submarine or the exact training cycle initiation date for the Blue crew of the eighteenth submarine.

Even the Steering Task Group, as it meets bimonthly year after year, is beginning to reflect the torpidity of advancing age and diminishing challenges. Its members recall somewhat affectionately the early STG meetings when crucial program boundaries were being established and quick decisions were needed. Today, when discussion at the meetings often turns to logistics problems, the excitement of participation seems lost.[78]

To the outside observer, then, it seems that it is the new development, the Poseidon project, that keeps the Special Projects Office functioning and its contracting team intact.[79] Without responsibility for the Poseidon, the Special Projects office would be hard pressed to maintain its independence in the face of conflicting organizational claims over the jurisdiction for Polaris operational support. Without responsibility for the Poseidon, the Special Projects Office would find it difficult to maintain the interest of the type of person (both in terms of skills and organizational level) that has distinguished the organization within the government.

But the shift to the Poseidon has important consequences of its own. The Poseidon is not simply an extrapolation of the Polaris technology, a bigger and better missile system. The Poseidon will, if the development objectives are achieved, possess strategic capabilities in terms of targeting options that are different from those of the Polaris.

77. Ints VI-79, 80, 81, 82, 83.
78. Ints VI-84, 85, 86, 87, 88.
79. Int VI-88A.

The strategic mission of the Polaris series of FBMs, the initial "targets of naval opportunity" smokescreen notwithstanding, was simple, precise, and necessarily well advertised. The development of Polaris was to guarantee that the United States would have the capability to destroy so large a percentage of the urban population and industrial capacity of an aggressor nation that the self-destructive futility of a nuclear attack against the United States would be obvious to that nation. Unhesitatingly, thousands of naval personnel and civilians have devoted years of their lives to obtaining and maintaining this strategic capability for the United States and, unhesitatingly, the nation and its representatives have paid for the Polaris.

The strategic mission of the Poseidon, however, is neither simple, precise, well advertised, nor even widely accepted. The decision for a successor to the Polaris came at a time when neither the national threat nor the means to counter it were clear. Top defense officials in the early and mid-1960's were concerned about both an apparent buildup in Soviet strategic offensive missiles and the prospective deployment of a Soviet antiballistic missile system (ABM). In November 1963, the Special Projects Office was authorized to proceed with the definition of a Polaris follow-on (known initially as the B-3) that would enhance FBM penetration of defended urban-industrial targets. Just as work along these lines was beginning in the summer of 1964, the concept of multiple individually targeted warheads (MIRVs) launched from a single missile was proposed by an Air Force contractor. MIRVs, by their number and spacing, increase significantly the ABM penetration capability of incoming warheads. Combined with possible improvements in guidance systems, MIRVs offer the potential for attacking hard military targets (for example, missile launches) as well as soft city targets. Faced with continued strategic uncertainties, defense officials directed the Special Projects Office in November 1964, to include the MIRV concept and advanced guidance systems in its B-3 designs, giving the next generation FBM the potential for both a hard-target (described often as "time urgent") and soft-target capability. This change in strategic emphasis for the B-3 (designated by the President in January 1965 as the Poseidon) was said at the time to be an insurance measure, though precisely what the insurance would buy in strategic terms was not extensively discussed with or among Special Projects Office personnel.[80]

Although the President's Poseidon announcement did, in fact, mention increased target flexibility for the missile, and subsequent statements of the Secretary of Defense discussed a damage limiting role (necessarily a capacity to attack hard or time urgent targets) for the FBM force, apparently only a few persons involved in the FBM Program and even fewer in the general public were fully aware of the possible alteration of the original B-3 mission.[81] Since the delivery accuracy needed to attack hard targets is much more stringent than that needed to attack city targets, there had to be some consultation between strategic planners and developers of the B-3; it just was not possible to accept the Polaris follow-on system being considered in 1963–64 and expect it to perform satisfactorily in both countercity and counterforce roles. But as there was great uncertainty about the strategic need for a new FBM mission, the discussions were apparently limited to the technical issues and included only a handful of naval officers and contractor personnel.[82] Since the Defense Department had decided in its Poseidon action neither to relax certain technological constraints, such as the ABM penetration capability and the use of a new reentry vehicle common with the Minuteman (this requirement was later rescinded), which it had imposed on the Polaris follow-on development, nor to increase substantially the funds and move up the delivery date for the new FBM, the Technical Director of the Special Projects Office agreed to take on the task of providing increased accuracy for Poseidon only if the specific missile accuracy desired were treated as a development goal rather than a

80. *Final Report: Study of Poseidon C-3 Contract Definition* (SRD). Ints VI-89, 90.

81. President Johnson's Defense Message to the 89th Congress, *New York Times* (January 19, 1965), p. 16, and the Secretary of Defense's Posture Statement in U.S. Congress, Senate, Subcommittee of the Committee on Appropriations and the Committee on Armed Services, *Hearings, Department of Defense Appropriations for Fiscal Year 1967*, 89th Cong., 2nd Sess. (Washington: Government Printing Office, 1966), Pt. 1, pp. 1–252. Note also Ralph E. Lapp, *Arms Beyond Doubt* (New York: Cowles Book Co., 1970), esp. p. 21.

82. *Final Report, Study of Poseidon C-3 Contract Definition*, p. 33 (SRD).

development requirement.[83] Nevertheless, in late 1964 the Polaris follow-on, the Poseidon, had been given a second strategic mission without most of the FBM Program participants and certainly most of the public being aware of the change.

As a result of the quasi-secrecy with which the hard target counterforce capability was added to the B-3 proposal, the Poseidon development has brought two burdens into the FBM Program, one short-term and one long-term. The short term burden has been analyzed in a report on the Poseidon contract negotiations prepared for the Special Projects Office by Harbridge House, Incorporated.[84] It was discovered that most of the military officers and civilians representing the government in the negotiations and most of the contractor personnel had been generally unaware of or misinformed about the Poseidon's newly designated dual mission. Given the additional fact that there are distinct system trade-offs between a countercity and a counterforce weapon (such as warhead yield, range, force level), the probability that there was considerable wasted motion and inaccurate structuring of the incentives in these negotiations seemed quite high to the Harbridge House investigators.

In terms of its potential impact, the cost of the Poseidon's long-term burden could be even more difficult to bear. Without a knowledge or belief in what they are building men work without commitment. Without commitment to the organizational purpose men may not be able to marshall the political support needed to maintain the organization in the face of a serious challenge. And today's political environment is just likely to offer that sort of challenge to a major technological undertaking. In short, the Poseidon, and with it the Special Projects Office, is politically vulnerable.

THE NEW POLITICS OF DEFENSE

The current FBM Program is a potential victim of its own past success. Established to thwart what was perceived to be "a clear and present danger" to the national security, within a few years the program produced a weapon system whose con-

83. *Ibid.*, p. 35, and Int VI-89.
84. *Ibid.*

tinued invulnerability now makes it extremely difficult to arouse the nation to what some in government believe are similar current dangers to the national security. In the years since the FBM force first became operational, the Chinese Communists have gained nuclear weapons, our world alliances have tended to fragment, and the Soviet Union has begun to deploy a number of advanced missile systems that could make at least the land-based portions of our offensive forces obsolete; yet there is no visible national sentiment for new weapon projects. Action in national security matters is, of course, the complex result of a mixture of potential foreign threats, threat perceptions, technological opportunities, and domestic politics, both bureaucratic and partisan, but behind it all today lies the knowledge that a significant part of our strategic retaliatory force, the FBM submarines, is essentially invulnerable to a surprise attack. Thus, attempts to improve the existing FBM force can run into both indifference and opposition.

That the current political environment for weapon programs is quite different from that of only a decade ago is easily demonstrated. The Defense Department is beset today, just as it was a decade ago, by large cost and time overruns in military development projects, but the treatment of these overruns in the press and in Congress today is quite different than it was then. In the late 1950's and early 1960's, editorial writers and politicians were concerned that the overruns, which they attributed to a decentralized and inept military procurement establishment, would prevent the United States from obtaining the important weapon systems before the Soviets did; in the late 1960's and early 1970's, many of the same editorial writers and politicians are concerned that the overruns, which they attribute to a centralized and insatiable military-industrial complex, will prevent the United States from obtaining important domestic reforms.[85]

85. See, for example, the *New York Times* editorial entitled, "Escalation in Overkill" (April 9, 1969), p. 46; and James Reston, "The Decline of the Pentagon," *New York Times* (May 28, 1969), and news headlines, "Defense Budget and Policy Face Broad Senate Attack," *New York Times* (May 14, 1968), p. 1ff; "Growing Number in Congress Seek Arms Spending Cut," *New York Times* (May 18, 1969), p. 19, and "Forty-Five in Congress Seek Rein on Military," *New York Times* (June 2, 1969), p. 19. The list is easily extended.

Throughout this period the FBM Program has possessed the highest official priorities and substantial annual budgets, but it has, in fact, been gradually losing its claim on national resources. The public's concern for missile gaps faded after the 1960 election. Missile firings and submarine launchings were soon lost in the back pages of the newspapers. National goals were shifting and new priorities were being established. First came the Apollo program, then the domestic war on poverty, and finally the war in Vietnam to hold the attention of the nation and its political leadership. The FBM firings at the Eastern Test Range had to wait for those of the National Aeronautics and Space Administration.[86] The FBM paperwork in Washington must now wait for that of the Vietnam effort and domestic problems.[87] In 1968, for the first time in the history of the program, relevant congressional committees, citing the press of other business, refused the opportunity to be given a special classified briefing on the plans of the FBM Program. The days of automatic priority to missile programs are gone. Even within the Special Projects Office, a certain longing to be involved in the "new challenges of the time" can be detected.

The decision to move on to the Poseidon development was, as has already been noted but cannot be overstressed, an internal bureaucratic decision. There was no attempt to marshal public support for the advanced missile system. There was no attempt to explain the need for the investment in new FBM equipment even within the program, let alone within the nation. The political support for the Polaris has been so visible, particularly in the period after its greatest technological accomplishment, that a presumption of continued support developed among the leaders of the FBM Program. Moreover, the reorganization of the Department of Defense had produced a widespread but mistaken belief that national security decisions were no longer "political"; the calculations submitted to higher authority and framed in the proper cost-benefit style alone would prove the case, it was apparently assumed. Finally, the real changes in the FBM Program, basically limited as they were to the front end of the missile (for example, decoys, multiple warheads, and radiation hardening) are not the kind

86. Int VI-91.
87. Int VI-92.

easily discussed in the news media, comprehension as well as classification being the barrier.[88]

Thus, when the Poseidon conversion bill was presented to Congress, it met what was to some surprising opposition in the Senate. Unconvinced of the technical viability of the proposal and extremely skeptical of the systems analysis studies that lay behind it, the Senators on the Defense Appropriations Subcommittee refused to permit the conversion of more than two FBM submarines to the new missile in fiscal year 1970, thereby disrupting extensive scheduling plans that had been prepared for a thirty-one-boat program. Production repercussions of the conversion decision necessarily will be felt throughout the Poseidon effort in the coming years.

This Senate-initiated action was the first congressional cut consciously made in an FBM appropriation request (the preceding year there had been an accidental cut in an FBM-related measure). It came, however, not because there was a new hostility to the FBM concept, but rather for just the opposite reason. Throughout the subcommittee's discussion of the Poseidon conversion, strong concern was evident for the maintenance of the Polaris deterrent. No one was prepared to advocate risking the reliability of the existing FBM force by converting a large number of the submarines to an untried missile and warhead system. The congressional commitment to the Polaris was clearly too firm to break.[89]

There exists, however, no similar commitment to the Poseidon. In fact, others in the Senate of a quite different political stripe than their colleagues on the Defense Appropriations Subcommittee and many in the scientific community, arguing that any missile incorporating MIRVs is inherently destabilizing, have also had serious reservations about the desirability of moving ahead with the Poseidon deployment.[90] An accurate MIRV, they point out, could be used not only to limit the damage to one's own forces and cities after a nuclear attack has begun, but also to strike first to eliminate an enemy's capacity to attack. A nuclear-armed adversary confronting us in an international crisis, they claim, may, when MIRV-equipped

88. Ints VI-93, 94, 95.
89. Ints VI-96, 97, 98, 99, 100.
90. See the editorial, "Moratorium on MIRV," *New York Times* (June 12, 1969), p. 46.

missiles are deployed, fear that his own forces are in jeopardy and attack first in self-defense. Since the concern is necessarily with an adversary's perception under stress of our intentions and capabilities, and since MIRVs are hidden in warheads and thus not detectable through passive observation techniques, it matters not, in the view of these critics, that our national leaders have stated the United States neither wants nor will be able to obtain an actual first strike capability.[91] The arms control implications of the Poseidon are in question.

Although the members of the Senate Defense Appropriations Subcommittee might favor it, an attempt now to initiate a new FBM submarine construction program such as would be required in the Trident proposal would almost certainly fare worse than the Poseidon conversion request. For the first time in a generation, there is an informed and organized public opposition to increases in defense spending. And since this opposition is based, as the ABM debate reveals, in large part on an essentially unchallenged belief that existing nuclear delivery systems, particularly the Polaris force, are invulnerable enough and large enough to compensate for any threat to the Minuteman force, it seems unlikely that major new strategic offensive systems will gain easy approval.[92]

91. A statement of Secretary of Defense Melvin R. Laird denying U.S. interest in or intention of developing a first strike capability was reported in *The Washington Post* (November 11, 1970), p. A1. Fears that new weapons will decrease our security no matter what the interests or intentions involved are expressed in Herbert F. York, "ABM, MIRV, and the Arms Race," *Science*, 169 (17 July 1970), pp. 257–260, and his *Race to Oblivion* (New York: Simon and Schuster, 1970). See also U.S. Congress, Senate, Subcommittee on International Organization and Disarmament Affairs of the Committee on Foreign Relations, *Hearings, Strategic and Foreign Policy Implications of ABM Systems: Anti-Submarine Warfare, Multiple Independently Targeted Reentry Vehicles (MIRV)*, 91st Cong., 2nd Sess. (Washington: Government Printing Office, 1969), Pt. 3 (May 16 and July 16, 1969). For an analysis which argues that Poseidon deployed MIRVs would be a stabilizing influence, see the statement by John Craven, former Chief Scientist of the Strategic Systems Project Office, "An Invited Comment on Poseidon and the MIRV," distributed by the M.I.T. Faculty Advisory Group.

92. Note the argument in Abram Chayes and Jerome B. Wiesner, editors, *ABM: An Evaluation of the Decision to Deploy an Antiballistic Missile System* (New York: Harper and Row, 1969); Jeremy J. Stone, "The Case Against Missile Defenses," *Adelphi Papers*, No. 47 (London: Institute for Strategic Studies, April 1968); George W. Rathjens, "The Dynamics of the Arms Race," *Scientific American*, 220 (April 1969), pp. 15–25; George W. Rathjens, *The Future of the Strategic Arms Race:*

SCANNING A DECADE

In summary, the 1960's have brought two important changes to the FBM Program: bureaucratization and political vulnerability. In 1960 the program was at its height, having just completed, with the launch of a Polaris missile from the submerged USS *George Washington,* a most amazing technological feat. It had both organizational independence and political support. Yet, as the 1970's begin, the program chafes under what are, for it, unique administrative restrictions and finds that its very future is in doubt.

The Poseidon project, despite the fact that it is being conducted by nearly the same government-contractor team as built the Polaris and the fact that it involves basically an extension of the Polaris technologies, is clearly not going to be as successful as the Polaris development. The contrast between them will be sharp. Whereas the Polaris effort is remembered for meeting an accelerated schedule, returning a surplus and winning management accolades, there are already problems in the Poseidon development schedule, indications of large cost overruns, and hints of unfriendly congressional investigations.[93]

The Poseidon labors under special handicaps. Unlike the Polaris, it is being developed in an era of constrained defense budgets and, thus, it can neither benefit from forgiving supplemental appropriations nor expect to have its initial estimates forgotten. Unlike the Polaris, it is being developed without the promise of expanding procurements and the guarantee of succeeding versions that permit the correction of errors and absorb their costs. Unlike the Polaris, it is being developed by organizations now long tenured in weapon procurements that are as much concerned with the stability of their relations as they are with assuming the risks of innovation. And, unlike

Options for the 1970's (New York: Carnegie Endowment for International Peace, 1969). An important assessment of Polaris invulnerability by Rear Admiral Levering Smith is reported in "A Sub Invulnerable, Polaris Chief Says," *The Washington Post* (May 12, 1969), p. 1.

93. Orr Kelly, "The Navy's Blues: Poseidon's Rising Cost Stirs Senate Scrutiny," *Washington Evening Star* (December 27, 1969), p. A1; "Proxmire Sees A \$3.6 Billion Poseidon Overrun," *New York Times* (January 1, 1970), p. 12; " 'Production' Problems Cause Poseidon Installation Delay," *U.S. Naval Institute Proceedings* (April 1971), p. 107.

the Polaris, it is being developed when some inside and many outside the program are uncertain of its strategic need and fearful of its strategic impact.

Some limitations in freedom of action, of course, had to be expected with the maturity of the FBM Program. Deployment on the scale of the FBM force necessarily brings with it administrative formalization not appropriate for a development effort. Moreover, arguments supporting independence and priority were bound to lose their persuasiveness once a basic deterrent force was in place. The Air Force ballistic missile program had a similar organizational experience.[94]

But bureaucratization has been as much a result of reorganizations and policy changes in the Department of Defense and in the Navy as it has been of FBM Program maturity. When the FBM Program was in its initial stages of development, defense policy was being established decentrally. Competing groups both within the service departments and within the Department of Defense fought to gain national support for their favorite programs. FBM proponents in the mid-1950's simply were not given all the formal authority needed to build a ballistic missile for the Navy; rather, through a variety of political strategies, they seized the necessary authority from others. In a real sense they were poltical entrepreneurs as well as technological innovators. The times permitted, even required, the combination of roles.

The organizational changes that took place within the Department of Defense during the McNamara era did not completely eliminate the competitive instinct of the FBM Program. They did, however, severely limit the room for political maneuvering, thus forcing adjustments in the operations of the Special Projects Office. The Special Projects Office's concern in the 1960's was discovering the minimum degree of conformity to Department of Defense-imposed regulations that would permit the uninterrupted continuation of the FBM development program rather than maximizing the program's political support as it had been previously. The adjustments were not trivial; the Special Projects Office changed its finan-

94. *An Analysis of Management Effectiveness in the Ballistic Missile Program* (U), prepared by the Ballistic Systems Division of the Air Force Systems Command (Norton Air Force Base, California: 30 April 1962) (SRD, Group I) (Number BSL-68) and Ints VI-101, 102.

cial management procedures and its relationship with contractors. But neither were the adjustments particularly onerous. Since the FBM system was held in high regard within the Office of the Secretary of Defense, the FBM force was rapidly expanded, and system development was continued.

With the Poseidon decision, the Special Projects Office traded general public support for specific Department of Defense support. It was apparently assumed at the time that bureaucratic success—the maintenance of the organizational team—equaled program success. Attention naturally focused on the gap in development activities that would follow the completion of the Polaris A-3 effort rather than on the gap in the public's understanding of the agency's mission which was then developing. The Poseidon proposal, by satisfying Department of Defense trade-off analyses, brought the Special Projects Office and its contractors further development appropriations and a long-term task. It was sufficient for the acceptance of the proposal that high-level officials thought both that further guarantees of target penetration and flexibility were needed for U.S. strategic missiles and that Poseidon was the most cost effective means of obtaining such guarantees. Since the formal structure for defense decision making had changed, there appeared to be no need or any way to garner broader support.

Yet political tides have also changed. Even if by groups that are quite antagonistic to one another, the policy making process within the Department of Defense and the defense policies that are its product are now being challenged on a broad front. Dependent on the Department of Defense Secretariat for its political support, the FBM Program has become vulnerable. The broad political support used to initiate the Polaris development was not required to initiate the Poseidon development. Without this type of support, however, it may be impossible to complete successfully the Poseidon development. Certainly it will be harder to begin Trident.

8 | Success and Its Secrets

For the partisan, goal attainment is the only appropriate standard by which to measure the success of governmental programs and oroganizations. A partisan has a cause; he seeks the implementation of particular ends to the exclusion of others. Therefore, by definition, a partisan is concerned with the performance of governmental programs and organizations only in so far as they affect the implementation of goals he supports.

The FBM proponents had a set of well-defined goals. They sought to have the nation build a solid-fueled ballistic missile and a fleet of missile launching submarines. They sought also to have the FBM Program, once established, managed as a completely independent activity within the Department of the Navy. Given the experience that has been examined in the preceding chapters, there can be no question that the FBM proponents view the Polaris development and the Special Projects Office as outstandingly successful ventures.

The neutral observer, however, needs a more inclusive standard of success in order to evaluate objectively the performance of government. He must recognize that governmental programs invariably affect the interest of several partisan groups, each of which promotes a different set of goals. He must also recognize that governmental organizations are required to serve not only the goals of programs within their jurisdictions, but also the contextual goals of government, the goals of equity, due process, fiscal integrity, and the like which are the procedural norms of the society and which have their own partisans.[1]

1. Problems relating to the analysis of goals in governmental agencies are discussed in Robert L. Peabody and Francis E. Rourke, "Public

The very structure of the political system, allocating as it does power among several component institutions, guarantees that there will be different perspectives on every activity of government. Congress and the President, for example, are elected by different constituencies and, thus, represent different interests.[2] Congress, elected by small districts, is said to represent special interests. The President, elected by a national constituency, is said to be the champion of principle. No one can demonstrate, though many might assert, which set of interests should predominate in an assessment of governmental performance.

What is needed, then, is a standard that considers all goals or interests as equal. The appropriate standard would be one that defines success in terms of the satisfaction of those affected by governmental programs and organizations. This, of course, would be a difficult standard to employ since it would require that all affected groups and persons be surveyed to discover the degree of satisfaction that exists for each program or organization. Just the identification of affected groups alone would pose important methodological problems.

There is, however, an operationalizable surrogate. The option to complain is fundamental to the functioning of democratic government. Each participant in the American political system is assumed to be the best judge of his own interests and is expected to express his dissatisfactions with government. In national politics, at least, those who carry a pressing grievance against a governmental program or organization—who feel their own goals have been frustrated or ignored by government—can always find a forum for their anger in a

---

Bureaucracies," in James G. March, editor, *Handbook of Organizations* (Chicago: Rand McNally and Co., 1965), pp. 802–837. The most thorough summary of the literature on goal achievement in all types of organizations is James L. Price, *Organizational Effectiveness: An Inventory of Propositions* (Homewood, Ill.: Richard D. Irwin, 1968). See also Charles Perrow, "The Analysis of Goals in Complex Organizations." *American Sociological Review* (December 1961), pp. 854–866; and Herbert A. Simon, "On the Concept of Organizational Goals," *Administrative Science Quarterly* (June 1964), pp. 1–22. I found an unpublished paper by Lawrence B. Mohr, "The Concept of Organizational Goal" (Institute of Public Policy Studies, University of Michigan, August 1970) to be quite helpful.

2. Willmore Kendall, "The Two Majorities," *Midwest Journal of Political Science* (November 1960), pp. 317–345.

congressional hearing, a General Accounting Office report, or a newspaper column, even if they cannot affect the direction of public policy. Absence of criticism, therefore, can be taken as a mark of success, for it means that no one views the operation of a particular program or organization as inimical to his own interests or goals and that some may even perceive it as beneficial.[3]

By this standard, the FBM Program and the Special Projects Office have been very successful; they have been virtually without critics. One cannot, for example, find a single scathing congressional investigation, a really incriminating report from the General Accounting Office, or a truly hostile newspaper comment on the Polaris and its developing agency. To be sure, there are congressional committee hearings, General Accounting Office reports, and newspaper commentary on these subjects, but they are almost invariably favorable, or, at worst, restrained and apologetic for raising any objections. What one can find in abundance is praise—from Presidents, Secretaries of Defense, congressmen, defense strategists, management specialists, technologists, arms control experts, indus-

---

3. This standard of success complements what Alvin Gouldner has described as the natural-system model of organizational analysis. Instead of viewing organizations as mechanically converting inputs into predetermined outputs, the natural-system model suggests that organizations are adaptive social organisms seeking to survive in an uncertain and potentially hostile environment. By this approach a successful organization would clearly be one that meshes with its environment in such a way as to be able to avoid serious challenge. Alvin W. Gouldner, "Organization Analysis," in Robert K. Merton *et al.*, editors, *Sociology Today: Problems and Prospects* (New York: Basic Books, 1959), pp. 400–428. See also Amitai Etzioni, "Two Approaches to Organizational Analysis," *Administrative Science Quarterly* (September 1960), pp. 257–278, and James D. Thompson, *Organizations in Action: Social Science Bases of Administrative Theory* (New York: McGraw-Hill, 1967), pp. 3–13. Similarly, such a definition of success fits well with Albert Hirschman's analysis of the means by which firms, organizations, and states are renewed. As he reminds us, consumers in a competitive economy generally signal their dissatisfaction with a commodity or firm by exit, the switching of purchases to other commodities or firms. The citizen, he points out, has relatively limited exit possibilities and must rely instead upon voice, the articulation of his interest, in order to gain alterations in a political system's policies and organizations. The absence of criticism where opportunities for its expression exist is therefore an indication of the success of governmental programs and organizations. Albert O. Hirschman, *Exit, Voice and Loyalty: Responses to Decline in Firms, Organizations, and States* (Cambridge, Mass.: Harvard University Press, 1970).

trial contractors, and scientists. With near unanimity, the FBM is said to be one of the most outstanding and desirable achievements in weaponry since the Second World War, and the Special Projects Office is regarded as the model of development effectiveness.[4]

The degree of success that the FBM Program, especially its Polaris component, and the Special Projects Office achieved was greater than that achieved by the other ballistic missile development efforts and appears to be almost without parallel in government. Although the Air Force missile programs continue to receive significant appropriations, their management was sharply criticized in the Congress, first for allowing certain contractors to gain favored competitive positions and later for allowing those contractors to live lavishly.[5] Within the arms control community both the scale of the Air Force Minuteman deployments and their vulnerability have been challenged. The more modest Army missile program was generally thought to be strategically worthless and was eventually canceled.[6] Attempts by the Army to initiate an antiballistic

4. This is not to say that the strategic doctrines, particularly deterrence theory, upon which the military value of the FBM is based have not been continually subject to criticism. Note, especially, Philip Green, *Deadly Logic: The Theory of Nuclear Deterrence* (Columbus: Ohio State University, 1966). More recently, there has been a growing concern within the Navy that U.S. naval strength has deteriorated due to an overreliance on the FBM force and strategic weapons. The attacks against the FBM are always muted, however, for the real concern is with the overall national strategy and not with the weapon system itself.

5. U.S. Congress, House, Committee on Government Operations, *Report, Air Force Ballistic Missile Management,* 87th Cong., 1st Sess. (Washington: Government Printing Office, 1961); U.S. Congress, House, Committee on Armed Services, *Report, The Aerospace Corporation,* 85th Cong., 1st Sess. (Washington: Government Printing Office, 1965). See also U.S. Congress, House, Committee on Government Operations, *Report, Organization and Management of Missile Programs,* 86th Cong., 1st Sess. (Washington: Government Printing Office, 1959); Harold L. Nieburg, *In the Name of Science* (Chicago: Quadrangle, 1966); Roy Neal, *Ace in the Hole: The Story of the Minuteman Missile* (Garden City, N.Y.: Doubleday and Co., Inc., 1962); Ernest G. Schweibert, *A History of the U.S. Air Force Ballistic Missile* (New York: Praeger, 1964); and Robert L. Perry, "The Atlas, Thor, Titan, and Minuteman," in Eugene Emme, editor, *The History of Rocket Technology: Essays on Research, Development and Utility* (Detroit, Mich.: Wayne State University Press, 1964), pp. 142–161.

6. The fate of the Army's program is analyzed in Michael H. Armacost, *The Politics of Weapons Innovation: The Thor-Jupiter Controversy* (New York: Columbia University Press, 1969). See also Herbert York,

missile program were long resisted by the Department of Defense. When such an effort was finally begun, it drew crippling congressional and public criticism.

The Manhattan Project, conducted under wartime secrecy, was, of course, protected from criticism.[7] However, once its activities and management arrangements were revealed, both the Manhattan Project and its successor, the Atomic Energy Commission, were targets of outspoken opposition.[8] The National Aeronautics and Space Administration clearly achieved its Apollo moon landing objective, but not without being subject to constant attack from those who thought the funds and manpower it consumed should have been allocated for other purposes.[9] The Federal Bureau of Investigation, the perennial favorite of congressional appropriations committees, police chiefs, and the nation's movie producers, has acquired the animosity of certain ethnic groups, several attorneys general, and most intellectuals in the execution of its programs.[10] Even

---

Race to Oblivion: A Participant's View of the Arms Race (New York: Simon & Schuster, 1970), and Major General John B. Medaris, Countdown for Decision (New York: G. P. Putnam's Sons, 1960), p. 148.

7. Secrecy was no bar to criticism in the case of the Polaris. Competition among the services guaranteed that sufficient information upon which to base judgments was always available to the public. I have compared the official classified chronology maintained for the FBM Program with a chronology gleaned from public sources, especially the New York Times, and found that classified items relating to the program appeared regularly in the press either the day they happened or at most a day or two later.

8. See Richard G. Hewlett and Oscar E. Anderson, Jr., The New World, 1939/1946, History of The United States Atomic Energy Commission, Vol. I (University Park, Pa.: Pennsylvania State University Press, 1962); and Richard G. Hewlett and Francis Duncan, Atomic Shield, 1947/1952, of a History of The United States Atomic Energy Commission, Vol. II (University Park, Pa.: Pennsylvania State University Press, 1969); Alice K. Smith, A Peril and A Hope: The Scientists' Movement in America 1945–1947 (Chicago: University of Chicago Press, 1965).

9. Note, for example, Amitai Etizioni, The Moon-Doggle: Domestic and International Implications of the Space Race (Garden City, N.Y.: Doubleday and Co., 1964). A complete history of the Apollo decision is provided in John Logsdon, The Decision to Go to the Moon: Project Apollo and the National Interest (Cambridge, Mass.: M.I.T. Press, 1970).

10. See "'Mr. FBI' and his 'G-Men': Near Legends Since 1924," Congressional Quarterly Weekly Report (December 26, 1969), pp. 2697–2711; Tom Wicker, "What Have They Done Since They Shot Dillinger," New York Times Magazine (December 28, 1969), p. 4ff.

Smokey the Bear and the Forest Service have been challenged within their well-protected domain.[11]

Other programs and organizations established with less widespread support have found success completely elusive. The Office of Economic Opportunity, for example, began its operation in a hostile environment and managed to generate additional opposition with its effort to stimulate community participation.[12] Similarly, the supersonic transport project, controversial even within the aerospace industry, discovered that its lobbying effort stimulated only disastrously negative results at a time when aerospace activities were out of favor.[13]

The task for the partisan obviously is to have the implementation of his goals viewed as being in the interests of nearly everyone, or at least not against the interests of many. What factors favor such a situation is the question that remains to be examined.

A FAVORABLE ENVIRONMENT

An almost Marxian technological determinism tends to prevail in current popular interpretations of the relationship between technology and society, especially the relationship between technology and national security policies. The lure of technological opportunities and the economic pressures such opportunities generate are said to force the direction of policy. As Ralph Lapp puts it, there is a "technological imperative—when technology beckons, men are helpless."[14] And thus, the

11. Ashley L. Schiff, *Fire and Water: Scientific Heresy in the Forest Service* (Cambridge, Mass.: Harvard University Press, 1962); Charles A. Reich, *Bureaucracy and the Forests* (Santa Barbara: Center for Democratic Institutions, 1965); Joint Northern Region-Intermountain Station Task Force, *Management Practices in the Bitter-root National Forest* (Washington: U.S. Forest Service, 1970).

12. James L. Sundquist, *Politics and Policy* (Washington: The Brookings Institution, 1968), chap. 4; Daniel P. Moynihan, *Maximum Feasible Misunderstanding: Community Action in the War on Poverty* (New York: Free Press, 1969); Robert A. Levine, *The Poor: Lessons from the War on Poverty* (Cambridge, Mass.: M.I.T. Press, 1970).

13. Harry Lenhart, Jr., "Transportation Report: SST Foes Confident of Votes to Clip Program's Wings again before Spring," *National Journal* (January 9, 1971), pp. 43–58. The SST was terminated by congressional action in March 1971.

14. Ralph E. Lapp, *Arms beyond Doubt: The Tyranny of Weapons Technology* (New York: Cowles Book Co., 1970), p. 178.

ballistic missile is said to follow inevitably from the V-1, and the MIRV-equipped Poseidon from the Polaris.

The challenge to this view is the long list of canceled and curtailed weapon projects compiled during the past twenty-five years.[15] To be sure, some of the projects were casualties of rapid shifts to new technologies. The Regulus cruise missile, of course, fell victim to the Polaris ballistic missile. But more seem to have been caught in complex twists of economic and strategic policies that have left both technologists and contractors unfulfilled. There was, for example, still a gleam in the eyes of the project engineers when the nuclear-powered aircraft effort was canceled,[16] and, if it had not been for Vietnam, we might well have built the Fast Deployment Logistics ship and bought all the C5A's initially envisioned. Moreover, though it may be difficult to believe, not every technological opportunity has been pursued. As weapon contractors well know, many development proposals are technologically feasible but economically and politically infeasible.

An opposite interpretation of the relationship between technology and society is one that some economists, most notably Jacob Schmookler, have advanced. Schmookler, who long studied the pattern of patent behavior in the railroad industry, argued that technological progress is demand-pulled rather than supply-pushed.[17] Converted into public policy terms, this means that national needs as expressed in dollar allocations determine the direction of technology rather than technology determining the direction of dollar allocations. This view, though modified by Schmookler and other economists to consider the interaction of supply and demand forces, has in recent years apparently been held in a simplified form by the

15. A partial listing that includes 60 weapon projects canceled during the period 1953–1965 appears in United States Senate, Committee on Appropriations, Subcommittee on the Department of Defense, *Department of Defense Appropriations for Fiscal Year 1967*, 89th Cong., 2nd Sess. (Washington: Government Printing Office, 1969), Pt. 1, p. 476.

16. See W. Henry Lambright, *Shooting down the Nuclear Plane* (Birmingham: University of Alabama Press, 1967).

17. Jacob Schmookler, "Changes in Industry and in the State of Knowledge as Determinants of Industrial Invention," in *The Rate and Direction of Inventive Activity: Economic and Social Factors* (Princeton, N.J.: Princeton University Press, 1962), and *Invention and Economic Growth* (Cambridge, Mass.: Harvard University Press, 1966). I am indebted to Frederick Scherer for reminding me of this argument.

advocates of pollution control, ocean exploration, and urban development who envision a technological renaissance as the result of any national political commitment to pursue their goals.

Complicating a need or demand determining view of the relationship between technology and society is the fact that the society and particularly its government, the prime source of funds for technological advancement, seldom makes clear-cut choices among available policy alternatives. The national agenda is always crowded with contending needs or demands that are ordered differently by advocates of different policy positions. Whether the issue is technological or not, the basic political question is: What should be done? This question is usually met with indecision.

The consequences of indecision are clearly revealed in the weapons acquisition process. The choice among weapon projects is the choice among defense strategies. Conflicting views on defense strategies abound, their number and intensity no doubt influenced by differing perceptions of technological opportunities, but also by differing value orientations, organizational loyalties, and, perhaps most importantly, perceptions of enemy threats. Projects to develop new weapons are initiated or adopted by the supporters of a particular strategy, but these projects often fail to gain full development, production, or deployment approval because there is no general agreement on strategy. Most weapon projects languish in uncertainty, with no guarantee that funds will actually be appropriated or procurements will actually be made. An evaluation of the costs of overcoming inevitable technical obstacles to weapon development or the costs of buying the production tooling has to be made in terms of the contribution to a national strategy. Without an agreement on strategy, however, it is impossible to agree on the evaluation. Is it worth two billion dollars to develop and deploy a new Main Battle Tank? The answer depends, at least initially, on the perceived desirability of maintaining a significant conventional warfare capability. The usual answer to such a question appears to be: We are not sure; some (in this case, the Army) think it is desirable, but others (in this case, the Office of the Secretary of Defense) do not.

Where there is strategic disagreement or indecision the

usual result is a conscious or unconscious compromise to keep options open. The project gets just enough resources to drag along, but not enough to make much headway. The project management team gets just enough authority to request the assistance of others, but not enough authority to command their attention. With the ebb and flow of the strategic debate, the project's opportunities shift. The greatest uncertainty in the project becomes the political uncertainty over its own future. To both observer and participant the research and development effort looks inefficient; there are likely to be cost overruns because of underbidding, schedule delays because of irregular funding, and inadequate technical performance because of a failure to gain a concentrated effort.

There is within the FBM Program an excellent illustration of the fruits of strategic indecision. For years the submarine communications area has been a problem for the program. It is not that communications cannot be maintained with the FBM submarines; several basic systems have been in operation since the first patrol. Rather it is that cumulatively expensive long-range projects designed to improve FBM communication systems have yielded few tangible benefits.

Effective communication was recognized early in the Polaris Program, if not in the joint Army-Navy Jupiter program, as an important element in the weapon system. The Task One final report of the Steering Task Group, which presented recommendations in the spring of 1957 on the Polaris system design, described command and control communications as a potential "Achilles heel of the entire Polaris operation."[18] A two part R&D program was soon begun. The first part, development oriented, was to provide reliable (not subject to jamming) and secure (not likely to reveal the location of the submarine or the contents of the message) communications equipment for the submarines, and the second, initially research oriented, was to seek exotic solutions to weaknesses revealed in the basic systems.[19] Jurisdiction for FBM communications was shared by the Special Projects Office (which

18. Polaris-Submarine Special Task Group, Task I—*Final Report, Recommendations for Polaris-Submarine Envelope*, SP #2912, 1957 (SRD). Note also SP 20 Secret Memorandum to SP 00, 29 November 1956 (Secret).
19. Int VII-1.

supplied the funds) with the Bureau of Ships and the Director of Naval Communications. Although this troika-like management arrangement caused innumerable difficulties, the Special Projects Office never sought to assert its primacy in this area, apparently deciding that the inevitable battle would jeopardize more vital relations with the Bureau of Ships and the naval policy staff.[20] Nevertheless, the development part of the program was completed successfully, and a satisfactory set of FBM communications equipment and facilities were ready for the deployment of the first FBM submarines.[21]

The long-range research program involved work on many problems, but concentrated on improving the FBM communications systems' response time (decreasing the elapsed time between the issuance of an order to fire and its receipt by all deployed submarines) and survivability (assuring that a surprise enemy attack against the communications facilities themselves would not destroy the command link). The effort, though relatively modest in any particular year, absorbed substantial resources over time. It produced a number of seemingly workable concepts, but as a review panel (whose report was aptly titled "Where did the $100 million go?") noted in 1964, and it is apparently still true today after the investment of even more dollars, there has been little development payoff in the long-range program.[22]

The fault lay not in the organizational arrangements nor in the intensity of the effort. It lay rather in a persistent conflict over strategy. The concepts advanced by the program,

20. Ints VII-1, 2. As might be expected, jurisdictional overlaps are common in naval communications research. See, for example, the discussion on airborne radio in *History of Communications-Electronics in the United States Navy*, prepared by Captain L. S. Howeth, USN (ret.) under the auspices of the Bureau of Ships and Office of Naval History (Washington: Government Printing Office, 1963), pp. 422–431.

21. Ints VII-1, 3; Polaris Command Communications Committee, *Where did the $100 Million Go? Polaris Command Communications R&D Yield Summary* (U) (Washington: Special Projects Office, May 11, 1964) (Secret). Also, *Proceedings of the Special Projects Office Steering Task Group, Task II—Monitor and Sponsor the Fleet Ballistic Missile Development Program* (U), 22nd Meeting, 1, 2 December 1960, pp. 89ff (SRD) and *Proceedings of the Special Projects Office Steering Task Group, Task II—Monitor and Sponsor the Fleet Ballistic Missile Development Program* (U), 39th Meeting, 26, 27 September 1963, pp. 179–181 (SRD).

22. Polaris Communications Committee, *Where Did the $100 Million Go?* (Secret).

particularly those designed to improve response time and survivability, had no attraction for advocates of an assured destruction strategy. In their view the message would get through. ("After all, the basic systems are already very redundant.") It seemed to matter little whether or not it got through to all submarines in one hour or ten. ("Does the threat of nuclear destruction deteriorate over time?") The concepts did, however, gain the support of those advocating a damage limitation strategy since enemy missile silos are time sensitive targets. ("You shoot at empty holes if there is even a short delay in receiving the order to fire.") Without a real resolution to the dispute over which was the more desirable strategy, there could be neither major new investments in FBM communications hardware (the implementation of the concepts would have been expensive; several were in the multibillion-dollar category) nor a termination of research, and thus the research program languished halfway between initiation and deployment.[23]

Another episode in the continuing strategy dispute led, in 1967, to the complete separation of all FBM communication research from the Special Projects Office. An independent communications project office was established on the initiative of those who sought the deployment of advanced FBM communications systems. They have pressed forward with several major concepts.[24] Decisions are pending, but the strategic dispute is still unresolved.[25]

In contrast, the Polaris program as a whole did not suffer from such strategic indecision. By the time the Polaris was conceived, the nation was committed to a rapid expansion of its ballistic missile programs. Soviet ballistic missile tests had confirmed long-standing though unheeded estimates that ballistic missiles were feasible and had convinced defense officials that the United States would soon be threatened by a Soviet missile capability. The obvious counter to that danger was for the United States to acquire as quickly as possible its own ballistic missile capability. The launching of *Sputnik* strongly reinforced the perception of danger and the direction of

23. Ints VII-4, 5.
24. Ints VII-6, 7, 8.
25. Ints VII-4, 7. See also, "Navy Lets Public in on a Secret," *New York Times* (February 12, 1969), p. 10.

national policy. By the time the Polaris was ready for production, there was no question that the United States would deploy ballistic missiles in large numbers.

The Polaris and the other ballistic missile programs were thus clearly the beneficiaries of an unusual convergence between technological opportunities and a consensus on national needs, a convergence with parallels perhaps only in the Manhattan and Apollo projects. In the mid- and late 1950's the United States had a sharply defined defense problem and a compelling desire to pursue a given technological opportunity as it appeared to offer a solution to that problem. Earlier ballistic missile projects had been restricted in scale despite frequent claims by their proponents that rocket technology was ready for exploitation.[26] The breakthrough that permitted the rapid development of ballistic missiles was political rather than technological. When the consensus was reached on the direction of national policy, however, the technological opportunity was there to exploit. This convergence between technological opportunity and consensus on national policy was, I argue, a facilitating factor in the success of the Polaris program since, with it, came potential access to unlimited resources and a favorable political environment.

I would be the first, however, to acknowledge that the ballistic missile experience is rather unique. Most government undertakings, whether civilian or military, are apparently not the beneficiaries of a convergence between technological opportunities and political consensus.[27] The urban policy area is one example: there is no consensus on either a definition of the urban problem or on the appropriate direction for public policy, and there is no obvious technology (solution) to apply. Is the urban problem substandard housing, environmental pollution, inadequate educational programs, or the lack of modern community services? Is it crime, the coddling of the poor, or the decline of moral standards? Is it the concentration of lower-class (mainly black) populations unprepared for and

26. Robert L. Perry, *The Ballistic Missile Decision*, RAND Corp., P-3686 (October 1967).
27. A thoughtful analysis of the roles technology and politics play in guiding the direction of social policies is contained in Wallace S. Sayre and Bruce L. Smith, "Government, Technology and Social Problems," an Occasional Paper of the Institute for the Study of Science in Human Affairs, Columbia University, 1969.

isolated from job opportunities in obsolete core cities? Or is it
all of these taken together? Without agreement on what con-
stitutes the problem it is, of course, difficult to discuss solutions. And solutions to the urban problem are scarcely less
controversial than definitions. Even if there were an agreement, say, to provide massive federal aid for the urban poor,
disagreement would exist over whether the aid should be in
the form of cash payments, jobs, or services. Each approach
has its proponents, and none is without challenge on grounds
of technological and political feasibility. Lacking the benefits
of a convergence between technological opportunities and a
political consensus, every urban project operates in a hostile
environment.

A WINNING SKILL IN BUREAUCRATIC POLITICS

Access to unlimited resources and a favorable political environment, however, are not enough to guarantee success.
Problems of jurisdictional competition and interagency coordination will still plague a project even after a consensus has
been reached on its utility and feasibility. Within government
there are always a dozen or so agencies that can claim partial
or complete jurisdiction over another agency's project for legal,
technological, financial, or administrative reasons. And a
project of any significant size necessarily will utilize skills and
facilities that are the functional preserve of various autonomous governmental agencies.

Officially established priorities or an appeal to hierarchy
can do little to alleviate a project's political uncertainties.
Government is too complex. Laced throughout its structure are
many independent sections, bureaus, agencies, commissions,
and the like that demand the right to set their own priorities
and that have the power to do so. The Air Force's priorities
are seldom the same as those of the Army and the Navy, nor
are the Department of Defense's priorities binding on the
National Aeronautics and Space Administration, the Civil
Service Commission, the Office of Management and Budget,
the General Accounting Office, or Senator Fulbright and the
Senate Foreign Relations Committee. Timely intervention by
the President to save a project through a reassertion of priori-

ties, even his own, rarely succeeds since the President's political resources are always limited and frequently overextended.[28]

Clearly the success or even the survival of the Polaris program was not assured at its establishment. The three armed services were then competing for a role in strategic offensive missiles, and it was certain that one, or perhaps two, of them would be denied. The organizational risks involved in developing ballistic missiles had generated opposition to the venture within each of the services. The initial years of priority development, when the ballistic missile programs were vying for official support, were precarious ones for the FBM proponents.

Although the decisions to accelerate the development of ballistic missiles assured Polaris' survival, they did not guarantee success. Even after *Sputnik*, the ballistic missile programs were not free from potential restrictions. The lower levels of the bureaucracy, as Parkinson predicts, tended to back away from the responsibility of reviewing what had become the largest projects in the Department of Defense, but the highest levels did not. On the contrary, they were continually concerned that the projects would be faulty in some way and were quite prepared to intervene directly in their management.[29] Several technical committees were asked periodically to scrutinize the projects' progress and report on management arrangements. Frequent formal presentations were required. Negative comments from whatever source—outside experts, competitors, White House staff members—brought immediate requests for detailed explanations. With the investment of substantial resources in the development of ballistic missiles came much advice and many questions.

It has become fashionable in recent years for scholars and former defense officials to reconsider the arms race and to decry the apparent manipulative practices of certain projects.[30] There is almost a theory of "the good projects" and "the bad projects" (and with it a cast of "good guys" and "bad guys").

28. Norton E. Long, "Power and Administration," *Public Administration Review* (August 1959), pp. 257–264, and Richard E. Neustadt, *Presidential Power* (New York: Wiley, 1960).

29. Int VII-8.

30. See, for example, Herbert York, *Race to Oblivion: A Participant's View of the Arms Race* (New York: Simon and Schuster, 1970), and Ralph E. Lapp, *Arms Beyond Doubt.*

The bad projects are the ones that are alleged to have used political promotion techniques to gain support and that are said to have forced the nation to build more arms than it needed. The good projects, usually including the Polaris, are not charged with political manipulation and are cited instead as examples of the rational allocation of defense resources.

If, however, the Polaris experience has any lesson it is that programs cannot be distinguished on the basis of their need to be involved politically in order to gain support and independence. The success of the Polaris program depended upon the ability of its proponents to promote and to protect the Polaris. Competitors had to be eliminated; reviewing agencies had to be outmaneuvered; congressmen, admirals, newspapermen, and academicians had to be co-opted. Politics is a systemic requirement. What distinguishes programs in government is not that some play politics and others do not, but, rather, that some are better at it than others.

The FBM proponents had two basic objectives: to gain approval for the development of a solid-fueled ballistic missile for submarine launch and to gain the degree of organizational autonomy within the Navy that they thought the development effort required. Their determination to obtain these objectives was matched by their skill in bureaucratic politics. Every opportunity to promote and protect the FBM was seized.

Consider the use of science advisors in the history of the FBM Program. In the mid-1950's when a firm program had not yet been established, the proponents, in effect, used science advisory committees as a way to circumvent the bureaucratic hierarchy. Information passed to the Killian Committee (the Technological Capabilities Panel of the President's Science Advisory Committee) in 1954 led to the statement that a requirement for a naval ballistic missile existed at a time when the Navy itself was officially hesitant to make such a statement. Similarly, the fortuitous calling of the NOBSKA Conference permitted the Polaris missile concept to be put forward as a replacement for instead of a successor to the joint Army-Navy Jupiter missile at a time when few in the Navy were prepared to risk a request for an independent missile development effort. It was not the ideas of outside scientists that contributed to the program; rather, it was their ability to articulate and legitimize at the highest levels ideas generated by the

FBM proponents and hitherto suppressed within the bureaucracy.[31]

Once the FBM Program was established, however, a different and less open relationship developed between the outside scientists and the proponents, even though the scientists generally remained strong supporters of the FBM. The managers of the development program, who had rather definite ideas about the direction they wanted it to take, felt that scientists were too inclined to favor continuous changes in the system design. Thus, they resisted the suggestion of a permanent outside science advisory committee for the FBM Program, fearing that if one were established they would lose control over the development effort.[32] Nevertheless, the endorsements of outside scientists, particularly those with national reputations or who had served on Defense Department review panels, were still needed. The tendency was to fund research on any remotely relevant topic that a scientist might suggest, but to keep this work completely separate from the main development effort. Some of the technical branches in the Special Projects Office had contingency funds for this purpose although they were not officially acknowledged as such. Scientists were co-opted to protect the program from potential criticism. Assured that their ideas were being considered, scientists would pass on favorable reports about the overall technical program. It was, from at least the proponents' perspective, a quite advantageous if tacit exchange.[33]

Discernible in the effort of the FBM proponents to promote and protect the Polaris were four bureaucratic strategies— differentiation, co-optation, moderation, and managerial innovation. Through the pursuit of these strategies the FBM proponents were able first to generate a unique demand for the development of the Polaris and then to gain autonomy for the Polaris development agency, the Special Projects Office. Since the generation of demands for the Polaris reduced the number of potential critics of the program and since autonomy for the

31. Vincent Davis in "The Politics of Innovation: Patterns in Navy Cases," The Social Science Foundation and Graduate School of International Studies, Monograph Series in World Affairs IV, 3 (Denver, Colo.: University of Denver Press, 1967), p. 55, makes a similar point in an analysis of what he calls the vertical political alliance.

32. Chapter Two, above; also Int VII-9.

33. Chapter Five, above.

Special Projects Office meant that the program was invulnerable to attack by whatever critics remained, the pursuit of these strategies in effect secured the success of the Polaris program.

The point to remember is not that those particular bureaucratic strategies guarantee success. Environmental factors unidentifiable in a single case study could conceivably dictate the use of other strategies at different times. The point, rather, is that success requires skills in bureaucratic politics. Only through the exercise of such skills does a favorable environment yield sustained support for a program.

One strategy, however, that of managerial innovation, deserves further attention here because its by-products, especially PERT, seemed to many to be the key to the program's success and, in fact, the prime lesson of the Polaris experience. Though the program's innovativeness in management methods was, as I have tried to show, as effective technically as rain dancing, it was, nevertheless, quite effective politically. The Special Projects Office quickly learned that a reputation for managerial efficiency made it difficult for anyone to challenge the Special Projects Office's FBM development plans. With PERT, PMP, the Management Center, and the other management innovations, the FBM Program had a protective veneer that allowed the program's technical staffs to continue their frantic work relatively unhindered by concerned but disruptive outside officials. It mattered not that the management innovations contributed little directly to the technical effort; it was enough that those outside the program were willing to believe that management innovation had a vital role in the technical achievements of the Polaris.

By now, almost everyone is aware of the limitations of the Polaris management innovations, and their use is fading. A problem that remains, however, is why the management myth was so enthusiastically received. The management innovations not only helped to ensure the autonomy of the Special Projects Office, but they also had, as was noted, systemic consequences. Polaris competitors quickly produced their own management innovations. The ritual of PERT became a Department of Defense contract requirement. And civilian agencies and private firms eagerly sought to apply the management lessons of the ballistic missile programs. The gullibility of important officials in this case seems too great and the diffusion of the Polaris management innovations, especially PERT, too rapid to attribute the success of the myth simply to the effectiveness of the Special Projects Office's public relations activities, extensive as they may have been.

What appears to have happened was that the Special Projects Office and the Polaris program were the fortuitous beneficiaries of a general management malaise: the disposition of high-level executives to accept the claims of omnipotence offered for management systems. Faced with the necessity of making decisions in situations of great uncertainty, responsible officials can be expected to search for some system that will guarantee them wisdom. Their occupational concern for remaining in control of the silent bureaucracy below could also lead them in the same direction, hoping for some system that would provide unbiased and timely information on the activities of subordinates. Finally, their own political problems, the need to impress others, the need to look modern, the need to look busy, could make them eager to endorse and utilize magical management cures, whether or not they actually believe in the efficacy of the systems.

The tendency of organizational executives to reach for management straws is encouraged by the many management system salesmen that they encounter and exacerbated by the bureaucratic apparatus that they lead. Money and position can be made by placing dull objects in shiny packages and by limiting the sales description to the product's expected virtues, especially when the customers are gullible or desperate. Management consulting fortunes lie in championing management innovations since the standard management systems have already been absorbed (and subverted) by the bureaucracy. Staff aides can gain recognition and reward by learning the esoteric systems that are the latest management fad.

Despite its reputation, the bureaucratic apparatus need not be considered the automatic opponent of management systems changes. Within most bureaucracies there are those who see their opportunities in zealously carrying out the perceived wishes of the boss. Moreover, bureaucracies seem to have a facility for converting the boss's management preferences into rigidly prescribed management rules. At the higher levels of the bureaucracy it is easier to process elaborate reports on adherence to management procedures than it is to evaluate their impact on actual organizational performance. For example, the Department of Defense prepares many charts describing the growing adoption of incentive contracts, but few studies of the effectiveness of incentive contracts.

Ironically, the problem with the Special Projects Office management innovations lies in their virtue. The myth of management system effectiveness helped protect the independence of the FBM development, but it also came to limit the flexibility of other development efforts when, on the basis of their supposed role in the Polaris program, the innovations were made the model in government and industry.[34] The innovations produced considerable political benefits for the Special Projects Office, but these benefits were dependent upon a unique application. When such innovations are diffused throughout society by requirement or imitation, no one can claim any special competence because of their application, and, thus, no one can gain their political benefits.

As Perry points out in his penetrating studies of major Air Force weapons programs, there are a number of widely accepted military research and development doctrines that are based on unexamined premises.[35] But it seems that, as soon as one doctrine is proven false, another takes its place. Warnings about the seductive and distractive lure of management systems go unheeded.[36] A Defense Department industry review panel recently complained that there were 934 different management systems, many of dubious value, being applied in the weapons acquisition process and recommended that the Assis-

34. U.S. Congress, House, Committee on Government Operations, *Hearings, Systems Development and Management*, 87th Cong., 2nd Sess. (Washington: Government Printing Office, 1962), Pt. 2, pp. 577–594.

35. Robert L. Perry, *The Mythography of Military R&D*, RAND Corp., P-3356 (May 1966). See also his "System Development Strategies: A Comparative Study of Doctrine, Technology, and Organization in the USAF Ballistic Missile and Cruise Missile Programs, 1950–1960," (U) (RAND Report RM-4853-PR, August 1966) (Confidential).

36. See, for example, the report of a speech by Dr. Robert A. Frosch, Assistant Secretary of the Navy (R&D) in the *Electronic News*, 14 (March 31, 1969), p. 1, and an article by James W. Grodsky, Staff Assistant to the Assistant Director of Defense Research and Engineering (Engineering Management), "Flexibility in Management of Research and Development," *Defense Industry Bulletin*, 5 (June 1969), pp. 13–16.

tant Secretary of Defense (Comptroller) coordinate their use.[37] Other groups, most recently in the Congress, have complained about the mammoth overruns that continue to plague weapon procurements. The Comptroller himself, however, sought the answer to both the proliferation of management systems and the inefficiencies of the procurement process in a new performance accounting system based on fixed work packages.[38] We are still offered the management system cure because the uncertainties involved in managing major technological developments are so great and because the political rewards for claiming to have devised a truly effective management system are so large.

AN ABILITY TO MANAGE
TECHNOLOGICAL COMPLEXITY

A favorable environment and the skillful application of effective bureaucratic strategies, however, were not in themselves enough to gain the Polaris program permanent success. At some point in time major technical problems, had there been any in the program, would have caught up with the Polaris and its promises. An element in the formula for success had to be the skillful implementation of effective policies for the management of the technical development effort.

Despite appearances and assertions to the contrary, the management of the FBM system development did not require the invention of entirely new management techniques. Rather, the secret of the technical success of the program seems to lie in some rather prosaic and easily overlooked management policies. The unusual management features of the program

37. The panel was the Department of Defense-Council of Defense and Space Industries Association Advisory Committee for Management Control Systems and their report and recommendations are discussed in Arnold J. Rothstein, "DOD-Industry Efforts Pass Milestone toward Management Systems Control," *Aerospace Management,* 3 (Spring–Summer, 1968), pp. 5–20. See also, "The Pentagon Builds a Monster," *Business Week* (February 18, 1967), pp. 198–199.

38. The performance accounting system is discussed in: "DOD Stalks the Weapon Systems Tiger," *Government Executive* (June 1969), pp. 65–66. Officially it is described in DOD INSTRUCTION 7000.2, "Performance Measurement for Selected Acquisitions," December 22, 1967.

were: the fact that the development team was given the opportunity to apply these policies without interference, and the fact that the development team had enough self-confidence in its own abilities to follow through and apply them.

The FBM development problem centered on the uncertainties of system integration. Whereas progress in each of the component subsystems could be generally anticipated, it was difficult to predict far in advance the moment of effective synchronization for all the subsystems. The development team's approach to this problem involved the application of a number of related policies that might be summarized as disciplined flexibility. The only dimensions that were permitted to be firmly fixed at the beginning of the development were those forced by the requirements of submarine construction, the basic physical boundaries of the system. Within the system's physical constraints, all performance options were kept open to allow for the collection of sufficient information upon which to base decisions. There were in each subsystem backup (parallel) developments and fallback (minimum acceptable performance) positions. Having control over the system's military requirements, FBM developers could, with the advent of accelerated schedules, select values for subsystem performance that the development data indicated would add up to a viable and achievable weapon system. All further subsystem advances were saved for consideration in the next version of the system. The existence of a planned series of system improvements—A-2 and A-3 and the various submarine classes—was important for it meant that the development team was relatively free from the normal pressures to make a given system perfect, the kind of pressures which drive up program costs and lead to significant schedule slippages. The development effort's discipline therefore was in the physical constraints of the submarine and in the determination to meet accelerated deployment schedules; its flexibility was in avoiding a premature commitment to any particular performance goal.

These management policies were buttressed by two important organizational policies, decentralization and competition. The structural decentralization was initially an awkward expedient of the Jupiter project, but it was consciously extended in the Polaris development. Thus, the burden of approving contractor design changes within a subsystem was placed on the field offices, the staff units closest to the actual development. The central technical staff and the technical branches in the Special Projects Office could then concentrate their attention on controlling system interfaces and making selections among subsystem alternatives. To have utilized a more centralized arrangement would have run the risk of burying the central units in a level of detail that they could not have effectively handled.

Decentralization in a complex system development, however, has its own risks. Independent subunits, for example, could seek to gain advantages for themselves to the detriment of the entire system. More importantly, they could be tempted to suppress information on subsystem problems in order to maintain control over their own operations. In the FBM Program these dangers were avoided through intense internal competition. It was generally not the formal request-for-proposal type of competition that was found in the program. Rather it was a more subtle type of competition, stimulated by personal and organizational ambitions and based on large prizes and an absence of rigid jurisdictional boundaries. Everyone had an actual or potential rival and no one was assured of a monopoly. Thus, within the program everyone had a strong incentive to watch for problems in the designs offered by others while working diligently to avoid any of their own. Decentralization assured a manageable division of labor and competition assured the honesty of the laborers.

Given technological uncertainties, these policies—disciplined flexibility, decentralization, and competition—seem, as several analysts have argued, to be eminently well suited to serve as management guides in major development projects.[39] Given the political uncertainties usually encountered by such

39. See the conclusions of Perry, *The Mythography*, and "System Development Strategies"; Burton Klein, "A Radical Proposal for R&D," *Fortune*, 57 (May 1958), pp. 112ff, and "The Decision-Making Problem in Development," in Universities-National Bureau Committee for Economic Research, *The Rate and Direction of Inventive Activity: Economic and Social Factors* (Princeton, N.J.: Princeton University Press, 1962), pp. 477–497; Richard R. Nelson, "Uncertainty, Learning, and the Economics of Parallel Research and Development Efforts," *Review of Economics and Statistics*, 43 (1961), pp. 351–364, and Albert O. Hirschman and Charles E. Lindholm, "Economic Development, Research and Development, and Policy-Making. Some Converging Views," *Behavioral Science*, 7 (April 1962), pp. 211–222.

projects, however, it is unlikely that project managers would have an early opportunity to apply these policies. Rather, their first need may be to reduce the political uncertainties, perhaps by devising some management system that gives the appearance (asserts the claim) of having eliminated the technological uncertainties. A reduction in a project's political obstacles is required before its technical obstacles can be approached effectively.

The formula for success I have outlined in this chapter can be best summarized in terms of James D. Thompson's analysis of organizational uncertainties.[40] Thompson argues that uncertainties are presented to complex organizations from three sources, two external to the organization and the third internal. The external sources are generalized uncertainty caused by the lack of clarity in cause and effect relationships in the society, and what he calls contingency or the uncertainty caused by the fact that the outcomes of organizational action are in part determined by the actions of elements (for example, other organizations) in the organization's environment. The internal source is the interdependence of components or the uncertainty caused by the coordination requirements of the organization's technology. In Thompson's view uncertainty control is the fundamental organizational problem and all complex organizations seek self-control or the ability to act independent of environmental forces.

The discussion of the convergence between technological opportunity and a political consensus described the conditions for avoiding general uncertainties. With such a convergence society provides a clear indication of the desired direction for organized action and the means to accomplish such action. Similarly, the discussion of bureaucratic strategies and the political involvement of the Special Projects Office described the efforts of the Polaris proponents to control environmental uncertainties. The autonomy the Special Projects Office achieved protected the FBM Program from the disruptive interference of potentially uncooperative organizations and groups. The support rallied for the concept of a submarine-launched ballistic missile assured the program the resources

40. James D. Thompson, *Organizations in Action* (New York: McGraw-Hill, 1967), pp. 159–161.

it needed to develop such a missile. Finally, the internal organizational arrangements devised for the Special Projects Office and the technical maxims employed by its leadership provided the coordination needed to control the uncertainties of the FBM's technical tasks.

The Special Projects Office was clearly successful in achieving the independence of action it sought, and its autonomy clearly facilitated the success of the Polaris program. Focused narrowly on a single mission and free from a reliance on the functional bureaucracy, the development team built the Polaris to an exacting schedule. It would, however, be a mistake to attribute the success of the program simply to the structural independence and product orientation of the development agency. Just as there are no magical management system cures, there are no magical structural cures in the administration of government.

Of course there are those who wish there were such magical cures. Defense officials, apparently on the basis of the ballistic missile experience, required the service departments to establish project management offices to oversee the development of critical weapon systems with the implication that this structural change would assure programmatic success. As early as 1962 the Navy had set up 58, the Air Force 47, and the Army 28 project management offices. And today it is common to hear political leaders and social commentators calling for the formation of project management offices similar to those established for the Manhattan project, Apollo, or the ballistic missile programs to conquer cancer, to develop low-cost housing units, or to solve the "environmental crisis." There is evidently a belief that certain structural arrangements automatically produce results.

As the Polaris experience demonstrates, however, the formula for programmatic success is somewhat more complicated. Useful first is a convergence between technological opportunity and a widely accepted policy need. Next there must be committed to the project people who are extraordinarily skillful in the art of bureaucratic politics. Project independence, except perhaps in time of war, cannot be assigned, but rather must be continually won. Finally, there needs to be available people who are knowledgeable in the effective management of technology and who have the self-confidence to apply their skills. The supply of such people is likely to be short.

Moreover, there are reasons to be cautious about urging the adoption of project management arrangements even when the conditions for programmatic success are present. As the Polaris experience also demonstrates, conflicts exists between programmatic success and bureaucratic success and this conflict grows as a program nears completion. The tendencies toward suboptimization inherent in a project management arrangement are exacerbated when the urgency of the mission declines. Organizational maintenance needs can easily replace the original concern with accomplishing the organization's mission. Society has yet to learn how to control the very bureaucracies which it establishes to save itself from impending disasters. Though their names are now different, the Special Projects Office, the Manhattan District Project Office, and the Apollo Project Office persist.

Index

Strategic Offensive and Defensive Systems, Director of (Navy), 200–201
Strategic Systems Project Office, see Special Projects Office
Submariners: attitudes of, toward FBM, 18; influence of, in FBM Program, 52–54; relationship of, in Special Projects Office, 52–54
Submarines: attack, 35; as missile platforms, 3; nuclear-powered, 3. See also FBM submarines
Subsafe, 170, 191
Success: costs of, 161; of FBM Program and Special Projects Office, 11, 160, 230, 232–234; formula for, in government, 230–254; lessons of, 181–184; official priorities and, 14, 34, 42; rareness of, in government, 1, 241–242; standards of, in government, 230–235; technological, 38. See also Bureaucratic politics; Bureaucratic strategies
Super Carrier vs. B–36 Controversy, 5–6, 17, 21
System for Projection and Analysis (SPAN), 105, 217

"Targets of naval opportunity," 44
Technology: breakthroughs in, 29–30, 136–138; management of, 249–254; supply and demand forces on, 235–237; uncertainty inherent in, 139–148, 204, 252–253
Teller, Edward, 29–30
Thomas, Charles, 20, 23

Thompson, James D., 252–253
Thor missile, 24
3Ts (missiles), 170, 177
Thresher, USS, 71, 191
Titan missile, 21
Transit satellite, 70
Trident: plans for, 11; prospects for, 226, 229
Triton missile, development of, 16, 25; victim of Polaris, 35, 168

ULMS, see Trident
United Kingdom: ballistic missile submarine program of, 10, 53; view of, on Polaris management, 87, 130

V–2 missile, 4–5
Vanguard Program, 21
Vitro Laboratories, Incorporated, 82, 93, 146, 154. See also Polaris contractors
Von Braun, Wernher, 24

Weapon acquisition process: contract forms in, 205–214; problems in, 61–77, 180–181, 223, 237–241; reforms in, 205–214; role of contractors in, 77–82; role of operational staffs in, 140–141; role of research in, 134–138, 141–145. See also Arsenal system; Contractors
Westinghouse Electric Corporation, 91. See also Polaris contractors
Wiener, Anthony J., 138
Wilson, Charles E., 33

Young, Richard, 115